Transgender Voices

TRANSGENDER
VOICES *Beyond Women and Men*

Lori B. Girshick

University Press of New England | Hanover and London

Published by University Press of New England,
One Court Street, Lebanon, NH 03766.
www.upne.com
© 2008 by University Press of New England
Printed in the United States of America
5 4 3 2 1

Library of Congress Cataloging-in-Publication Data

Girshick, Lori B.
Transgender voices : voices beyond women and men / Lori B. Girshick.
   p. cm.
Includes bibliographical references.
ISBN−13: 978−1-58465−645−6 (cloth : alk. paper)
ISBN−10: 1−58465−645−X (cloth : alk. paper)
1. Transgender people—Interviews. 2. Transgenderism. I. Title.
HQ77.7.G57 2008
306.76′8—dc22   2007049350

 University Press of New England is a member of the GreenPress
Initiative. The paper used in this book meets their minimum
requirement for recycled paper

This book is dedicated to kari, writer and gender activist *extraordinaire*.

Contents

Foreword

Generalizations of femaleness and maleness have long served as tools to enforce social order. Regardless of the details, which would certainly differ from tribe to tribe, from culture to culture, through language, and be influenced by geographic and economic conditions, the categorization of sexed human bodies and the interpretation of gendered identities and expressions have benefited some people and oppressed others for as long as human beings have told the stories of their lives. It is astounding to me that it has taken our society so long to listen to these stories. I can't imagine that they weren't being told, but I can imagine that they were suppressed, and that this was likely often done with great violence.

From the mid-nineteenth to the mid-twentieth centuries, the nascent sciences of sexology and psychology/psychiatry held sway over the definition of "normal" sexual and gendered behavior in Europe, America, and everywhere their influence could reach. By naming and classifying behaviors, and by creating a system of "deviations," and even criminalizing variance ("deviations" that caused no harm to person or property), the masters of these belief systems exerted a new level of control with which they intended—consciously or unconsciously, benignly or officiously—to shape society. In the same period, medical scientists confronted intersex and gender-variant infants, toddlers, adolescents, and adults, and contrived to enforce sex and gender "norms" on them as well. But in the mid- and late twentieth century, people who lived outside these binaries began to speak up, to assert their own integrity, and to demand respect for their bodies and their psyches. Lori Girshick is one of the academic social researchers who have been listening.

Girshick's previous work on same-sex domestic and sexual violence, homophobia and heterosexism, and abused women in prison has prepared her well for hearing the stories of sex- and gender-diverse people. She knows how to listen for the systematic oppression and for the damage to selfhood that occurs when gender-diverse people interact with a hostile world, and she understands how to convey to others just why that damage and oppression must be stopped. As Girshick says (in chapter 4), "Policing artificially rigid identity boundaries creates a false sense of security." She is speaking in this instance about lesbian unease with female-to-male transitions, but the statement is true in every demographic. When we create barriers to seeing other people as equal human beings, we not only circumscribe our own world; we also create psychic—and often physical— damage that reverberates through our social environment and erodes the very principles of freedom, morality, and justice.

In *Transgender Voices*, Girshick takes on the difficult task of describing and explaining the complexity beyond the common labels that transpeople have been struggling with for the past century or more, ever since the early sexologists, psychiatrists, and criminologists began their ascendancy. She offers readers transpeople speaking in their own voices about identity, coming out, passing, sexual orientation, relationship negotiations, and the dynamics of attraction, homophobia (including internalized fears), and bullying. She exposes the guilt and the shame that "gender police" (bullies and fearful people) use in their attempts to exert control. She points out the viciousness with which the gender binary is reinforced in order to protect the sanctity of gender-segregated bathrooms and the moral and ethical folly of that approach. She illuminates the hypocrisy with which transpeople are bludgeoned by an ignorant and vengeful society. It is not always a pretty picture, but it is still an intriguing one, one that needs to be seen, with a chorus of voices that need to be heard.

Girshick also explores the notion of a gender continuum, promoting the helpful concept of parallel continua, though the nature of the English language and the logical structures it imposes on our collective thinking makes it somewhat difficult to get across as something larger than a string running between two poles. This difficulty notwithstanding, she endeavors to illustrate, by showing us a variety of descriptions of diverse real lives, that there is nothing *inherently* binary about gender, that the way each of us experiences our own gender and our own gender variance is, in fact, normal and natural. "Normal" is not the same as "conforming." Girshick's analysis of gender as perceived, experienced, and expressed by her 150 study participants shows that the "common denominators" of male/masculine and female/feminine may be illusions, stereotypes invoked so that society doesn't have to bother with a much more complex reality.

Girshick says (epilogue), "Gender diversity is the liberation issue of our times and should be put at center stage." I agree. As in every other liberation movement, there is an oppressor whose tyranny must be exposed; in the case of trans and intersex people, that oppressor is anyone who believes there is only one way to be, and that way is the way they want you to be, NOT the way each individual feels her- or him- or eir-self to be with respect to their own gender and sexuality. Further, the oppressor in this case also believes that gender and sexuality are fixed and immutable, and wishes to ensure that everyone remains fixed the way the tyrant sees/perceives/desires them. The fact that trans and intersex people are apparently a minority makes this oppression that much easier—for now. But as more people raise their voices, and as more scholars, activists, and allies take these issues on, social change is inevitable, and social justice for all grows more achievable.

Jamison Green
Oakland, California
July 27, 2007

Acknowledgments

It's hard to know where to begin to appreciate the many people I've met and the experiences I have had that led me to write this book. I have been privileged to find creative spaces, whether at gender conferences, in books I've read, during discussion with friends, or even in my reaction to reports of daily discrimination and the horrors of hate crimes, that helped me form my opinions and commitment to gender equality in its fullest scope and form.

I am grateful to the writer of the letter I refer to in the introduction, who challenged me to rethink my ideas of the category of "woman." This man, who had been born with a female biology, asked me questions that made crystal clear to me how narrow my ideas really were. Trans and intersex issues were invisible to me, and I am grateful to have been jolted awake and spurred to action.

Ever since then I have integrated my growing understanding into my writing, my teaching, and my own life. As a member of the lesbian, gay, bisexual, and transgender (LGBT) communities—I identify as lesbian and queer—I hope to make some small contribution to the social and political equality we deserve. Understanding the consequences of the gender and sex binaries, and working against that rigid system, have enriched my life. Thank you to every trans-identified and queer person who has helped me on this path. Thank you to the non-trans allies I have worked with, especially while I was at Arizona State University and working on the Safe-ZONE program. We kept the issues alive and visible, and these great folks continue to push for social change and justice around LGBT issues.

Surveys and interviews of 150 trans-identified individuals form the basis of this work. I have full gratitude to these people for sharing their life experiences and thoughts with me. I have been lucky to meet over 40 of them personally, and I cherished each meeting. Many of the people in this book have kept in touch with me over the years, and many I consider friends. Numerous people from the Phoenix support group in Asheville, North Carolina, where I was living when I first started this research, helped me enormously. Thank-you to the five volunteers (Holly, Jessylynn, Beth, Marc, and Andrea) who formed the focus group that guided me in my survey construction. I also appreciate the support and encouragement I received from faculty and the dean while I was at Warren Wilson College.

A few people deserve special mention by name for their support over the years in terms of feedback, networking, and encouragement. Thank you to Holly Boswell, who answered my numerous questions when I was starting out, and to Jamison Green for his support, our many conversations, and for writing the foreword to this book. These two individuals are exemplary activists who have worked for decades to end trans invisibility in public policy and to support people at different stages of their journeys with gender identity. Many others supported me by just talking with me at conferences over the years (such as Kelley Winters, Mara Keisling, and Marsha Botzer). Thanks to my Kick Ass Sister, April Summitt, who has inspired me daily to keep writing and has listened to my writing woes, real and imagined. Peggy Coulombe and Karyn Riedell, friends and fellow writers, also encouraged me to keep on going through the various revisions.

When it came time to find a publisher for this work, I could not have been luckier than to be accepted by University Press of New England. Phyllis Deutsch, editor in chief, was so excited about the importance of the work that it fed the enthusiasm I already had for it. Her energy has been infectious, and she has challenged me repeatedly to make this the best manuscript possible. I am very appreciative to the readers of my draft manuscript who gave perceptive and thoughtful feedback and, again, pushed me to be as clear as possible with a complex and provocative subject.

I regret that this book took me longer than I'd intended to research and write. I had significant interruptions that included moving across the country, several job changes, and a diagnosis of breast cancer. I am sure that many people in this book have forgotten about the project and may think I never followed through. But my commitment was always to those who were willing to give of themselves. Ventures like these involve years of work, deep reflection, and the will to make a difference. I thank you, the many who shared with me, the many who listened, and the readers who I hope will challenge themselves to work toward understanding gender in new and revolutionary ways—outside the binary.

Transgender Voices

Introduction: Identity Boxes

I want to reiterate that I don't see myself as a gender transgressor, I see myself as a gender transcender. I dream of a world where the gender binary is transformed, with grace and peace, and with genuine respect for all current forms, from two genres to an infinite number. I fear that a socio-political program of transgression only serves to reinscribe the binary system by not really ever escaping what is perceived to be the gender continuums: a line between two supposedly opposite poles. My spiritual home is off the continuum. I believe the particular quality or cluster of qualities in each of us that makes us unique is also, at least partly, off that continuum. (Julian, ungendered)

Aims

In 1999 I was working on my book on woman-to-woman sexual violence. The outreach for participants in that study called for lesbians, bisexual women, and transwomen (individuals born male-bodied and now living as women) who had experienced sexual violence at the hands of other women. In the course of my research, I received a letter from a female-to-male (FtM) transsexual who asked me if I was interested in the abuse experiences of FtMs. At the time I held a rudimentary understanding of who transsexuals are (individuals born with anatomy defined as male or female but who identify as women or men, contrary to what their biology indicated), and I had a simplistic, traditional understanding of the category "woman." I thought of transwomen as people who considered themselves women in the same way I thought of lesbians and bisexual women as women—people self-defined as women. In other words, I wasn't considering the influence of male biology for MtFs or of male identification for FtMs. Because my outreach yielded only one transperson—and she identified as a lesbian at the time of the sexual violence—I did not feel a need to investigate the much more profound complexities bound up in the notion of gender identity and gender-variant people.

While the terms gender and sex are often used interchangeably, such usage is incorrect. *Gender* is the conceptual category (labeled masculine or feminine) that a culture assigns to a wide range of phenomena. People (man or woman), actions or attributes (a manly grip, a feminine walk), physical objects or phenomena (Mother Nature, Father Time, her [a ship's] maiden voyage)—virtually anything can be "gendered" in a given society. Gender is a binary system: it neatly divides the world in two. It does not necessarily have anything to do with sex (the masculine or feminine nouns in French grammar, for instance). However, when people are gendered, their gender designations (men or women) are expected to correlate with their biological sex. *Sex* refers to the biological characteristics of genitals, internal reproductive organs, gonads (ovaries and testes), hormones, and chromosomes. Male and female are the labels for these clusters of biological traits.

Gender identity is an individual's internal sense of gender (whether that person feels masculine or feminine, a bit of both or neither, or however that person self-identifies, notwithstanding the traditional categories). This self-identity may or may not correspond with that person's anatomy as traditionally understood. We communicate our gender identity through gender roles and gender presentation, which often follow the gender norms of the culture. *Gender roles* are the behaviors, and ways of thinking and feeling, that the culture teaches are appropriate for the two genders. *Gender presentation* or *expression* is the way an individual chooses to present his/her gender to others through dress, speech, actions, and grooming. *Gender norms* are the acceptable cultural behaviors, ideas, and values associated with different genders. In this book, I use trans, transpeople, or trans-identified individuals to encompass the collective of people who are gender variant in some way, who experience a disconnection between anatomy, gender identity, gender expression, gender presentation, or gender roles that puts them outside the norm.

Gender identity is often confused with sexual orientation, but they are not the same. Gender identity refers to an internal self-identification; sexual orientation refers to physical attraction to other people. An individual's sexual orientation label is based on that individual's gender identity and the gender of the person(s) that individual desires. Labels in this category include gay, lesbian, bisexual, heterosexual, pansexual, and asexual. Occasionally the term sexual identity is used, but it is much less common than sexual orientation. Furthermore, "orientation" helps us understand that sexual attraction is how we feel toward other people.

I realize now that my original understanding of the meaning of "woman" was problematic. It actually favored, and helped to perpetuate, a one-dimensional gender binary—a traditional cultural conception based on the widespread assumption that the terms "man" and "woman," and "male and "female," are mutually exclusive categories, polar opposites. According to the gender binary, males and females are defined by incontrovertible and fixed biological and psychological characteristics that distinguish them from one another. These biological and psychological characteristics turn them, inevitably, into people of the expected gender (men and women), who reaffirm their (obvious) differences from one another in dress, speech, manner, behavior, interests, and passions.

Given what we know about the remarkable diversity of human beings, it is astounding that this gender binary continues to prevail, and to impair (if not devastate) the lives of millions of people. Because of nonstandard chromosome or hormone combinations, millions of people cannot and do not relate to the binary's polar opposites of male/female. Offered two identity boxes from which to choose—male or female—where do people who identify with neither place their X?

How Many People Are We Talking About?

How many people in the United States are "trans-identified?" It is difficult to know. First we must ask: Who fits this potentially vast category? Transsexuals who have had a certain kind of surgery? Individuals whom psychologists diagnose as having gender identity disorder (GID)? What about intersex people, butch women, male cross-dressers, androgynous people, and other gender variants? And then: Who could be relied on to do the counting? Doctors, therapists, sociologists, law enforcement agencies, social service providers—all have their own agendas for including or excluding people who themselves may or may not trans-identify. The psychological diagnosis of GID captures only those who seek counseling. Female-bodied male-identified people may never come to the attention of a data collector, as there is some level of tolerance for women who publicly present in a more masculine-defined way. And cross-dressing males may be the most hidden of all, as the majority cross-dress in the privacy of their homes.

At this time, there is no reliable way to obtain a head count. Given the nature of the problem—the wide array of gender expression and the understandable reluctance of many stigmatized transpeople to come out of the closet—we may never be able to come up with accurate numbers. And even if we were able to somehow create a standard definition for gender variance, and all those who fit it raised their hands, we'd have to ask ourselves why the head count is so important. Do we want to show that gender variance is extensive and natural and not aberrant? Do we hope to win legal rights and protections for gender-variant people? Does our count serve to legitimize (and render insurance-worthy) certain medical services? Or, alternatively, will these numbers be used to prove there is a serious threat to traditional gender norms, to marriage between a man and a woman, and the like?

Nonetheless, some groups of gender-variant people are easier to count than others. Because intersex people (individuals with a variety of nonstandard reproductive, chromosomal, or sexual anatomies) are likely to come in contact with the medical system, some records of them exist. However, estimates based on these records are imprecise; there is a wide range of intersex conditions, and not all intersex people visit doctors. Researchers have estimated that one newborn in 100,000 is a true hermaphrodite—a person who has gonads with both ovarian and testicular tissue (Fausto-Sterling 2000). One in 10,000 males is born with hypospadias: the penis opening is on the underside rather than at the tip (Kessler 2000). According to the Intersex Society of North America (ISNA) website, one in 1,666 births involves a child who has neither an XX nor an XY chromosomal pattern. One in 500 to one in 1,000 males is born with an extra X chromosome (Klinefelter syndrome). These boys have male-looking genitals but fail to masculinize at puberty. Androgen Insensitivity Syndrome (AIS) occurs in one in 20,000 individuals: the child either partly or fully fails to respond to produced testosterone. These children lack internal female organs but also don't develop along external male lines. They are raised as girls, and often the syndrome is not discovered until puberty. When these and other intersex conditions are counted, one in 100 births "deviates" from what we expect in terms of male and female bodies.

There are also medical records for transsexuals who opt for sex change surgery. These estimates too are quite variable. Lynn Conway estimated the number of male-to-female sex reassignment surgeries performed over forty years by doctors in the United States at 40,000. Dividing by the number of males at that time (approximately 80 million between the ages of eighteen and sixty) gives a figure of one in 2,000 males who are postoperative MtFs. Conway suggests that adding in the non- and pre-operative transsexuals yields a number closer to one in 500 people who are transsexual MtFs (Roughgarden 2004, p. 285). Being transsexual, therefore, is certainly not a rare occurrence and hardly a genetic defect, countering the argument that transsexual people are "abnormal." The International Foundation for Gender Education (IFGE) estimates that cross-dressers constitute 6 percent of the population. According to Garber (1997), only 1 percent are transsexuals.

As a sociologist, I have been influenced by the dictum of sociologists William I. and Dorothy Thomas: "If men [and women] define situations as real, they are real in their consequences," penned in 1928. The simplicity of this statement captures a profound truth of social life: that we are in charge of our perception of reality and that we hold the means to create, reinforce, or alter that perceived reality. Therefore, we have enormous power to interpret, understand, and define what is "normal" and what is outside the norm. And, as the Thomases note, what we perceive to be real becomes real in the sense that it has real consequences, whether or not it is the truth.

I believe in the social construction of reality. What we believe—how we think about ourselves, our relationships, our social world—has less to do with scientific or biological "facts" and more to do with profound familial, cultural, and social training that reinforces what is considered "normal." Whether or not "normal" defines real experience for a few, many, or anyone doesn't much matter. What does matter is that "normal" maintains sets of hierarchical political structures, economic systems, and social conventions that benefit those at the top of the pyramid. Because of this, the idea of "normal" remains powerful, and "normal" for gender still means male or female, man or woman. The general public regards this mainstream gender system—one or the other, but not both or neither—as an accurate description of how people do, or should, self-identify themselves and how most, if not all, people live. This assumption guides all sorts of interpersonal interactions and dictates a vast range of social and political policy. When an individual's experience does not fit the binary and deviates from the norm, the individual is criticized, not the system. To force individuals to manage their appearance or behavior in ways that feel untruthful so that others feel comfortable inhibits everyone from exploring and experiencing the full range of human self-expression.

I believe that the gender binary does not work as a framework for people's life experiences. It does not work because gender expression *as it is lived* is far more colorful and creative than two identity boxes, male or female. It does not work because some people are shamed, stigmatized, and discriminated against for who they are. The question is not simply whether gender is biological or socially constructed; extensive research has demonstrated that both are influential, and that we attach social and cultural meaning to otherwise neutral biological givens. The really important questions are whether we can stop assuming that genitals = gender, whether we can overcome our knee-jerk tendency to think of masculinity and femininity as polar opposites, and whether we can honestly investigate how our language and ideas create and sustain two oppositional sets of identity boxes in which millions of people do not fit.

I am a sociologist by training and a social activist at heart. As the former, I have framed this book in the sociological method known as grounded theory, described below. As the latter, I wrote this book to give voice to people whose stories must be heard. I have intentionally privileged these voices over the work of gender theorists and other scholars and academics who work in the broad field of gender/queer studies. For the purposes of this book, complex theoretical work on the cultural construction of gender takes us too far from the life experiences of the 150 trans-identified people interviewed for this project. These people are my experts. This book is their book: it charts their lived experiences, feelings, and relationships. It shows the limitations and challenges of living with, adapting to, or breaking away from the gender binary in terms of family, work, and community. It shows the courage and personal integrity of people who, no matter what their choices, cannot be easily channeled (or mainstreamed) into male or female, man or woman.

This book is a radical call. Because sex, gender, and sexuality are at the core of our individual identity, to question the binary is to question the very essence of how we see and define ourselves. The interviews open a door. The book invites you to walk through it.

Methodology

As I began my research on this book, I started with one question: What does it mean to say "I feel like a boy" or "I feel like a girl"? Other questions flowed from this one. How do individuals express their sense of masculinity, femininity, both, or neither? How do individuals manage their sense of discomfort and the discomfort of those around them as it relates to variable gender expression? What is the relationship between gender identity and sexual orientation? What are the consequences of gender constructed as a binary, and should/can this construct be changed? Is a person's sense of gender identity genetic, or is there an element of choice? Why is gender conceived as a binary?

I generated questions for my survey from a focus group with five trans-identified people. The conversation of that focus group confirmed significant topics, experiences, and viewpoints, while adding nuances I had overlooked. I followed the method of grounded theory, in which theory is generated from data to ensure a fit between the two. According to Glaser and Strauss (1967), categories determined by examining the data are more easily understandable to the non-researcher, and the resulting theories are more enduring than those determined by logical deduction. Conceptual categories come from the data, as opposed to the data being selected to prove ideas. Themes consistently mentioned determined the chapter titles and subheadings. I stopped interviewing at 150 participants. By then I had sampled a wide range of gender identities and experiences, and responses had become repetitive, representing saturation.

Using the approach of grounded theory with a range of trans-identities, I was able to discover where life experiences of trans-identified people are similar or different. In this way I could discern categories of experience and show the properties of the categories, increasing their generality and explanatory power. The gender and sexual orientation continuums I present in the epilogue also emerged in direct response to what I learned from the data. Grounded theory allowed me to generate a better way to capture gender identifications, a scheme that encompasses but goes beyond the two categories (man, woman) of the gender binary.

My outreach for research participants began in 2002. I mailed a flier (appendix 1) to lesbian, gay, bisexual, and transgender (LGBT) community centers across the United States, Tri-Ess groups (an international organization that serves heterosexual male cross-dressers), trans support groups nationwide, and feminist bookstores. I distributed fliers at gender conferences. Numerous websites posted the call for participants. The title of the flier, in bold, asked "Are you a gender transgressor?" and was followed by these questions: "Are there times when you are too female or not female enough? Too male or not male enough? Do you feel you're not male or female? Or maybe you feel male *and* female?"

Because I framed the questions in terms of "gender transgression," those who responded were more likely to self-identify in this way. Clearly, individuals who did not identify with the label of "gender transgressor" were less likely to respond to this appeal. I chose the word, out of many others (including the word "transgender"), in consultation with some of my trans friends. After realizing that whatever label I chose would meet with resistance from some people, I had to make a decision. I felt that the follow-up questions would appeal to people beyond those who saw themselves as a "gender transgressor." I believe that I was correct, since a few responders said they did not like the term but filled out the survey anyway. In my mind, what made these individuals "transgressors" was not that they might label themselves specifically transgender or transsexual but that they nonetheless challenged the gender binary in terms of self-definition and how they lived their lives. Participants defined "gender transgressor" in their own way. Not all those who accepted the term were "out" as trans. But all the people in this book felt that their anatomy, gender identity, gender expression, and/or gender role was different from the norm.

Those willing to be interviewed contacted me via e-mail, by phone, or through my website, where they could download the survey and consent form (appendix 2). Participants returned the consent form and survey, and in most cases participated in a follow-up phone interview. Of the 150 people in the study, more than one third nearly half (69) learned about it on the Internet. Almost 20 percent (29) heard of it from me; about 17 percent (25) got the information from a friend. The rest learned about it from support group outreach, newsletters, and postings at their local LBGT community center. Participants ranged in age from seventeen to seventy-one; the average age was forty-two. Most were non-Latino white (85 percent). Nine people identified as multiracial. Four identified as Latino. One each identified as African American, Asian American, Asian/Pacific Islander, and Native American. In the "Other" category I had one human, one person of color, one Italian American, and one French Canadian. Although I targeted people of color LGBT organizations, these did not yield any significant results. This was disappointing. I had hoped to be able to discuss differences in self-perception and attitudes associated with race and ethnicity; yet because my participants were mainly white, my narrative lacks the variations in child rearing, adolescence, and marriage that are created by ethnic difference. On the other hand, this largely white sample created a baseline homogeneity from which significant differences in social class, educational status, and personal attitudes came into sharper focus.

Participants lived in thirty-two states, the District of Columbia, and four countries outside the United States (Canada, Ireland, Australia, and England). More (47) lived in the Southeast than any other region, with the Pacific West (28) being the second most common region.

In terms of relationships, 60 participants were single, the largest category. Thirty-nine were married, 36 had partners, 13 dated, and 2 were separated. This category counting is complicated by the fact that many married or partnered individuals had relationships on the brink of dissolution. Many marriages of long duration were in turmoil as cross-dressers came out to their wives and transsexuals decided to live in their true gender full-time or have sex change surgery. Partners of the participants in my study were deciding whether the gender-nonconforming behaviors and traits of those they were dating or living with meshed with their views of gender, including their own gender identity. Participants who were single or about to be single hoped they would someday find someone accepting of who they were, so that they would no longer need to hide these significant aspects of themselves. However, experience showed that this would be a painful personal challenge, and would not be easy.

This was a highly educated group. Of the 150 participants, only 2 had less than a high school education, and 13 had a high school diploma or GED. Forty-eight had some college, 40 were college graduates, and 47 had advanced degrees. Eleven also claimed graduation from other certificate programs. In this sense, as with race/ethnicity, the participants were more homogeneous than the wider population, most likely because high education levels may increase the likelihood of responding to surveys. Individuals who have been to college are probably more comfortable with surveys than those who have not been to college and probably better understand how such studies might benefit them or promote social change. Hence, my recruitment method may have slanted the education profile of those who responded.

It is very telling that, in spite of the participants' high levels of education, approximately one-third had an income under $19,999 (twelve of whom had no earnings), compared to men's yearly full-time median earnings of $42,743 and women's yearly full-time median earnings of $32,903 in 2005 (De Navas-Walt, Proctor, and Smith 2007, p.6). This speaks to the challenge of being accepted by others in the workplace. Even with high levels of education, many found their jobs eliminated after their gender transition or met with difficulty in getting past the interview stage when trying to secure new employment. Furthermore, class variations among participants illuminated the especially difficult struggles of low-income transpeople in gaining access to medical care, hormones, therapists, and transportation to support groups or gender gatherings.

Occupations varied widely. Some participants held more than one job. Professional fields such as medicine, computers, and engineering were represented more than any other category (29). Twelve participants were artists, musicians, actors, composers, or in broadcasting; 7 identified as writers. Nineteen were in business/managerial careers. Fifteen worked in education, and 22 were students. Eight worked in social services, 3 in farming, 4 in security, and 17 held a variety of blue-collar jobs. Thirteen were semiretired or retired, 10 were unemployed (including 2 housewives), and 5 stated they were self-employed without mentioning what they did. Trans-identified individuals are found in every kind of occupation and setting, increasing the exposure of people who believe in the gender binary to individuals who live outside those norms. Unfortunately, resistance from employers and coworkers is one of the major types of discrimination that transpeople face.

The survey offered a series of gender identity labels for participants to select. However, checking one or many of these boxes created problems for some of the participants—not even this variety was sufficient to encompass all types of self-identification. Many people checked or listed more than one identity, so the numbers total more than 150. Adding to the complexity, labels were interpreted differently from person to person. For example, one participant checked off cross-dresser but wrote in, "more complex than that." The list below offers a superficial look at how participants identified themselves, but the richer truths of their identities must be gleaned from their interviews.

A final note on naming: Most studies use pseudonyms for participants, but many transpeople are already using second names—second names on the Internet, and/or legally changed names as part of their transition, or second names they go by without legal change. Transpeople are accustomed to many names, labels, and forms of self-identification. When I asked participants what name they wanted used in the book, only a minority chose a name that was not one they go by in some arena. It is also important to keep in mind that, since the interviews, any number of individuals in this study may be using a different name, a different pronoun, or be presenting as a gender other than the one presented when I first met them. This fact alone shows the fluidity of gender or, for some people, the length of time a gender transition can take.

GENDER SELF-IDENTIFICATIONS OF STUDY PARTICIPANTS

Male-to-female (MtF) transsexual (not all necessarily living as such full-time, and individuals at various stages of transition): 57
Female-to-male (FtM) transsexual (not all necessarily living as such full-time, and individuals at various stages of transition): 30
Male cross-dresser: 26
Female (including transsexuals and non-transsexuals): 21
Male (including transsexuals and non-transsexuals): 16
Transgender along with other identities: 9
Butch (including labels of butch lesbian, stone butch, dyke, soft butch, and masculine woman): 8
Intersex: 8
Genderqueer: 6
Transgender as the single identity: 4
Femme: 2

There was also one each in the following categories: woman-born transsexual, androgyne male, femme androgyne, ungendered, bigendered, metagendered, intergendered, tranny boy, human, genderqueer boy, transman, gender variant, trans male performing butch, trans, femme dyke or transdyke, and tranny fag, tranny, or trans.

In terms of sexual orientation, participants identified as follows (numbers add up to more than 150 because some checked more than one option): heterosexual (47), bisexual (37), lesbian (29), polyamorous (17), queer (13), gay male (8), none of these (6), not sure (5), pansexual (4), asexual (3), autogynephilic (1), tranny chaser (1), gay (1), and not active (1). These were not static identities, as some said their sexual orientation was fluid and likely to change and some transsexuals felt that they would identify differently after transition.

As you can see, despite the fact that most of the participants were white and well educated, my sample showed great diversity in terms of age, region of the country, social class and income, and gender identity. There were other types of diversity as well. I interviewed people with visual impairment, hearing loss, and learning disabilities. A few were wheelchair users or on crutches. Some participants were closeted; others served as public advocates for transpeople. A few examples of the latter: MSNBC interviewed Melissa, a male cross-dresser. A Discovery Channel special featured Angela's sex reassignment surgery. Male-to-female transsexual Tina consulted for the movie *Normal*. Robyn is active in the National Transgender Advocacy Coalition; Holly and Jill run a support group; and Lonny volunteers for the local LGBT paper.

In addition, and perhaps most important of all, there was passionate disagreement on the key issue of the gender binary. Most participants acknowledged that traditional views of gender are based on the two categories of man/woman. Many participants viewed the traditional binary as inhibiting, however, and identified with neither of the two. Like Julian, quoted at the beginning of this introduction, they sought to turn two genders into "an infinite number." At the same time, though, many participants actively sought to reaffirm the gender binary through hormone replacement therapy or surgery. Those who had chosen (or would eventually choose) to make a transition yearned to make their physical body conform to their strong feeling of being either male or female, man or woman.

My own bias in this book is to advocate for liberation from the binary gender system, which for many people artificially restricts the fullest expression of self. At the same time, though, I deeply respect people who wish to identify with "male" or "female," "man" or "woman," and are willing to undergo expensive and painful medical treatments to achieve physical correspondence with who they feel themselves to be *given the cur-*

rent gender system. In fact, I would argue that the entire process of a "sex change operation" itself questions and challenges the binary at its root by suggesting that what people feel their gender to be does not always match their genitals, reproductive organs, or hormones. The choices of those who undergo hormone therapy or sex reassignment surgery are as radical, given the strictures of the traditional binary, as the choice of those who accept the body in which they were born. Other trans-identified people, who are not transsexual and for whom transition is not an issue, present their gender as neither clearly man nor woman. They have my highest admiration for they stand as living proof that we do not have to choose between two categories. I envision a society in which their personal truths do not put them at risk for harm.

Terms and Concepts

What language can be used for those who are not-male and not-female? For over two hundred years, historians and anthropologists referred to alternatively gendered individuals as hermaphrodites and sodomites (both seen as negative), confusing gender roles and presentation with biological conditions or sexual behavior. Europeans used the terms berdache, homosexual, transvestite, and transsexual interchangeably to describe Native North Americans. They misunderstood the multiple gender system that existed in countless tribes, contributing not only to misinformation but also to an incorrect framing of gender in binary terms (Roscoe 1998).

Prior to the mid–twentieth century, cross-dressing and/or cross-living came under the category of "inversion," associated with homosexuality. The writings of early researchers in the fields of sexology and gender issues employed this framework, which still exists in the public mind. Dr. David Cauldwell and Dr. Harry Benjamin first used the term transsexual, associated with sex change, in the late 1940s and early 1950s in their medical writings, a usage followed by the press coverage of Christine Jorgensen's sex change surgery in 1952 (Meyerowitz 2002). Commenting on the legacy of scientific discourse on gender variance, Nakamura states:

> There is no such thing as a complete break, a totally new and revolutionary articulation that will liberate us all from the shackles of sex/gender. Even as transsexuality challenges the biological basis of gender, it comes out of the discourse created by sexologists surrounding sex. We may realize the nature of the machine that inscribes on us who we are, but we cannot escape it.
> (1997, p. 84)

As Roughgarden has pointed out (2004), entire academic disciplines frame gender variance in the limited framework created by scientific language. The diversity found in nature has been suppressed through the labeling of difference as negative rather than natural. Same-sex mating behaviors in birds and other animals are framed as deviant or anomalous, rather than as functional, natural, and widespread. Gender-changing animals, fish, and birds are marginalized in the literature rather than incorporated into a fluid gender schema. Biologists still disagree as to whether gender or sexual diversity within a species is inherently good or reflects "impurities."

As for gender-variant people, no conceptual framework fits their experience, and no individual words adequately describe it. Reid (FtM), in his frustration when trying to communicate his identity, stated: "I now say that, rather than transitioning female to male, I've transitioned female to not-female. English is inadequate to the task!" The lack of an adequate conceptual framework also gives rise to specific (and painful) phenomena, such as the feeling that one is "trapped in the wrong body" (Cromwell 1999, p. 105). Glen, who identifies as human, told me:

I thought for forty years that I was the proverbial "a female/woman trapped in a male/man's body." What I eventually realized is that I was a human being trapped in a society that wanted me (and still does) to live a life of limitations as EITHER *"a man" or "a woman" but* NEVER *as a complete, unique and total human being.*

Furthermore, the "wrong body" concept opens up the question of what is the "right body"? Is it the surgically constructed body? The body in which the individual is born, socialized as a man or a woman? Which body carries the truth (Garber 1997)?

Transpeople have created from scratch words, phrases, and concepts that resonate with their experience. These include such terms as gender variant, gender gifted, and gender nonconforming. Sex reassignment surgery may be referred to as gender confirmation (a term first used by surgeon Milton T. Edgerton—see Edgerton 1984) or even corrective surgery (if biological difference is viewed as a birth defect). Female-to-male transsexuals may refer to their breasts as their chest or pecs—before or after surgery. What is commonly called a double mastectomy may be called, for an FtM, chest reconstruction.

Writing this book, I was immediately constrained by the limitations of the English language, which does not capture the wide diversity of sex and gender characteristics of the people I interviewed. Although languages change over time, people tend to use language in an unproblematic way, as if the terms "woman" and "man" had unified and agreed-upon meanings. A strange, unwritten consensus about such words reinforces the binary and renders invisible possible nuances that might open these terms to wider definition. These shortcomings—both in the words that exist and in how we interpret them—are widespread and present profound challenges to transgender individuals. As Dan (FtM) stated:

How do you make things thinkable when you don't have the words for them? . . . Language is not just a reflection of reality, and gendered language is not just a reflection of gendered reality but it is productive of it. You need linguistic tools to be able to think.

And Helen (androgyne-leaning femme) raised an excellent point:

To put it another way: not only is there no "standard," generally accepted model for fitting anywhere outside the usual gender binary but there is ALSO *no generally accepted model for the process of questioning that binary, or for the process of formulating one's own "labels" or identity outside of that binary. . . . What are some possible alternatives to the usual labels, even if the "usual labels" are themselves drawn from some of the various transgender communities already accustomed to challenging binary concepts of gender? If none of the labels we hear "feel" right to us, how do we go about creating a new label that does? How do we know whether we've "found" the right identity/label for ourselves because it really* IS *the right one, or whether we've "found" the right one mostly through default?*

On another note, I also will not be referring to the "opposite" sex, as I do not want to reinforce binary thinking. We need to be mindful and offer alternative expressions leading to the vision of a more fluid gender conceptualization.

Below I define some basic terminology fundamental to the discussion of gender identity. As Helen says, even these generally acknowledged terms are fuzzy in the sense that their meanings are unstable; people use them with reluctance or to mean different things. It is difficult to use words when I know the words themselves are problematic, but we must start somewhere.

Terminology

The term *transgender* is most commonly used as an umbrella term for gender-variant individuals. *Gender variance* refers to individuals whose gender

BEVERLY

expression and behavior do not match the expectations associated with the gender binary. The term transgender is widely used on websites, in support groups, in self-identity labels, in political writings, and in general conversations about the "LGBT community" where "T" stands for "transgender." As an umbrella term it includes transsexuals, male cross-dressers, masculine women, androgynous people, intersex individuals, bigendered, ungendered, and genderqueer people. Boswell states, "the word 'transgender' describes much more than crossing between the poles of masculinity and femininity. It more aptly refers to the transgressing of gender norms, or being freely gendered, or transcending gender altogether in order to become more fully human" (in Bullough et al. 1997, p. 54). Beverly (MtF) echoed, "I use the term just for anybody who feels somewhat—something of the other gender inside of them whether or not they ever act upon it."

However, despite its wide usage, many find the term unhelpful, in part because it covers too much territory. Namaste writes:

> One of the potential strengths of the term "transgender" is its ability to include a wide variety of individuals who live outside normative sex/gender relations. At the same time, such a catchall category fails to recognize the differences between transsexuals, cross-dressers, drag queens, FTM transsexuals, and gender atypical lesbians. While the term "transgender" has entered into public discourse within certain Anglo-American academic and activist contexts, its use is challenged by transsexuals. What does it mean to

group the very different identities of FTM transsexuals and heterosexual male cross-dressers? How does this term function to define a specifically *transgendered* social movement? What kinds of issues are overlooked within such a perspective? What important differences within this category are being excluded? Are some bodies rendered invisible within this debate? (2000, pp. 60–61)

The people in my study had mixed feelings about the term. Kand preferred transgendered to describe her identity as a masculine female, while Gwyneth, a male-to-female transsexual, said that the term "is misapplied as a catch-all" and that it "arbitrarily and perhaps unfairly groups together unrelated phenomena and behaviors." Stephe, an androgyne male, preferred "to stay away from the term . . . which has been co-opted by so many groups it's almost useless."

A *transsexual* is an individual who feels that his/her gender identity does not align with his/her physical body, as traditionally defined. This individual will usually take steps to alter his/her gender role, gender expression, and body to feel greater psychological harmony—measures that are perceived as contrary to one's gender assignment and physical body at birth. This process, known as *transition*, involves many options and choices. A person may or may not take all the steps (hormones, different types of surgery, electrolysis, among others) associated with *sex reassignment surgery* (SRS). SRS is also known as genital reassignment surgery (GRS) or gender confirmation surgery (terms used for "lower" or "bottom" surgery) or as double mastectomy, breast augmentation, or chest reconstruction (for "top" surgery). The medical, psychological, and legal changes required for transition are expensive and time-consuming. Shorthand references of pre-op (pre-operative), post-op (post-operative), and non-op (non-operative, one who rejects surgery) are widely used in the transsexual communities to refer to where someone is in the transition process.

A *transgenderist* is a non-operative transsexual. Virginia Prince coined the term in the late 1980s to describe individuals like her—male-bodied individuals who live full-time as female without undergoing any surgery. Transgenderists are non-ops, not pre-ops, because they do not intend to have any genital surgery, though they might take hormones, undergo electrolysis, or have cosmetic surgery.

Cross-dressers are individuals who dress in clothing of another sex for fun, self-expression, erotic stimulation, or some combination of reasons. Generally the term refers to men who wear feminine clothing; women who wear men's clothing are rarely labeled cross-dressers. (Women in "men's clothes" such as pants and suits have become socially acceptable and generally don't cause much stir. But men in women's clothes present a greater challenge to male authority and are subject to ridicule or worse.) Cross-dressing is not connected to sexual orientation; most male cross-dressers are heterosexual and are expressing their femininity.

The terms *drag king* and *drag queen*, commonly used in LGBT communities, refer to people who cross-dress for entertainment and performance. The term *transvestite*, which is outdated (and pejorative), has been replaced by cross-dresser, except in medical texts. Prince created the term *femmiphile* to describe the cross-dresser's love for the feminine and to give "three-dimensional, real-time 'life' to his own inner 'girl within'" (1976, p. 3). Because cross-dressing and drag involve men in women's clothing, they constitute visible "in your face" challenges to traditional gender norms. Dressing up is risky business. And for most cross-crossers, it is not just a matter of putting on "female" clothing (Feinberg 1996). Cross-dressing is part of one's core identity.

Gibson and Meem (2002, p. 3) trace the term *butch* to the 1890s, when it referred to a female butcher, a traditionally male occupation. Lesbians (women sexually attracted to other women) were first referred to as "mannish inverts" who dressed and acted in ways considered masculine. Sexologists, and lesbians themselves, were slow to define the *femme* as a lesbian, seeing her only as a woman who was not attractive to men and so turned to other women. In common usage, butches are masculine lesbians and femmes are feminine lesbians.

Butch/femme identities are best known in terms of the 1940s and 1950s lesbian subculture. Butch and femme lesbians often see themselves as unique—that is, distinct from male or female genders. Butches were more confrontational vis-à-vis the gender norm and for that reason threatened the invisibility of femme lesbians, who could pass in society. On the other hand, butches also defended femmes and all lesbians from harassment.

The feminist movement of the 1970s was ambivalent about butch-femme presentations and criticized them for imitating male-female gender roles. Butches and femmes were viewed as standing in the way of women's liberation, which emphasized the goal of women freeing themselves from male dominance. As a result, the androgynous look of lesbians gained in popularity (Halberstam 1998), and butch/femme relationship roles went underground. But in the 1980s, with increased tolerance around sexual behaviors and expression, the butch/femme subculture reemerged. By the mid-1990s, opportunities for transition existed for butches who identified as men. Thus there arose a different kind of split in the lesbian community—between female-bodied masculine butches and female-to-male transsexuals. Today we add queer-identified females to the possibilities of gender identification among those who spend part or all of their lives within the lesbian communities.

Lesbian communities display a wide range of attitudes toward butches who transition to a male identity (FtM or transman). As Cromwell writes, "From some FTM/transmen's perspectives, butches are transsexuals in denial; from some butches' perspectives, FTM/transmen are misguided lesbians. It is not always possible to make clear distinctions" (1999, p. 28). Femmes may worry that transition steals the butches out of their community, while butches may worry that femmes will be attracted to FtMs. Insecurity on both individual and community level is the result (Green 2004).

KT (butch lesbian and transgender) wrote:

Since I've taken on my identity as butch the biggest challenge has been and still is simply getting people to understand what it means that my gender identity is butch, not female (or male). Even other gays and lesbians, who have had to prove themselves to society as outside the norm in sexual orientation, are not always very accepting or understanding to variations on gender. Like heterosexuality, the gender dichotomy is rigidly reinforced, and people are reluctant to challenge it. So my biggest challenge is getting them to look at gender as more than two categories. Sometimes I am successful and often I am not.

Johnny, who identified as FtM in a butch/femme lesbian relationship at our first contact, wrote:

I am looking for a support group now. Or even for just someone who "packs" regular. Or even feels like me. I didn't know there were people who felt like I do until I started surfing the internet. Started with gay sites. Then butch sites. Then stone-butch sites and found out that lots of butches "pack." I was beginning to think I had some mental problem or sick fantasy. And then I found the trans sites. I knew men had the sex reversal surgery. Didn't know women could.

Johnny has since transitioned, and his relationship mutually came to an end since his partner wanted to be in a lesbian relationship.

Although butch identity is not necessarily an early stage of transsexual identification (Halberstam 1998), most of the FtMs in this study identified as lesbians or butch lesbians before deciding to transition. This is primarily because, before transition, the lesbian community is the most comfortable fit—it allows a greater range of masculine expression for a female-bodied person. However, this works only up to a point. According to the FtMs and butch women I spoke with, the basic difference between

KT

the two is that while they share a sense of masculinity, FtMs are not content to be in a female body or to be perceived as female.

Intersex people are individuals born with physical variations—such as a micropenis or an enlarged clitoris, both types of gonads, or internal reproductive organs that do not match external organs—and/or a variety of chromosomal combinations other than XX or XY. At birth the genitals may be ambiguous; at puberty the child may not go through anticipated physical changes. There are scores of medically defined intersex conditions. Some intersex people feel that intersexuality has no connection to gender, while some transsexuals feel that being transsexual is a form of intersex. This is a highly contested area within the transgender community. Because their conditions are seen as medical abnormalities, many intersex people have access to medical intervention that transsexuals do not have, but intersex people often have surgical procedures at birth or in adolescence without their consent.

Several of the participants in my study identified as queer or genderqueer. For example, "I'm not a big fan of 'androgynous' because the palette of gender expression is much wider and wilder than that scholarly word would indicate. I like genderqueer and gender outlaw and genderfuck much more. There's an edginess to those that is very appropriate" (Kosse, FtM). Gunner (genderqueer boy) stated, "Genderqueer works better because it describes my gender, not as traditional or straight, more fluid, and my sexual orientation [as] 'not straight.'"

Generally the term *genderqueer* (or *queer*) refers to people who feel that their gender identity and/or sexual orientation are outside the binary. In the mainstream, the term queer refers to a status or a person who is shamed and isolated. When LGBT-identified people reclaimed the word queer, resulting in Q sometimes being added to LGBT (for LGBTQ), the idea was to reclaim difference as positive. Clare makes this observation:

> *Queer* has accomplished a number of things for the l/g/b/t individuals and communities who have embraced it. The word names a reality. Yes, we are different; we are outsiders; we do not fit the dominant culture's definition of normal. *Queer* celebrates that differentness rather than hiding or denying it. By making *queer* our own, it becomes less of a bludgeon. We take a weapon away from the homophobes. (1999, pp. 96–97, emphasis in the original)

Queer is used to capture the notions of transgressive sex and gender, and the fluidity of sex and gender, in a way no other word does. Genderqueer allows a person to identify with multiple communities at once. Dylan (FtM) used the term queer to name his attraction "to butch women, trans men, anything in that spectrum." As Nicholas (FtM) said, "For me, dating a butch dyke makes me a homosexual, dating an FtM makes me a homosexual, because I'm riding that line, I'm really between those two communities, somewhere between passing butch and FtM, and it's all queer. It's all really queer."

Other terms similar to queer include gender bender and gender fuck. *Gender bender* refers to individuals who challenge gender notions through their gender expression and appearance, usually done quite deliberately and sometimes as farce or play. This behavior is also known as *gender fuck*.

The term *androgyny* has multiple meanings. To some it means qualities of both male and female within one person; to others it means that the person's gender is ambiguous or unclear. Laura (MtF) said: "Androgynous is a term others have used to describe me. Others have used that term because they cannot tell my sex by looking at me." Cris (male cross-dresser) added, "The term androgynous, to me, means a person who presents themselves in a physical way so that their sex cannot be determined by physical appearance and that appearance could be defined as either male or female." Gelsey (male cross-dresser) echoed, "An androgynous presentation leaves everyone totally confused." And Karen (MtF) pointed out another issue: "The androgyne gets the worst of both worlds, being subject to suspicion and contempt, not accepted by either men nor women, a target for derision or pity, at best on the fringes of society but never part of anything."

Julian, an ungendered individual, explained that he disliked the term because it reinforces binary thinking:

Androgynous as a word does not work especially well for me as it is comprised of the roots for man and woman, and so the term, to me, perpetuates the binary. Like the term blue-green doesn't really escape the notions of blue and green. That's just how it feels to me, and I can well imagine it working just fine for someone else. I have made comments though, like "I'm attracted to androgynous guys." So it's not so problematic to me that I won't use it on occasion. But even when I do, I find my meaning of it is not necessarily communicated to the person I'm talking to. For example, they might respond, "Do you mean she-males?" and that's not at all what I mean. I mean someone like David Cassidy in the Partridge Family.

Phillip preferred the term "metagendered" to androgyny because "it goes beyond the idea of either combining genders or crossing/changing between two options; it opens a whole world of third, fourth, and one-hundred-eighty-sixth options, which I like better!"

Nonetheless, many of the people I interviewed identified as androgynous. Jon, an intersex person, felt that as a genetic 47XXY he was "definitely a combination of two sexes." Babz, an androgynous butch female, thought of herself as "both m/f and neither. I am me, who happens to have a female body." Dawn (hermaphrodite) wrote: "I really consider myself androgynous. I don't try to be male or female; I just go with what I feel."

Some Native Americans use the term *two-spirit* to replace berdache, a label dating from colonialism, and found in the writings of explorers, early missionaries, and anthropologists, who used it to refer to Native people living outside the gender binary. According to Roscoe (1998), the expression two-spirit came into use in 1990 during a sun dance gathering in Winnipeg, Canada. Although Native American FtM Gary Bowen does not himself use the term, he wrote:

In my understanding of Spirit, Spirit is not divided in itself, but is an integrated whole. It is not a thing in balance, as implied by dichotomies of male/female, gay/straight, and black/white so prevalent in the white way of thinking; but a complete and complex thing which includes an entire rainbow of possibilities—not just the opposite ends of a spectrum. That is why there are seven cardinal directions: east, west, north, south, up, down, and center, as the Native viewpoint embraces dimensions not normally noticed by the dominant culture; so too does Spirit embrace dimensions of humanity not normally accepted by the dominant culture. (Quoted in Feinberg 1998, p. 65)

Two-spirit people live as individuals whose gender presentation and gender roles do not match their physical body. Roscoe documented third genders (male two-spirits) in 157 North American tribes and fourth genders (female two-spirits) in about one-third of those tribes. He recorded a wide range of regional and tribal gender variations and degrees of acceptance by other tribal members based on records dating back to the early 1600s. Two-spirits were quite variable. Some cross-dressed, others did not; some did the work of both males and females, others of only one gender.

In tribal cultures prior to the European invasion, two-spirit people held high-status positions such as warriors or shamans. They often married (or partnered with) individuals of the same biological sex but were not considered homosexual. It was an honor to partner with a two-spirit person. However, Europeans forced two-spirit people to wear the clothes and hairstyle "appropriate" to their biological sex. They jailed many and killed others. Government officials, missionaries, teachers, and Indian agents hounded two-spirits underground, and third- and fourth-gender people virtually disappeared. Although two-spirit is an identity that is only slowly being reclaimed within contemporary Native American cultures, the existence of two-spirits in Native American history as honored tribe members demonstrates that gender variance can be successfully integrated into family, community, and culture.

Intergendered is a term gaining in usage. Unlike bigendered, which refers back to a twofold binary system, intergendered rejects any sort of gender system. According to Gabriel, who identifies as intergendered, the term signifies "that within-ness," a natural and internal gender that is not a socialized construct. Gabriel doesn't want to be a man or a woman but both man and woman; not he or she but "Gabriel."

The Social Construction of Biological Facts

I think that my transgenderism was caused by a prenatal misprogramming of my posterior hypothalamus, just as I know, medically, that my Intersex condition was caused by a congenital misprogramming of my anterior hypothalamus and adrenals. (Raven, transgendered FtM intersexual)

To the best of my knowledge I wasn't diagnosed as hermaphrodite at birth. The medical records I have been able to obtain only indicate unusual genitalia, but not the word hermaphrodite. I don't see any scarring on my body that would indicate infant surgery. Keep in mind I was born in '69 in a tiny rural town in the Deep South. When I was taken to the doctor at age 7 for precocious puberty is when doctors really noticed I was "different." My family didn't have money for doctor visits, plus my mom being mostly raised by her Native American grandmother didn't believe in "white medicine." So for those reasons I think I escaped the doctor's scalpel. After the doctors paraded me around to their other doctor friends and nurses as a circus freak, I begged mom not to take me to the [doctors] again and she never did. (Dawn, hermaphrodite)

The physical differences between the sexes are in themselves of little relevance to the human capacities required in most of life's undertakings—except for reproduction. In the face of the fact that some infants are born with some combination of "male" and "female" reproductive and sexual characteristics—"incontrovertible evidence"—doctors still cling to the idea that there are only two "natural" options (Kessler 1990, p. 4). This makes the questions asked by Erving Goffman (1977, p. 319) all the more compelling: "How in modern society do such irrelevant biological differences between the sexes come to seem of vast social importance? How without biological warrant, are these biological differences elaborated socially?"

When I use the term *sex* or *biological sex*, I am referring to an individual's chromosomal makeup, external genitalia, internal reproductive organs, hormone levels, and gonads (ovaries and testes). As we shall see, even biological sex manifests differently from person to person. Doctors observe these differences, and many step in to decide, for example, what is an acceptable size for a penis or clitoris. As intersex individuals have learned, doctors may surgically transform an appendage labeled a "micropenis" into a vagina; they may reduce the size of an "enlarged clitoris." What biological "fact" made the penis too small or the clitoris too large? None. Instead, doctors and other medical/scientific personnel have interpreted a set of biological traits to fit their notion of a binary gendered reality: penises should be large, and clitorises should be small. But as we shall see, biology itself defies the binary.

The presumption that two genders correspond to two sexes is shown to be false when we realize that there are more than two sexes and, therefore, more than two genders. According to Roughgarden (2004, p. 27) bodies are sexed according to only one biological fact: the size of the gametes (sperm and eggs) of the species. Sperm are small and eggs are large. Period. This gamete binary (small and large) does not correspond to anything else in the body such as body type, behavior, or life history; it is a minor "sex marker" in a much wider constellation of biological sex traits. In the course of extensive research, Roughgarden has found that most kinds of plants, and half the species in the animal kingdom, consist of individuals that can be male and female at the same time or at different times in their life span. Goby fish, for example, crisscross their sex for the purpose of reproduction.

Variations in mammals can involve the presence of gonads (ovaries and testes) and/or the making of gametes (sperm and eggs). These variations are intersex combinations. For example, 10 to 20 percent of female grizzly bears, brown bears, American black bears, and polar bears mate and give birth through the tip of a clitoris rather than having a separate uterus. All female spotted hyenas of Tanzania have a clitoris that resembles and functions like a penis, and fused labia that form a scrotum. This spotted hyena gives birth through the penile canal. In Europe, male old world moles have testes, but females have both ovarian and testicular tissue. Among marine mammals, some striped dolphins have external female genitals with testes and internal male plumbing. Some bowhead whales have both

external female parts and internal male parts, including male chromosomes (Roughgarden 2004, pp. 34–42).

Turning to humans, Roughgarden observes:

> Apart from gamete size and associated plumbing, nearly every male trait is
> naturally possessed by some female, and nearly every female trait is natu-
> rally possessed by some male. Claims of a gender binary in humans based
> on small statistical differences against a background of great overlap
> amount to social myths. (2004, p. 325)

Influences of Hormones and Brain Development on Gender Identity

In the late nineteenth century, when scientists identified sex hormones, they shifted from defining gender according to physical features
(genitals, reproductive organs, gonads) and chromosomes, focusing instead on hormones as the origin of sexual development. They labeled
these hormones male or female (Meyerowitz 2002).

During the sixteenth week of gestation, the human fetus reaches a sexual crossroad. At that time the presence, absence, or quantity of hormones—or interfering drugs or chemicals ingested by the pregnant
mother—can all influence the fetal hypothalamus, the part of the brain
that governs gender identity. If a hormonal imbalance prevails, gender
identity may not develop in sync with genital development (Brown and
Rounsley 1996). Because it is chemicals that influence brain cells to take
on a male or female neural network at this stage of fetal development
(Devor 1989), a change of gender identification after birth is unlikely.

These "brain characteristics" eventually manifest as behavioral traits
we label masculine and feminine. They also show up in how males and females differently process visual and spatial information, mathematical
reasoning and verbal skills (Moir and Jessel 1991; Walworth 1999). Moir
and Jessel argue that hormones influence the brain and body far more
than chromosomes. Brains influenced by testosterone are somewhat
larger and have denser concentrations of neurons in some areas. Males
have more gray matter in the brain's parietal and cerebral cortices, which
handle computation, while females have more white matter, which spe-
cializes in connecting brain cells with each other (Crenson 2005, p. A7).

Aside from the question of which has the greater influence, it is clear
that both chromosomes and hormones influence parts of the brain, the
central nervous system, and reproductive organs. The hypothalamus, as

the endocrine center of the brain, regulates the cyclical release of hormones later in life, thereby affecting secondary sex characteristics such as body hair and breast development. A hormone spurt in the first few months after birth and then again at puberty suggests that the development of gender identity—primarily the result of prenatal hormone exposure—continues under the influence of the body's hormonal environment, in conjunction with the culture's gender socialization. But hormonal development is not straightforward or clear-cut. Devor discusses the complexity of hormones: "Chemical pathways in the body often convert one sex hormone to another before the hormone is actually used by the body. As well, all of the sex hormones are quite similar in chemical structure and can cause similar effects. The situation is further complicated by the fact that the action of sex hormones in combination can either be inhibitory or enhancing" (1989, p. 10).

Many of the participants in my study had absorbed a good deal of information about hormonal research, and some found it useful in coming to grips with their own situation. Karen (MtF) said:

I am sure that transsexualism has a biological basis, and there is some preliminary evidence suggesting this. Biology cannot be denied, and Mother Nature cannot be fooled. I can believe that I initially developed along the female line probably because testosterone was deficient in the first few weeks of embryonal life. Then testosterone appeared and I became a chimera.

The Influence of Chemicals on Gender Identity

Other chemicals that affect gender identity may enter the body from external sources. Synthetic estrogens, for example, can change the way the endocrine system functions by mimicking what hormones do and by blocking or triggering natural hormones. Natural estrogen and other hormones bind to receptor molecules in different cell tissues (brain, breast, prostate, etc.) in order to influence the body to develop in particular ways. Mimics also bind to receptor molecules and produce estrogen-like effects on the development of the brain, male and female organs, and breasts, causing a variety of disorders, which can include feminization of males, infertility, and early breast development (Endocrine Society 2002). The use of these endocrine-disrupting chemicals (EDCs) became widespread in agriculture during and after World War II to eradicate insects that affected crop yields (Johnson 2004).

In 1938, diethylstilbestrol (DES), a synthetic estrogen, was discovered to be even more effective than the female hormone estradiol for treating a multitude of female hormonal problems and prostate cancer in men. In the 1940s the Food and Drug Administration (FDA) approved this sex hormone for use in pregnant women to prevent miscarriages. DES did not, in fact, prevent miscarriages; by 1952, studies were showing that it did no better than bed rest or sedation, and during the years it was used it may actually have increased the number of miscarriages and premature births. Yet three million to five million women in the United States used it between 1941 and 1971, when it was taken off the market. (It had been discovered that "DES daughters"—girls born to mothers who had taken DES—were at high risk for clear cell adenocarcinoma, a rare vaginal cancer.)

In the 1980s and 1990s, studies of "DES sons" disclosed increased risks of testicular cancer, a variety of structural abnormalities of the reproductive system, benign cysts, undescended testes, micropenis, and hypospadias (these last two are seen as intersex conditions). Because of the hormonal imbalances it creates, DES exposure may also affect psychosexual development, sexual orientation, and sexual differentiation in later years. Too much estrogen or not enough testosterone—conditions that exposure to DES can influence—cause de-masculinization in males (Johnson 2004; Kerlin and Beyer 2002).

Audrey, a transwoman, shared with me her suspicions of having been exposed to DES:

Although medical records from 60 years ago are no longer available, there is a good possibility that my mother was given DES while she was pregnant with me. The salient facts are as follows: The estrogenic properties of DES were first reported in 1935 six years before my birth. Mom had a history of stillbirths and miscarriages. She told me, before she passed away, that she was given medication to prevent a miscarriage while pregnant with me. Her father was a medical doctor who took an interest in her pregnancy. Mom probably received the most advanced medical treatment available for that era, which probably included being administered DES.

Another chemical that can affect hormonal development is the pesticide dichlorodiphenyltrichloroethane (DDT). Johnson (2004, p. 28) argues that widespread use of DDT opened the floodgates to "chemicals in general and pesticides in particular" from 1945 to the early 1970s. After much ecological damage was done, we learned how plants and animals absorb these chemicals from the environment, how they are stored in human body fat, and how they find their way into milk and food. But DDT had protected U.S. troops from diseases carried by insects, and this immediate, obvious advantage outweighed its long-term harm, which took longer to understand and document.

More recently, high levels of phthalates found in women at the end of their pregnancies have been linked to less "masculine" baby boys. (Phthalates are chemical compounds used in cosmetics, plastics, detergents, medicines, and hundreds of other products.) The boys had smaller penises and scrotums, a higher incidence of undescended testicles, and shorter distances between their anus and genitals than boys born to mothers with lower levels of phthalates (Arizona Daily Star 2005a).

Additional studies continue to suggest new pathways of chemical influence on physical sex, gender identity, and sexual orientation. In 2003, a Canadian study found that boys with an average of 2.5 older brothers are twice as likely to be gay as boys with no older brother, while a boy with four older brothers is three times as likely to be gay. Researchers believe that male fetuses trigger a response in the mother's immune system to an antigen that is found only in males, and that this immune response plays a role in the next male fetus's sexual orientation (Sydney Herald 2003). The greater the number of older brothers a boy has, the greater the amount of the antigen his mother's immune system encountered during his gestation.

A study published in 2004 found that mothers who take the thyroid pill Thyroxine and amphetamine-based diet pills are more likely to have lesbian children. Mothers of lesbians were at least five times more likely to have taken the thyroid medication and eight times more likely to have taken the diet pills than mothers without lesbian children (Matthews 2004). Taken together, these and other research studies suggest that many aspects of ordinary life, such as using cosmetics, having several children, or taking medication for a common illness such as thyroid disease, can affect sexual orientation or gender identity.

Correcting the "Mistakes" of Biology

Apparently, bodies must conform to societal ideas of what males and females should look like. If this were not so, infants would not be subjected to surgery for intersex conditions, currently performed in the United States on one (or, as high as two) in every two thousand (Fausto-Sterling 2000; Preves 2002). Doctors impose cultural decisions on these infants by assessing their genitals and surgically creating a gender for them. But doctors don't see it this way. They believe they are "uncovering" something that was always there (Kessler 2000, p. 23). In other words, the doctors feel they can find the true gender that is there but isn't readily apparent.

Intersex conditions include a wide variety of physical organs, chromosomal arrangements, hormonal blocks, or adrenal gland malfunctions. Typically, individuals are born with a pair of sex chromosomes: one X, the other X or Y. An XX pair of chromosomes promotes the development of female characteristics; an XY pair is associated with males. But this is not always the case. Those with Klinefelter syndrome possess more than one X along with the Y (XXY or XXXY), a combination that manifests in male genitals, small testes, some breast development, and sometimes infertility. People with androgen insensitivity syndrome (androgens are male-associated hormones) have XY chromosomes but are highly feminized. Because testosterone is blocked, their bodies do not fully masculinize; they usually have internal male organs but female secondary sex characteristics. Congenital adrenal hyperplasia creates XX children who undergo masculinization at birth or at puberty. This is the only life-threatening intersex condition, caused by a disruption of salt metabolism. In other cases, immature reproductive organs (as with Turner syndrome, in which female ovaries do not develop, and breasts, uteruses, and vaginas underdevelop) and other biological differences blur the imposed male/female distinctions.

To doctors, genitals that seem different from the male/female norms are "deformed"; to the individuals with these genitals, they are "intact." Doctors may perform surgery to "correct" such genitals; the human beings undergoing this surgery may feel that their genitals are being damaged or destroyed (Kessler 2000, p. 40). As Kessler points out, infant genitals are "corrected" not because they threaten the infants but because they threaten the infants' culture (2000, p. 32).

If an XY infant has a small penis, doctors can decide that this baby is not a "real" male. Chromosomes, in other words, can be less of a determinant of a baby's sex than the size of his penis. This baby may be subjected to surgery to construct a vagina and be given estrogens at puberty to produce a female child. Why? Because someday the child with the small penis would have been ridiculed in the locker room. Likewise, if an XX infant is born with an enlarged clitoris, this infant may be viewed as male regardless of chromosomes, and doctors may recommend removing female internal organs, implanting testicles, and giving lifelong hormones so that she will be seen as a male. The common factor in these situations is the penis: a certain kind of penis is valued, as defined by gender-based cultural notions of appearance and function. Doctors and worried parents thus collude to produce and reproduce cultural notions of how sex organs constitute gender. Instead, they themselves create gender artificially (Kessler 2000).

People who identify as trans and intersex are often engaged in a struggle: how they feel internally about their gender often conflicts with the cultural imperative of how they "should" look and act. Yet their difficulties go beyond this internal struggle. Secrecy about medical procedures they have undergone, or about other medical records; shame about being paraded in front of doctors; confusion over whether their body is normal or abnormal; and difficult developmental experiences in puberty, in establishing sexual relations, or in attempting pregnancy—all contribute to major challenges for respondents in this research.

Participants in this study discussed these problems. Many had tried, with difficulty, to reconstruct their medical history. Dana, for instance, identified as a male-to-female transsexual with an intersex history. Asked what had happened to her at birth, she responded:

Well, it's hard to know. I had a surgical scar and my father at one point mentioned that they thought something was wrong at birth. And it affected my circumcision. So, there are those hints. . . . So, yeah, I knew, I mean I had serious problems and I knew they had to do with my reproductive system. I started bleeding through my penis so hard, that was pretty freaky. I didn't think that happened to most kids my age in my class. So that was the beginning of when I really knew something was wrong. . . . I say I'm intersexed because I have a uterine remnant and I've menstruated already and I have a female gender identity, so that's mixed with my male genitalia and my XY chromosomes, which I assume I have, so that makes me intersexed.

Jon, a married, intersex male with Klinefelter syndrome, told me:

I am one of those people who wish I had been surgically altered at birth. I get so frustrated because my balls are so small and my penis is so small, you could call it a turtle because ofttimes it's inside and you don't see it. And it's so frustrating. I mean I could go for amputation there, and it wouldn't bother me at all. . . . We couldn't have kids, we couldn't figure out why. So I went for tests and the doctor said you have no sperm count. But he forgot to tell me that I had Klinefelter's. That was in '83. And in '99 I find out, getting a DNA test. . . . I had no sperm, it was definite Klinefelter syndrome, 47XXY. But I found the paperwork in a file from the adoption agency. And I dig it out and I go, oh, my gosh. Because it affected me so incredibly much, my physique and everything. I mean, everything.

Raven (transgendered FtM intersexual) was born with congenital adrenal hyperplasia. He grew up female-bodied and a tomboy. He described puberty as hitting him with a "double-barreled shotgun—literally. I grew breasts and hips and began to menstruate—irregularly and painfully, but it was happening. My skin broke out and my voice started to crack, just like the boys in my junior high school class. Stubble began to show up on my chin, and my sex drive caromed upwards like a speeding car." Raven's mother brought him to a doctor, who diagnosed a hormone imbalance and placed him on estrogen. Although the hormones stopped the development of masculine secondary sex characteristics, they made him "dangerously hypertensive and psychotically depressed." Raven took hormones for a dozen years and finally stopped. Later, he married, took hormones to get pregnant, and bore a daughter. Looking back, he said: "coming to terms with my true sex [male], a sex barely recognized by humanity outside of freak shows and medical oddities, took years of work and soul searching. I finally ran across the budding transgender community and breathed a sigh of relief. Here was a roomful of bi-gendered people all together!"

On May 27, 2004, the Human Rights Commission of the City and County of San Francisco held a historic public hearing on the medical "normalization" of intersex people. Framed from a human rights perspective, its comprehensive report (Arana 2005) urges an end to so-called "normalizing" surgeries on intersex individuals without their consent. The report specifically states that the social discomfort of others (parents, medical personnel) is not valid ethical grounds to perform such surgery. Testimony from intersex people, family members, doctors, and researchers affirmed that the public needs to be better informed on a range of issues—for example, intersex conditions are not rare, genital variability is not the same as abnormality, gender identity is not determined by genitals, and surgeries often create scarring, loss of genital sensitivity, the need for repeated surgeries, and severe life trauma. Testimony from intersex people emphasized that only they can determine their gender identity and that gender identity cannot be created through socialization or surgical intervention. Their testimony directly contradicts the long-held medical view that one can be made into a boy or a girl.

As the commission hearings demonstrated, most intersex people do prefer that their bodies remain intact until they decide if and when to have surgery. Dale Lynn, MtF and intersex, is one study participant who was given no choice: she had "corrective" surgery as an infant. Later, she had sex reassignment surgery as an adult. But even then, the second time around, her doctors viewed it as corrective surgery!

I wish they had left me alone [the first time, as an infant]. I wish they had left my decision to me. I didn't have a choice. Now I'm left with scar tissue. And there's nothing wrong with a large clitoris. I mean, it feels great. There's nothing wrong with a small phallus if it works for you. . . . Now I can tell you that I'm probably the exception to the rule. Normally once a child reaches the age of 18 it's no longer corrective surgery, it's gender change surgery. Well, my documentation specifically says correction surgery. . . . The thing that kicked it up was I went and got out of the military [as a male] and went in for a gynecological exam. My documents said one thing and my body was something else. They sent back the claim, the insurance denied, wrong gender. Wrong! Went to my GYN, got an affidavit, sent that along. But it shouldn't take that.

The Made-up Gender Binary

If gender is assigned according to one's sex, and there are only two sexes, there can also be only two genders. This is the logic underlying the bigendered view of humanity. However, Jeremy (FtM) reminds us: "Equating sex with gender expression is stifling and, ultimately, limits a lot of wonderfully masculine women and feminine men in their expression of their humanity. We've lost a lot in this world because of these largely arbitrary restrictions."

According to traditional thinking, the idea that there are only two genders, men and women, is natural. Furthermore, gender is assigned based on genitals and is seen as unchangeable. That notion, captured in the concept of essentialism, also posits that biological sex has only two categories: male or female. Therefore, sex and gender are the same thing. These are unquestionable ideas; everyone "knows" them to be true. Should there be some variation in one's genitals or gender presentation that defies classification into one of the two "natural" categories, this is viewed as unnatural, pathological, or a joke. Membership in a man/woman category is not a choice; it is a natural and automatic assignment (Garfinkel 1967). But the "natural" premises of the gender binary, are, in fact, not natural. They are imposed. To accept that they are imposed contributes to the crumbling of the gender binary system.

Wilchins (1997) refutes the notion that the binary is natural: "the more we look, the less natural sex looks. Everywhere we turn, every aspect of sex seems to be saturated with cultural needs and priorities" (p. 51). In fact, she continues, "Gender is not what culture creates out of my body's sex; rather, sex is what culture makes when it genders my body. The cultural system of gender looks at my body, [and] creates a narrative of binary difference" (p. 51).

The conceptual separation of gender (as socially constructed) from sex (as biologically given) seemed like an important feminist contribution in the 1970s, but it did not challenge the notion that bodies fall into a natural binary. One's biology, in other words, could still be viewed as fundamental, and this basic binary might still be used to determine one's natural or proper gender. Such biological determinism, according to Feinberg, "is a theoretical weapon used in a pseudo-scientific way to rationalize racism and sexism, the partitioning of the sexes, and behavior modification to make gender expression fit bodies" (1996, pp. 110–111). Issues involving the strictly binary view of the body were neglected until transgender and intersex individuals defied theoretical perspectives and challenged the supposed alignment of genitals, gender, and sex (Davidson 2002).

Nevertheless, socialized in American culture, most people today still do not question the gender binary. This includes some transpeople. As Caroline (male cross-dresser) said, "I see myself in binary terms. I like to be either a man and behave as such, or be a woman and behave as such." And Theresa (MtF) commented, "Yes, rightly or wrongly, I am very comfortable with [the gender binary]. I grew up in a culture built around the paradigm of diametrically opposed gender poles. Feminine and masculine were constructed to sort out the attributes associated with those poles."

But for others, the binary is limiting. BJ (male cross-dresser) wrote: "It's so silly, when you stop to think about it, the idea that being man or being woman is determined by your body at birth and that you'd better not cross the line. I believe that to be fully human is to possess the capacity to cross all manner of lines.

Several individuals talked about a need to understand the "gray" areas as opposed to assigning only two discrete categories. "The fallacy inherent in the bi-gender system is its failure to recognize that we represent a continuum with a nearly infinite number of shadings or gradations," commented Joy (MtF). And for Gabriel, who identifies as intergendered, the binary doesn't work at all. "As an intergendered person I reject this binary system and do not associate characteristics or traits with a particular 'gender.' The ways in which people identify or express themselves are neither 'feminine' nor 'masculine,' they just are!"

A few people I interviewed felt that binary thinking was something innate. For example, Patric (FtM) said, "I think people are naturally in a binary [frame of mind] and are more comfortable with that. I think that it's socially reinforced but I think it's natural, too. I think a lot of it is how you're wired, who you are."

Yet whether or not we have an innate tendency to think in binary terms, those terms often obscure the fullness of reality. In fact, there are no accurate, empirical tests that yield a completely distinct biological or gender binary (Rothblatt 1995). Instead, real variation exists in every measurable attribute used to assign the categories of "male" and "female" to bodies. Facial hair, voice pitch, hormone levels, chromosome makeup, internal reproductive organs, external genitalia, as well as people who are intersex all prove that "biology" is not a clear-cut basis for category and offers faulty criteria for determining a gender binary (Fausto-Sterling 2000). Pushing to the logical conclusion of so many visible aspects of gender diversity, Clare states:

> Many trans activists argue for an end, not to the genders of woman and man, but to the socially constructed binary. Within this context, to answer the homophobes becomes easy, those folks who want to dehumanize, erase, make invisible the lives of butch dykes and Nellie fags. We shrug. We laugh. We tell them: your definitions of woman and man suck. We tell them: your binary stinks. We say: here we are in all our glory—male, female, intersexed, trans, butch, Nellie, studly, femme, king, androgynous, queen, some of us carving out new ways of being women, others of us new ways of being men, and still others new ways of being something else entirely. (1999, p. 128)

The social construction of biological facts has significant implications when it comes to gender identity. Countless individuals have physical bodies that do not line up in standard ways with their social roles and identities. However, biological facts *are* normal by definition—they exist in nature. It is the social construction and interpretation of gender norms that create the view that trans-identified individuals and gay or lesbian people are abnormal and stigmatized. This same social construction constantly reinvents and reinforces the gender binary.

Acting "As If"

The Thomases' comment that I mentioned in the introduction—"If men [and women] define situations as real, they are real in their consequences" (1928, p. 572)—explains a lot. It explains how people come to believe certain ideas without those ideas being true, and why, having embraced a false belief, they act in a way not based on reasonable evidence. We can make something false seem true, and make it have real consequences, by acting *as if* it is true. We may do this to build our self-confidence or for other personal reasons. But to build an entire societal structure on a binary system for which there is no scientific evidence is a colossal fraud.

Symbolic interactionism, a perspective in sociology, emphasizes that definitions of reality are socially constructed through interaction. We assume the perspectives of our larger social world and don't respond directly to reality but to our interpretations of it. These unchallenged perspectives frame how we define situations, which lead first to responses (or actions), then to interpretations and judgments. The resulting interpretations might then alter our perceptions and lead us to new definitions of the situation, and to different actions, and so on. This process is highly interactive, unconscious, and ongoing. Symbolic interactionism highlights the nature of interaction between people as they interpret and reinterpret meaning. It is the symbolic meaning we create through interpretation that defines reality; our reality is symbolic, not "real."

In determining who someone is and how we should deal with that someone, we assign or attribute an identity to that person and then act according to the societal rules governing behavior toward that type of person. We label others based on how they dress, act, or look, or what they say. Gender is one cognitive scheme, shared by nearly everyone, that assists individuals in interpreting others and deciding how to act toward them. Such shared frameworks are learned quite early: "children learn that gender is a legitimate way to classify the contents of the world and that others will readily understand them if they communicate through such a framework" (Devor 1989, p. 46). Such ideas as the gender binary, and the maleness or femaleness of people, objects, emotions, and ideas, are presented as "fact." He is a boy, we say, or that is a girl's toy, and so on.

Once society establishes gender categories for people to be fit into, they are assigned to those categories based on characteristics that individuals who belong to each category are believed to have. The characteristics that determine the fit are not inherently gendered, yet once socially constructed they are indeed seen as "essential" gender traits. For example, individuals utilize bathrooms for biological functions common to all people. Facilities do not have to be segregated by gender. Goffman writes:

> The *functioning* of sex-differentiated organs is involved, but there is nothing in this functioning that biologically recommends segregation; that arrangement is a totally cultural matter. And what one has is a case of institutional reflexivity: toilet segregation is presented as a natural consequence of the difference between the sex-classes when in fact it is a means of honoring, if not producing, this difference. (1977, p. 316, emphasis in the original)

Gender socialization is a cycle. We are born into society, where we are exposed to systematic training via myths, stereotypes, and selective information. This information is taught and reinforced by family, friends, teachers, religious institutions, government, media, and advertising. We internalize these messages as truth, and without question. This results in our perceiving everyone we see through the gender system, which then prescribes how we think of them and ourselves, how we treat others, and how we present ourselves to others. Finally, we receive societal validation if we behave appropriately for our assigned gender and don't challenge gender notions. At any step along the process we may feel confused, angry, hurt, or afraid, but the cycle functions to convince us of its rightness. In order to interrupt the cycle we have to unlearn the truths, learn new attitudes and knowledge, and act differently. These are challenging steps to take, for this gender system tells us "what our bodies can mean, regulates those meanings, and punishes transgression" (Wilchins 1997, p. 145).

One of the more remarkable aspects of the binary gender system is its supposed basis in genitalia. Men are men because they have male genitals, and women are women because they have female genitals. However, most people do not actually see the genitals of others with whom they interact. This speaks to the importance of gender presentation and role (Devor 1989). And gender cues, of course, change over time. Garber (1997) reminds us that before World War I, boys wore pink—a strong color—and girls wore blue—a dainty color. The red necktie taken on by politicians and professionals in the 1990s was formerly, in the early 1900s, a symbol of homosexuality and signaled men about other men (pp. 1–2).

A certain presentation or behavior leads to an assumption of certain genitals. Because we have some control over some of these gender cues, we engage in impression management (Goffman 1959). We play a part and hope the observers see what we want them to see. However, stigma or degradation may result if what a person presents is discovered to be different from what others expect such a person to present. Stigma "constitutes a special discrepancy between virtual and actual social identity" (Goffman 1963, p. 3). A known stigma, such as an observable physical impairment, means that you are discredited; an unknown stigma, such as a hidden heroine addiction, means that you are discreditable. Gender is such an important signifier in how people behave toward each other that when a denouncer discredits someone, the denouncer identifies with the community as a whole: "The denunciation is not his or hers alone, but conforms to what all reasonable human beings believe" (Charon 1989, p. 146).

To explore the issue of how we assign gender, Kessler and McKenna (1978) showed ninety-six different combinations of stick drawings to five adult males and five adult females. They asked their participants to determine the gender of the stick figures, assess how confident they felt in assigning gender, and describe what it would take to change their original gender attribution. To differentiate the stick figures, Kessler and McKenna used different combinations of typical gendered characteristics such as long hair, short hair, wide hips, narrow hips, breasts, flat chest, body hair, penis, vagina, and "unisex" pants and shirt. Given the wide range of variation among stick figures, the researchers were interested in how gender was socially constructed into a dichotomy of man and woman.

Their research disclosed that people attributed maleness whenever there was *any* indication of it—one strong, visual male marker outweighed several signs of femaleness. Thirty-two of the figures had their genitalia covered by non-gender-specific pants. Ten of these had nothing but observable "male" characteristics (e.g., no breasts, body hair, and slim hips), ten had nothing but observable "female" characteristics (e.g., breasts, wide hips, long hair), and twelve had an equal number of such male and female traits; yet more than two-thirds of the study participants saw maleness. Among all figures without genital clues, 69 percent were seen as male. Not surprisingly, drawings with a penis were overwhelmingly seen as male (despite female cues such as breasts), but figures with vaginas did *not* have the same rate of signifying femaleness. Fewer than two-thirds of the study participants assigned femaleness in those cases. In one-third of the cases people disregarded the vagina when other male cues were present. The power of the penis to elicit a male attribution was a full 50 percent stronger than the presence of a vagina to cue female attribution (Kessler and McKenna 1978, pp. 146–153).

Lest this seem like only a game, consider now that actual people, rather than stick figures, are being sorted and judged in such gendered ways. Devor reminds us of the far-reaching consequences to transgender and intersex people of gender assignment:

[Their social and legal status] can be determined by virtue of legislation, by virtue of the opinions of medical practitioners, by virtue of legal opinions, or by fiat of government bureaucrats. And no matter what any authorities may say, there will always be those people who refuse to accept that a person may ever change their sex, no matter what they may go through. Thus, although sex is commonly understood to be a biological reality, it is, in many ways, very much the result of largely invisible social negotiations. We engage in social and legal wrangling to decide what actually counts to qualify one to be able to legitimately claim membership in a particular sex category. (2002, p. 7)

The Standards for Social Construction

There is the body one is born with, and then there is the socialization one is exposed to. Participants in this study, when talking about major influences on their own ideas and presentations of gender, mentioned most frequently the media, family, religion, and societal pressures to conform to gender roles. Others included school, peers, the medical community, the military, and threats of harm.

Media

The media both establish acceptable gender behaviors and exaggerate gender roles and manifestations. Individuals are exposed to thousands of media messages daily in every conceivable way—visual images, print, radio, music, advertising, logos, and so forth. Talk shows such as *Geraldo*, *Oprah*, and *Sally Jessy Raphael* have offered scores of episodes on crossdressers and transsexuals over the years. Movies such as *Tootsie*, *Victor/Victoria*, *Yentl*, *Torch Song Trilogy*, and *Transamerica* have portrayed gendercrossers in a variety of ways, sometimes with sympathy, sometimes not. Jennifer (MtF) says she was exposed to gender information "constantly, through TV, movies, and the news media including my first introduction to the word transvestite in the movie *Psycho*. . . . I videotaped "The Christine Jorgensen Story" on TV but it was on a late night show called *Weird*."

Tina (MtF) believes that the media carry out a policing role:

I can give you a list of images the media has had about who and what I am. From Geraldine on the Flip Wilson Show to Gilligan dressing as a woman on Gilligan's Island, the media has tended to show men in women's clothing as a "joke." No man could seriously want to dress that way, right? Why would you want to "give up" your masculinity (read that to be superiority)? . . . The interesting thing is that the media not only impacted me by showing how society viewed the hidden me . . . the true me . . . but it also made me determined to never, ever reveal myself to others. Do not, under any circumstances, open up. You'll be scorned and ridiculed, and possibly institutionalized.

TV shows usually reinforce appropriate gender behaviors, as Kand (transgendered) points out:

I never had a role model. I remember the old sit-com Petticoat Junction. One of the daughters (Betty Jo, I think) was a lot like me. She played sports, could beat up on the *guys, ran the train, wore blue jeans. As she got older, she married a crop duster. I remember he proposed to her while they were under the plane, on their backs working on the plane. The second she accepted his proposal, she became a regular girl; wore dresses, stayed home and kept house, had a baby. I was very young and it was quite disturbing. The message I got from that was that it really was not ok to be different.*

This shared experience of media exposure creates a fairly common or stereotypical mind-set of expectations, including idealized notions of masculinity and femininity. Such notions are accentuated by the fact that much airtime and print space is devoted to selling products connected to masculinity and femininity, distorting gender once again into a binary. To Alex, a female-to-male transsexual, the media are "the biggest part of the problem in educating the general public as to what gender is really about."

Religion

Religion is powerful because individuals are generally first exposed to it at young and impressionable ages and for long periods of time. Parents and others tell us that the messages of our religious institutions are correct and not to be questioned. Furthermore, because major religions teach some of the most traditional versions of gender expectations and sexuality, they have a greater conservative influence than other mechanisms of socialization. According to many religious views, the consequences of *not* conforming to the gender dichotomy are severe. As AJ, a female-to-male transsexual, wrote:

Preachers and religious people are always telling us that "God made man and God made woman. There are no other genders besides that. If you try to change what God made you then you're a freak and doomed to hell. God don't make mistakes. . . ." I've grown up with the religious message that you're either male or female, and you must dress and act that way. When I went to the Baptist Church with my family, the preacher would actually pick me out of the whole church and preach on how girls should dress like girls. Anytime he would mention homosexuality, he would put cross-dressers, transsexuals and child molesters in the same category . . . preaching that they all were not going to heaven.

Jennifer (MtF) recited her own struggles with her church: "I have been through repentance, laying on of hands, [and] demon exorcism attempts under the belief that either I was involved with some terrible, sinful perversion or demonically possessed or influenced." Gail, a male-to-female transsexual who grew up on an Indian reservation, was an active member of a spiritual community until its members rejected her: "My spiritual leaders and all that, they just denounced me. I mean, I not only lost my family, my job, but I lost my community, and I lost the tribe that I was in and the right to take part."

Medical Commentary

Several of the people I interviewed had negative experiences with narrow-minded medical professionals. For example, Jessylynn (MtF) wrote: "I first came out to my family doctor, requesting hormones. He smirked and told me that I should not want to take them; they would 'Mess me up,' he said." A similar experience was echoed by Johnny (FtM): "Had a male gynecologist once that I could not come out to, though I tried, and he insisted I needed birth control, etc., so I wouldn't get pregnant. Couldn't get a hysterectomy." Transwoman Jennifer was also denied a wished-for medical procedure: "Recently a male dentist [failed] to understand why I wanted straight teeth in my bottom jaw and a male optometrist had [difficulty in] understanding why I might want contacts and pink tint on the lenses of my glasses. I was told 'you don't want. . . .'" And Max, a transgender stone butch, comments, "I have felt very emasculated by various doctors and medical procedures." Beverly reminds us that transman Robert Eads "is dead because he was denied treatment for ovarian cancer by 26 doctors or medical offices. He died needlessly. I miss him." Robert's story is sensitively told in the movie *Southern Comfort*.

Perceptions of Others

People frequently misinterpret the gender identity of transpeople. I received countless comments from my interviewees on this subject. Their comments reveal how deeply ingrained ideas about appearance (especially about hair, breasts, and clothing) result in their being misread. Glen, who identifies as human, relates this story:

A few years ago, I was at a bank in what I will refer to as my "dressed" mode. Make-up, wig, dress, heels, etc. and I was waiting for my turn with the next available teller. When the previous lady left, I proceeded to the counter. Suddenly I got a tap on the shoulder and the lady who had been at the counter previously said, "Excuse me, ma'am, but I forgot one item of business with the teller. Do you mind?" I said, "No, please go ahead." When she finished, she turned and said, "thank you, ma'am." Then as she looked at me closely, she got a funny look on her face. I responded with, "I hope you don't mind me explaining this, but I'm not a madam." Immediate anger on her face and suddenly with her hand on her hips asked, "So my dear how long has it been

GLEN

since we've had our operation?" I responded as nicely as possible with, "Oh, I've never had any operations." "So you're a man?" My response, "No, I'm just a human being who does happen to be male." With that, she let out a "humph," turned and as she walked away, mumbled, "Disgusting, just disgusting." I must admit I just don't know how people can get so upset just because I'm wearing human clothing. But I see and experience it all the time.

The unpleasantness of having one's gender identity misinterpreted is magnified when the person is in transition. Dan, a female-to-male transgender person, had this experience:

Once I had to retrieve a wallet that I'd lost in a bus and I went to the bus station and the woman got on the phone and she said, "I've got a young man in front of me who's lost his wallet and his last name is———," and then there's this lull on the phone and then she looks up at me and she says, "You are a male aren't you?" And I felt like saying, Can I get back to you? Can I mail that answer to you? Because I don't have one for you right now for that kind of question. It was a very, very difficult moment actually, it was extremely humiliating. . . . I said, "No, I'm a female."

These comments from Jeremy, a transitioning FtM, show another aspect of the gendered self:

I have a disability, so I'm perceived as asexual and gendered only to the extent a prepubescent child is gendered. When I was trying to suppress my awareness of myself as a man, I became hyper-feminine and got a lot of approval, but in the way little girls, not grown women, do. As I came to accept my male self-identity, I started attending a support group for FtMs, presenting as a man, but this time I didn't exaggerate my gender presentation to the point of stereotype. I felt comfortable with that, but I became discouraged and left the group for three years when one member of the group told me that I wasn't masculine enough and would never really be a man. I went back to that group last year, presenting the same as before, and the members now aren't so narrow-minded.

Jeremy wasn't the only transperson I interviewed who faced criticism from others in his community. Simon, a FtM tranny boy, shares: "[I was seen as a] slut, or too female, at 12 years old; a tomboy at 8–12 years old; out as a dyke, then butch dyke 16–21 years old. Still [identify] as a woman with family, but too masculine for them. At [True Spirit, a masculine-focused conference, I'm asked] 'When are you starting testosterone?'"

Gender assignment is relative to the context. As Nicholas (FtM) observes:

If I'm a girl and knitting, all my maleness is negated by people around me. They "know" it's just a short step to me turning into Donna Reed. When I'm knitting and a boy, I am transgressive. My maleness cannot be denied, but my feminine nurturing side is seen (doesn't matter what I'm knitting) and affirmed. That offends biomen. I'm ruining their ambient testosterone levels, but I never cared for them anyway. The women see me, all of me, at once.

Ian (male cross-dresser) can relate to the dilemma of being seen/not seen by others, because "if people look at you and don't see what you think is you that's kind of a painful experience. It's a denial of yourself. It's sort of like if you were wearing a mask all of the time."

For Casey, a butch lesbian, no traditional gender-identity box ever seemed to fit, no matter what the context:

I have always been perceived as too male and not female enough. Even as a child, although social convention was that I wore a dress, I would frequently be asked if I was a boy or a girl. Once I reached puberty, I was told I was too old to dress/act like a boy and I should learn to be more feminine. Even now, if I were to dress 'feminine' I look like a dyke in drag.

For most trans individuals I spoke with, gender assignment was fraught with problems for part or most of their lives. But Keven, a two-spirit-identified person, tries to stay centered on the fluidity of gender. Keven said:

I am perceived as who I am. However, some people have to add labels that don't fit me for their own purpose like to feel superior when they call me "young lady" or "miss." I hate very much that there are not enough words to describe people in the middle like me. Language is a battle. I do not care if someone considers me masculine or feminine because that is a fluid state for me. But some people see me as my gender, which is not true. They often try to force down my throat that I am a woman, which I am not. It is their issue but it hurts me in that I feel saddened for them and for me in the process.

KEVEN

Confusion with Being Gay

The social construction of biological facts is complicated by a tendency throughout the culture to confuse gender identity with sexual orientation. Since transgender individuals are still so poorly understood, for many people it is a short step to lump them into a stigmatized category with those who are lesbian, gay, or bisexual. Our homophobic society debates whether homosexuality is natural or a choice, and similar arguments, based primarily on religious grounds, view transsexuality as unnatural. Transgender cj reflects: "If homophobia is a more broad fear of transgressing the 'rules' of gender, it can easily encompass both fear of gay people and transpeople for the same reason. And it does seem that more homophobic people see the two as being indistinguishable while more open-minded people grasp the difference easily enough."

Everyone, of course, has a gender identity, and everyone has a sexual orientation. Although there is no basis for assuming that being trans also means being gay, the supposed association (if not equivalence) is one of the most common thoughts expressed by family and friends when someone trans comes out to them: "Does that mean you're gay?" This brings homophobic complications to an issue not related to sexual orientation. The assumption that transpeople are gay is reinforced through the media, jokes, and verbal comments. The notion is so ingrained in the culture that trans people themselves have had to grapple with it. For example, Lydia, a male-to-female transsexual, remembers her confusion about sexual orientation:

And the only models that I was aware of where men wore feminine attire was in conjunction with being gay. I read an article in Playboy . . . I remember one picture in particular, a really cute trans girl in a bikini and the caption was "This gay deceiver." And one other thing I remember was another Playboy cartoon, and it was around Christmastime and they showed this guy getting into a dress, and of course it was "donning on our gay apparel." So, cross-dressing equaled gay in everything I'd seen. . . . There was no other explanation for it, that I was aware of.

There is a history that explains how transgender and homosexuality became conflated. Some of the earliest writings about homosexuals included transsexuals in their discussion. In the 1870s Karl Heinrich Ulrichs wrote about homosexuality as both a desire for same-sex relations *and* a desire to be a sex different from what one was born as. Magnus Hirschfeld continued this association when he wrote in 1910 about different categories of people he referred to as intermediaries. His four categories included hermaphrodites; people with aberrant secondary sex characteristics; sexually passive men and aggressive women, who were placed in the same category as homosexuals; and cross-dressers and people who wanted to become the opposite sex (Califia 1997, pp. 12–13). These categorizations conflated gender identity with sexual orientation. By the 1950s most of the media were managing to distinguish transsexuals from intersex people, but the link between homosexuals and transsexuals remains to this day.

The link may be socially constructed, but the consequences of its persistence are real. Parents who send their gender-variant children to psychologists or psychiatrists often do so because they fear that their children are gay or lesbian (Green 2004, p. 14), and surgery on intersex infants is motivated at times because of the fear that the infant will grow up to be gay (Feinberg 1998, p. 91). Furthermore, sex change surgery has erotic implications—was the man who wanted a sex change a feminine gay male (Meyerowitz 2002, p. 82)? The supposed link between trans and gay/lesbian also means that someone's struggle with gender is seen as a sign of that person's "aberrant sexuality" (Halberstam 1998, p. 119). One of the long-held stereotypes of lesbians is that these are women who want to be men, though of course lesbians who are happy to be women are not the same as female-bodied individuals—lesbian or heterosexual—who feel that they *are* men. The confusion between sexual orientation and gender identity has thus obscured the very different identity dynamics that exist among different trans-identified individuals.

Gender presentation serves as a major cue for gay men and lesbians. However, not all feminine men are gay, or masculine women lesbian. Such single-focus perceptions of gay or lesbian signaling also demonstrate how people confuse gender identity and sexual orientation (Namaste 2000, p. 141). Gay bashings, which involve an assumption that a person is gay, often based on his/her gender presentation, show how people are at risk—regardless of their actual sexual orientation—in a homophobic society. Looked at from another angle, while feminine males are often assumed to be gay, there are also macho gay males who may well be mistaken for heterosexuals.

Genderqueers share these problems of perception, as Matt (androgyne, genderqueer) illustrates: "I also tend to be read as a swishy gay male, as opposed to a bi androgyne, which is equally annoying [to being seen as male or female when he/she feels neither/both]. I wish people would stop jumping to conclusions!"

Prince writes that when boys begin to cross-dress, they wonder if they are gay (1976, pp. 18–19). They use women's clothing to masturbate, and they know that the public views men in women's clothing as gay. Yet the vast majority of male cross-dressers are heterosexual. In fact, Tri-Ess, the largest social and support group in the United States for male cross-dressers, does not allow gay men in the organization. But often it takes a long while for cross-dressers—and the people with whom they associate—to sort all this out. SherriLynn, a male cross-dresser, said:

I shaved my moustache off. Plucked my eyebrows. And got rid of my body hair, more or less. Of course I didn't do those things at the same time. Little by little I did all that. And the girls I worked with just thought I was gay. . . . It seemed funny though, when I told them I was a cross-dresser, they wanted to know if I was gay. And I told them, "No." And that seemed like a big relief, although they couldn't understand it either.

Leslie, also a male cross-dresser, recalls:

When I was growing up, I'm talking 10, 11, 12, 13, and I was dealing with this, I kept thinking well, the only label, the only thing I know of that covers people like me are what we called then queers, homosexuals. And I said, I must be one of those. But I just didn't feel comfortable with that. It didn't seem somehow to click. And then the Christine Jorgensen thing came out [1952, a pioneering MtF sex reassignment surgery that was highly publicized] and I read in Time magazine the word transvestite, which, in fact I even memorized it back at 11, one that has a morbid desire to dress in the clothing of the opposite sex. And I said, "Wow, that's me. I don't have to be queer, I can still be heterosexual," even though that word wasn't in my vocabulary back then.

Living with the Gender Binary

The gender binary can make life deeply oppressive for those who don't conform to traditional standards of male and female; it is a shackle that limits and inhibits individual expression. Binary systems are inherently oppressive: to survive, they must stigmatize those who do not "fit." Binaries are also dangerous: they make it much easier for societies to marginalize, condemn, exclude, and even murder those who challenge social norms. As Bornstein has commented, "Either/or is used as a control mechanism, as in 'Either you live up to our high standards here in the club, or your membership will be revoked'" (1994, p. 102). Binaries divide people from one another, and these divisions, justified in biological and medical discourses, come to be seen as natural. But traditional standards of male and female make no sense to people like Glen (human):

For forty-three years (from the age of five to forty-six) I did believe in this binary. Call it "female and male," "girl and boy," or "woman and man," I tried to live within the context of these concepts. I struggled miserably with them psychologically; functionally, I did rather well. I learned how to "be a role" within the concept of "masculinity." But I openly admit, I spent decades experiencing a deep and irresolvable pain inside of me. . . . Gender (seems to be) an attempt by the majority of human beings in a culture to rationalize differences between each of the sexes (including intersexed people) that simply do NOT exist.

Keven (two-spirit) reiterates Glen's view, claiming "I have not transgressed gender; it has transgressed me. There is no such thing as gender in the first place. We may have different genitalia but gender is a social construction meant to control society."

Binaries depend on hierarchical systems, which are built on the belief that those in power deserve their privileged positions. According to those in power, those with less power have some innate characteristic that keeps them from the top rungs of society. These hierarchical systems are kept in place by language, socialization, laws, the media, custom, religious justification, and theories that justify the pecking order as natural. They are complex, institutionalized, and often taken for granted—so much so that they are invisible as systems.

Leslie (male cross-dresser) reflects on the nature of power in one of his columns in the *Tennessee Vals Newsletter* from January 2001:

So as I grew up, I wondered why would experimenting out of one's gender box be so serious that there would be laws against it? One obvious direction to investigate was to see what other groups also enjoyed protection from unlicensed imitation or impersonation. There were laws against impersonating a military officer, a law enforcement officer, a fireman, and a member of the clergy. A bit of thought would find most of those reasonable. More thought and I concluded that aside from potential disruption of society there was the power element. If anyone could go about impersonating a what-ever, then the power base of the what-evers would be eroded. If a group is powerful enough, then it can protect its power by limiting who can impersonate it.

Martine Rothblatt (1995) calls this "power base of the what-evers" the "apartheid of sex"—the system that entrenches the birthright of males (based on genital assignment) as superior to that of females. Tomboys (girls "trying to be boys") are acceptable, but sissy boys (boys "trying to be girls") are not. Feminine males are traitors to male dominance, while non-stereotypical girls are allowed greater leeway. Whether a transsexual, a cross-dresser, or presenting as ungendered, androgynous, or intergendered, male-bodied individuals who do not follow the typical masculine mold are highly suspect—what kind of man are they? "Sissyphobia," labeled by Tim Berling, is "a fear and loathing of men who behave in a 'less manly than desired' or effeminate manner" (2001, pp. 3–4). A sissy is a male who has failed at masculinity.

It is acceptable for women to wear men's clothes, but not for men to wear women's clothes. "Having a woman in men's clothes doesn't attack [other men's] manliness, a guy wearing a dress does," according to Kara (male cross-dresser). KT (butch lesbian, transgender) commented, "If I am out in public in men's clothes (which is what I always wear) and a man is with me in women's clothes, he is far more likely to be stared at or harassed than I am." "Women aren't going to be assaulted for wearing jeans; men in casual skirts, however, risk getting attacked," according to Shannon (genderqueer). In this context, MtFs threaten male privilege; they are "a disgrace, both to themselves and other men. I think men also see it as threatening to their own sense of status and masculinity," writes Kerwin (FtM).

Further, in a binary system in which men are privileged and women are viewed as less than men, male characteristics are the ones to adopt. Dustin (FtM) told me, "Femininity is encoded as weak of body and mind. Feminine men aren't 'real' men. Masculine women and FtMs are more accepted 'cause, well duh, everybody wants to be a man 'cause it's so much better." According to Tristan (FtM), "Males are seen as lowering themselves in status when they exhibit characteristics considered feminine. Conversely, women are seen as attempting to improve their stature when they exhibit characteristics considered masculine." Sonia (transgendered MtF) wrote, "Even my older sister, who is highly supportive of me, commented when I first came out, 'Why would you want to become a second-class citizen?'"

Second-wave feminism has created opportunities for (and, to some degree, acceptance of) masculine women, transgenders with masculine identities, and FtMs. In addition, the movement of women into a wide range of male professions has reshaped the cultural milieu in positive ways for those who are not and do not present as traditional females. But so far, there has been no complementary social movement for male cross-dressers or MtFs. The threat to the gendered status quo prevents it.

Bornstein discusses how enforcement of the gender binary is linked to sexism and is the key to patriarchal power; maintaining the male/female class system of male dominance requires sexism, homophobia, and misogyny (1994, p. 115). As Dylan (FtM) said, "[I]t's really hard to have sexism if it's impossible to tell who's male and who's female." The mandatory pairing of men with women as the only truly acceptable coupling also benefits from the binary framing of two distinct sexes and genders (Wilchins 1997).

This system is constantly reinforced. Wilchins reminds us that the gender binary is "not something 'out there' but a product of the way we see" (2002, p. 43). We are encouraged in this thinking through exposure to men's and women's bathrooms, through birth certificates, passports, and driver's licenses that require M/F sex identification, through marriage laws, and more, in a "vast and visible top-down structure" (Wilchins 2002, p. 26). "Names, IDs, badges, photos—all supposedly serve to make sure there is no 'innocent error or ambiguity'" (Goffman 1963, p. 60). We are all trained from birth in gender rules designed to prohibit, through "innocent error or ambiguity," any and all mistakes.

Most people have a deeply ingrained understanding of the stereotyped meanings assigned to traditional masculinity and femininity. Females should be soft, sensitive, delicate, nurturing, patient, collaborative, passive, beautiful, graceful, caring, gentle, and empathetic. Men are aggressive, physical, hard, detached, strong, controlling, loud, rough, insensitive, self-interested, and goal-oriented. (Although nuances associated with culture, race, class, and ethnicity exist, they do not alter the basic gender polarities.)

While Dustin (FtM) claimed, "None of my friends fit this model. It doesn't make sense; gender normativity enforces sexism and other forms of oppression," many participants in this study had absorbed these stereotypes. And indeed, many had experienced exclusion or oppression. Before transition, Gail, a Native American MtF, was involved in ceremonies and the sun dance. But she didn't actually perform the sun dance, because men pierce, and she knew she couldn't dance because she "wasn't a man." Kara (male cross-dresser) was excluded from "traditional" male activities when he was perceived as not "all male." For example, his coworkers did not invite him to a Super Bowl party until after he married. Says Kara, "So it was sort of like, 'Oh, I guess he is a guy, see, ok, yeah, you can come out now.'"

Although some accepted the gender binary and some even liked its either/or standards (see Caroline's comments earlier in this chapter), many rejected its traditional stereotypes. T.I., a naturally bearded dyke, insisted that her having a beard does not make her any less of a woman:

I think the reason I had such a difficult time with [my brother's decision to transition, as a female-to-male transsexual] is that especially in my role publicly as a lesbian and as a feminist and also as a naturally bearded lesbian—fighting for and struggling for women's rights to be different, and to be in fact—my appearance is entirely natural. To some people my appearance is very masculine. I just don't go there. I don't give it to them. It's natural, it's how I look.

Shannon (genderqueer) supports T.I.: "I think that behavior is either masculine or feminine based upon the person who is behaving that way. If a male feels that wearing a skirt is masculine, that is fine by me. (And I do wish that we'd have more men who thought that way!)"

Virginia Prince criticizes the underlying binary thinking: "Women don't lose their femininity because they wear pants. And likewise men don't lose their basic masculinity just because they wear a skirt and heels. They have simply added a new dimension to their total personality" (in Bullough et al. 1997, p. 476). And Jamison Green questions the notion that socially constructed femininity and masculinity rest on biological sex: "Plenty of penis-less transmen manage to engage in sex with penis-equipped gay men or penis-focused straight women, and these non-trans partners are often surprised to realize that a penis is not what defines a man, that the lack of a penis does not mean a lack of masculinity, manliness, or male sexuality" (2004, p. 121).

What will it take to change our ideas of sex, gender, gender presentation, and masculinity and femininity? Our ideas and theories about gender do not fit neatly with the real-life experiences of real people. Take Simon's (tranny boy) experience at the Southern Girls Convention in North Carolina in 2002:

We had to have a trans/intersex/genderqueer caucus because everyone was freaking out. Because they were, "oh, my god, everyone keeps putting these pictures of vaginas on and keeps calling them women's bodies, and I'm freaking out." This intersex woman said "I don't ever want to come to a place like this again." Even though she did two workshops, she was like, "I don't have a vagina. I am a woman. How many times do I have to say this?"

If notions of masculinity and femininity weren't widespread and entrenched, the binary construction would not be so rigid and so rigidly enforced. If the ideas that power and privilege rest upon were undermined, more people would be able to successfully challenge the sex and gender status quo. Transitioning male-to-female or female-to-male would not be traumatic; rather, it would be a choice, one among many. Gender would not divide people; its diverse manifestations would embrace differences. As Shannon (genderqueer) so clearly puts the case:

True, there are slight genetic differences between people whom we consider to be women and those whom we consider to be men. But 99.9% of the DNA between those two sets of humans is exactly the same. Why do we obsess about that 0.1%? It's ridiculous. Plus, thinking that men and women are opposites of each other, in whatever binary way, completely obscures the existence of intersexuality and intersexed people. There are way more than two sexes and way more than two ways to be gendered. It's just too, too bad that we live in a society where we try to force people into boxes (often successfully) based upon what's between their legs.

2

Self-Definition: Birth through Adolescence

I knew I was different from other children because I was a boy who desired to be a girl, but a strong sense of fear compelled me at that early age to conceal my desire. Perhaps this concealment predisposed me to identify with comic-book super-heroes, many of whom have two completely different identities, one of which remains a well-kept secret, which is sometimes threatened by exposure. I even invented my own comic book hero named Vov, on whom I happily conferred a secret identity. From what I knew of anatomy at a young age, I made a link between the letter "v" in Vov's name, and my wish to change my body: turned upside-down, the letter "v" encoded this wish. (Andrea, MtF)

Growing up I preferred dolls to sports. As boys attacked me I developed friendships with girls. One night I had a dream where I looked in the bathroom mirror and a pretty girl looked back. I felt my hair, my skin. I was certain I had turned into a girl. I was happier than I had ever known. Then I awoke and saw it was a dream and wept bitterly. I began two things: a lifelong study of dreams and cross-dressing. In both cases I was desperate to bring back the girl in the mirror. (Lynnea, MtF)

The doctor exclaiming, "It's a girl!" or "It's a boy!" is a well-known and comfortable image. As infants are dressed in pinks and blues, gender is foisted upon the newborns as a fait accompli. This is more complicated in the case of intersex infants, but the goal is the same: to establish gender before the one source of confirmation is available—the gender identity proclaimed by the child.

The visible biological evidence of sex will be interpreted within the gender frameworks of the culture. Devor (1989) feels that schemas are a natural product of the way our minds work but that a gender schema in particular is learned. While there may be other ways to organize the social world, gender is what children are encouraged to learn. They come to see gender as connected to behaviors, use it to form expectations of others, and plan their own behavior accordingly. Devor writes:

> Most societies use sex and gender as a major cognitive schema for understanding the world around them. People, objects, and abstract ideas are commonly classified as inherently female or male. The attributes, qualities, or objects actually associated with each class vary widely from society to society, but most do use gender as a most basic groundwork. Gender, then, becomes a nearly universally accepted early cognitive tool used by most children to help them understand the world. This means that children learn that gender is a legitimate way to classify the contents of the world and that others will readily understand them if they communicate through such a framework. Children also learn from those around them what to allocate to the categories of male and female, what elements of all things are considered to fall under the influence of the feminine principle, and which are classified as within the masculine sphere. In North American society, the gender schema most widely in use is biologically deterministic. (1989, p. 46)

The point that Karen (MtF) makes reminds us how early this training begins:

Children are encouraged to categorize everything around them, well, the first thing they categorize is other people or themselves in terms of, you know, are you a boy or are you a girl? And they turn that question on themselves, too. Am I a girl or a boy? And they explore that in terms of well, that's what girls do therefore because I'm a boy I shouldn't do that.

Family Influences

Parents, siblings, and other relatives are major influences on ideas of gender because family roles are strongly gendered. Mothers tend to act out woman/mother/wife roles, and fathers carry out societally reinforced man/father/husband roles. Children observe and learn to model these binary roles. They learn what is expected and what is acceptable. Toys, clothes, and chores are part of the gender socialization that occurs in the family setting. Male dominance is passed along, often in subtle ways; fe-

KAREN

male subordination is similarly reinforced. The teachings of the family are supported by the gendered environment of the broader culture and become part of the status quo of a gender dichotomy.

For the child or teen who feels uncomfortable with this status quo, there are few options: go along with the expectations and keep true feelings inside; rebel and pay the consequences of conflict; or act "normally" but have a secret, other life. Another possibility, of course—quite important when it does happen—is that the gender dichotomy in any particular family may be less rigid and allow some freedom. Transgendered Kand relates:

My older sister told me she would help me look more appropriate during the seventh grade. . . . One morning before school she tried to talk me into wearing this really flowery, lacy dress and I just couldn't do it. When I refused she shouted that I was a girl and if I couldn't accept that I ought to just see a doctor. I knew at that point I could never be what I refer to as a "typical female." I was going to have to just do it my way and take whatever shit came my way because of it. My parents had a hard time with the way I looked, but at the same time, allowed me to explore traditionally male activities (for example, I worked as a mechanic in my father's appliance store while I was in high school).

Glen (who dislikes any labels but will go with human), by contrast, shares this experience:

When [I was] 5, 6 years old, my uncle used to say to me all the time, "I'm going to make a man out of you. I'm going to make a man out of you. I'm going to make a man out of you." And when my father wasn't around he was always there, always hammering this home. And finally I said to him, I was about 8 years old, I said, "I don't want to be a man!" And that's when I got beaten up. I got beaten up because I didn't want to be a man. To him this is exactly what you need to do. And what he's really saying, he's saying, "I am going to turn you into somebody who is going to be suppressed and oppressed and control your emotions, and shut down so that you look real cool with everybody, so you look like you are in total control." In other words, you're going to be a control freak to the point that you're going to oppress yourself.

And Karen, a transwoman, felt that she was never masculine enough for her parents:

As a child I was constantly berated for not doing what boys do. My choices became limited and my tyrannical mother even told me what I was feeling and what my tastes should be. At school I was disciplined for playing in the girls' side of the playground. Notes were sent home and I was strapped by the principal (a man). I was an embarrassment and a disappointment to my parents, and I heard all about it often. My mother even put her grievances in alphabetical order.

Jeff (FtM) was unusual in having the parental support and upbringing he needed to address (and ultimately embrace) the transgender self:

Probably my parents played the biggest role in my—not who I am because I don't have a choice necessarily in who I am—but in how I was emotionally ready to adapt to the world living as a man. I credit my parents with being able to lay the groundwork when I was young about being who I was and about accepting yourself and about diversity, about not playing, just be yourself.

Mothers could be a strong influence on female-oriented boys. Gail (MtF) shares:

My mom and I were really close. I mean, she taught me how to cook, my grandmas and my mom taught me how to wash clothes when I was about 10. And that's what girls usually do. So that was a big influence, even though they didn't know. My mom didn't know until later on when my dad came home and found me dressed.

School Days

According to Human Rights Watch (2001, p. 18, based on the 1990 census), there are more than two million school-age children in the United States who are gay or lesbian (no data exist on the number of trans youth). These children spend an inordinate amount of energy plotting how to get safely to and from school, how to avoid the hallways when other students are present so they can avoid slurs and shoves, how to cut gym class to escape being beaten up—in short, how to become invisible so they will not be verbally and physically attacked. Too often, students have little energy left to learn. In interviews, lesbian, gay, bisexual, and transgender youth explained how teachers and administrators turned their backs, refusing to take reports of harassment, refusing to condemn the harassment, and failing to hold accountable students who harass and abuse. Some school officials blame the students being abused of provoking the attacks because they "flaunt" their identity. Other school officials justify their inaction by arguing that students who "insist" on being gay must "get used to it." And finally, some school officials encourage or participate in the abuse by publicly taunting or condemning the students for not being "normal." For gay youth who survive by carefully concealing their sexual orientation or gender identity, they learn that they will be protected only if they deny who they are—a message that too often leads to self-hatred and a fractured sense of identity. (p. 3)

Teachers reinforce gender stereotypes, as this comment from Aristotle (male) demonstrates:

In elementary school, when gender roles were being reinforced, the teacher would say something like, "Girls like music and art, boys tend to prefer sports. Girls like cats, boys like dogs." Whenever it came to distinctions like that, I found myself at least half the time on the girls' side. This didn't bother me until puberty.

And K, a male cross-dresser, remembers:

Grade school had (has) no provisions for other than the gender binary. If you do not fit, you become outcast. There was also no person educated enough to assist children who "did not fit." My white suburban grade school teachers and counselors were all too straight to understand or be sensitive to people like me. I felt tolerated but not understood.

Fellow students often mirrored, and acted on, attitudes they had learned from adults. K experienced threats of harm from grade school classmates if he didn't act as other males did. JT (FtM) says, "Throughout childhood I was picked on because I was 'too much like a boy.' I was socially isolated in junior high and high school because my gender preferences were too masculine (the way I talked, walked, dressed, etc.) for a 'female.'" Rachel (MtF) also had a difficult adolescence, owing to her poor performance in athletics. "This was between the ages of 9 and 14, after which I stopped playing sports to avoid humiliation. I embroidered when I was 7–8, I stopped doing it because it was too feminine but I don't remember why I felt that way. Playing clarinet at age 10, I was picked on for playing a girl's instrument."

Gender Socialization and Gender Roles

Learning how to behave in acceptable ways in one's own culture is a lifelong process. Children who are five to seven years old understand gender as a function of role rather than as a function of anatomy. Since learning to think about gender in an adult fashion is necessary to becoming a full member of society, as children grow older they learn to think of themselves and others in terms more like those used by adults (Devor 1989, p. 44). That is, they think of themselves in terms of physique, anatomy, sex appeal, and in terms of appropriate masculine/feminine behaviors.

Acceptable gender behavior is reinforced through inclusion and praise, while gender behavior or appearance deemed unacceptable is stigmatized by disapproval and harassment. This socialization occurs continually through a wide variety of mechanisms such as verbal comments; role modeling; jokes; laws; rituals such as weddings; harassment and violence, whether at school or on the street; segregated bathrooms; family roles; styles of clothing, hair, jewelry; and so on. Television delivers messages early in a child's life about how boys and girls are supposed to look and act. Parental roles serve as daily reminders of how a boy or girl should behave. School—especially immediately, in elementary school—reinforces boundaries between girls and boys, whether by lining students up, boys on one side and girls on another, by having segregated bathrooms, or by having segregated playground areas. Peer pressure begins at these early ages, and the child who feels "different" learns quickly to hide that difference.

Gail (MtF) tells us how one can pretend to go along, but that doesn't mean the gender lessons are truly internalized. On the gut-feeling level, none of this seems real: "I can play act it, but from the heart I haven't a clue. So it's been this great big pantomime or something, you know. Lip-synch. Gender-synch. As far as I can remember, since I was very young. But yeah it is kind of strange. I can relate sometimes when men are talking but the heart doesn't make sense."

Jessylynn, a male-to-female transsexual, comments on general gender socialization:

I can't tell you how many times I was told early in life from different sources: "Men don't cry," "Don't be a sissy," "A man's gotta do what a man has to do," "Gotta be tough, cuz it's a tough world," etc., etc. When I was young I really wanted to help my mom in the kitchen, and she would shoo me off, tell me to do something else, cuz she thought that males didn't have any place in the kitchen, cooking and cleaning, etc. It just wasn't allowed. Then, later, I would go to K-Mart (pre-transition) to buy sewing notions, buttons, zippers, and such. I heard the old sales-clerk woman say (under her breath) "Men ain't got no business sewing . . . that's for women."

Gender socialization is further exemplified by bunkey, a gay male, who remembers, "As a boy I was told men don't cry. I was called a sissy when I did. I refused to hunt and kill deer and my father and his peers degraded me as a sissy."

Childhood is a very influential time, since it is difficult for children to weigh the information they receive against their limited experience. For example, metagendered Phillip commented, "In both public education and in religious settings far too many things were set up in such a way that men/women and/or boys/girls were separated and distinguished, with no opportunity to question the norm and little tolerance for transgression."

Not fitting into traditional gender socialization can result in extreme mental and emotional distress. Here is how Tina (MtF) described it:

[The] combined feeling I got was a constant message, from everyone and every angle, that I was bad, wrong, immoral, and evil. I understood that, and constantly tried to portray that I was good. Being good meant hiding feminine traits at any cost. It meant praying at night that God would turn you into a girl, so that you would no longer be a freak, and waking up the next morning without an answer to your prayer. It means wishing you were dead, rather than going through another day in an alien body. It means feeling uncomfortable when the guys are talking about girls, anatomy, and so much else. It means feeling excluded from both the boys and the girls . . . feeling as if you are some kind of completely alien creature.

I Am Wrong

Several themes emerged from the study participants' recollections of childhood and adolescence. One theme that numerous individuals spoke to was the issue of feeling different, not normal, weird, or—in the ex-

TINA

treme, as Tina says above, like "some kind of completely alien creature." Virtually everyone has been in uncomfortable social situations at times, and can relate to the feeling of not fitting in, but usually that isn't because of gender identity—an element that is basic to who one is as a person. People who feel different because they have trouble fitting into their gender assignment feel *continually* weird; they feel wrong *as a person*. Participants in almost every category—MtF and FtM transsexuals, male cross-dressers, intersex individuals—addressed some variation of having this feeling.

The feeling that something is not quite right is common for transsexuals. kari (MtF) represents this experience:

I think it was around 7 or 8 that I sort of realized that something was up. And that's also when I started cross-dressing and also when I started getting beat up by my father for doing it. But it wasn't just my father. My behavior no matter what I tried to do was somehow apparent, because around 7 or 8 is when genders start to really, really segregate. And I was sort of expelled by the girls which was who I mostly played with, but at the same time was a target of the boys. So that formed a certain sense of isolation.

Jeremy (FtM) "felt freakish and inadequate"; Terry (MtF) said her transgender identity "made me feel like an outcast." Sandie (MtF) said her awakening to a new gender realization, different from the one she was assigned at birth, was "an out of body experience, feeling so misplaced, different. I loved who I was, but others didn't." And Leslie (male cross-dresser) commented about "learning to play a foreign role in an alien culture."

Dee's (MtF) confusion was only exacerbated by her parents' actions:

I started to question the fact that I was born with a penis but want[ed] to be a girl at a very early age. I knew early in life that girls did not have a penis. I tried to push it in a few times and even tried to pull it off. I was very confused. It was girls wear dresses and boys wear shorts. I wanted a dress but my mom said, "Honey, boys wear shorts." So I did what I was told. At one point in my childhood my mother forbid me from playing with my sister's dolls and tea set. I didn't want a truck and six guns. I had two older brothers so I was stuck doing what they told me to do or else they would tell mom and I would be brought in and made to go to bed or watch TV. In the mid-fifties my mother took me to a psychiatrist. He asked me to draw a boy and a girl. So I did. One with long hair and one with short. He asked me which was the boy. I pointed to the short hair picture. Then he asked me which one was me, and I pointed to the long hair picture. He said is that a girl. I told him yes. Then we talked about what I did when I played and stuff like that. After that I was asked to leave the room and my Mom and Dad went in for a while. When they came out we left the doctor's office. I remember my dad telling my mom it all sounded like a bunch of crap to him and I did not need to see the doctor again. From that day on until both of my brothers had died my father ignored me. My Christmas presents were androgynous. My mother picked out all my clothes and I no longer had to play with my brothers. I was left in a sea of confusion. I prayed to God to help but it never came.

Having body parts different from the expected was especially painful for Jon (intersex) and Dawn (hermaphrodite). Jon said nude swimming class in high school was "simply awful—humiliating" since he had "female breasts and small cock/balls while the rest were 'regular' guys. Had to endure the class from hell!" And Dawn wrote that she started to question gender at "3 years old when my mom kept insisting I was a girl. At 4 bathing with [a] female cousin realizing we were both supposed to be girls, but she didn't have all the parts I have. I just felt scared, not knowing why we didn't look the same."

Genderqueers, who come to see being queer as positive, represent an exception to this common experience of feeling "I am wrong." Although they, like others, recognize their misfit into traditional gender norms during childhood, and although this may initially make them anxious, they eventually conclude it is not they who are wrong but society. Matt (genderqueer, androgynous) wrote:

MATT

I remember being teased as a child for wanting a doll, wearing jewelry, and things like that. It wasn't until I started to dress in what was perceived as gender inappropriate clothing that others started to question my gender identity, and thus forced me to think about it myself, and come up with one consistent explanation for all of this. I was mostly confused by how my behavior didn't seem to fit society's expectations, although I was only doing what came naturally to me. Finally, with a sense of relief, I read a few web pages of people who identified as other than male or female, and I realized that this was a perfectly valid and natural way to be.

The Need to Hide

Children look to their parents, siblings, and peers for validation, for acceptance, for signs that they are okay. It is not surprising that confusing feelings about gender, or desires to cross-dress or to play with what are seen as cross-gender toys, are suppressed or, if not surpressed, acted out in secret. For what would the child do if rejected by her or his parents and friends?

Melanie (MtF) shared a common experience of suppression. When she was in kindergarten, she recalled, "I would try to play jump rope with the girls. My older brother, at the time he was in second grade, told me 'don't be a sissy.' So I learned not to do it." Kand, who identifies as transgendered, went into denial: "I do not remember a time when I did not feel like a boy. As a coping mechanism, I went into a deep denial about my gender identity situation that lasted for decades." Kara, a male cross-dresser, knew in kindergarten that he liked girls' clothes. "I also wore my underwear backwards so it would look like girls'. I went to bed hoping I would wake up a girl—and I didn't know there was a physical difference yet! While I do not have many problems with being male—it didn't make sense that I would think this way. I kept it all hidden." Female-to-male Abe related, "I questioned my gender most from ages about 5–9 years old but then gave in to peer pressure and fear of being different."

Parental approval was a major influence for many. As Beth (MtF) said, "Love by [my] parents was directly proportionate to my effectiveness in male role playing." A. (MtF) spoke of an early memory from age four:

I wanted a tea set at Christmas. . . . I got it, but it was pretty much the last feminine-type thing, I was not very approved of, but I wanted that so bad. It stands out really strongly in my mind. And I think that was my, pretty much the turning point for me. 'Cause from then on it was well, you're gonna get boy stuff. So, either you're gonna get approval by conforming or you're not gonna get approval. So, therefore, I chose that approval.

DakotaLynn (MtF) had dolls taken away from her and was given "first toy guns and then real guns and stuff like that that I started acting what [my father] considered more like a boy." Beth (MtF) had an article about Christine Jorgensen taken away by her parents, and "a shotgun was put in my hand, a rod and reel, baseballs, basketballs, and everything else." Felicia (transgendered), facing the same dilemma of self-expression versus approval, chose the same way as A.:

Since puberty I more or less felt like I was not, or am not, male even though of course that's what the world sees me as when I'm walking down the sidewalk or I'm working at the firehouse, whatever. I never felt that way. I always felt like I am a woman. I was a woman, or I am a woman, or I was meant to have been a woman at birth or whatever, but no one can see me. It's almost like I'm wearing a costume on the outside. This male body is not really me. And I'm screaming to get out but of course I can't get out because no one would really accept that, my parents especially.

It's not a surprise to hear Suzi (woman born transsexual) say, "It sucks as a child when no one believes you that something is radically wrong with your body and sex assignment."

More male-to-female transsexuals than other folks I interviewed mentioned feeling a need to suppress their sense of femininity, wanting to avoid humiliation or harassment, and pretending to be someone they weren't. This is attributable to the extreme rigidity of male gender roles in our society. Males must not exhibit femininity. And since there is no acceptable context for it, those who do are tormented until they stop. Kymberley (MtF) felt imprisoned:

When I was four years old, I knew something was not right. I knew I was a boy, but I felt like a girl. I didn't have a name for it at the time, and it was not until college that I figured out about "transgendered" people. I lived and grew up trying to copy what other boys in the neighborhood did so that my parents would think of me as a good little boy. It was like being trapped in a prison cell. My own description is that this cell has no doors or windows and after 35 years of life, the walls beginning to crack just a bit so I can escape and become the woman I am.

Early Discovery

As revealed in the experiences cited above, notions of gender variance frequently occur at very young ages. This is true across all identities. Male cross-dressers most often are attracted to feminine clothing by kindergarten, or certainly by puberty. Transsexuals often start cross-dressing at young ages, before they have the language and knowledge that they are transsexual and that there is something called sex change. And for others—butches, androgynous people, transgenders—not feeling quite male or female is typically an attitude of long standing. This is not to say that *everyone* knows by age five, but that is a common occurrence. Families and peers are often doing everything they can to enforce gender conformity, yet these contrary feelings persist for gender-variant individuals.

Children feel certain ways about gender before they can even discuss it. As a youngster, NiseyLynn (MtF) says she "used to eat M&Ms" and "used to pretend they were female hormones." AJ (FtM) talks about always being at odds with his assigned female gender—and with his female body:

I started to question my assigned gender very early. I was at least five when I first understood that I was female. Until then, I thought I was a boy. Everyone kept telling me that I can't do certain things because I was a girl. Later on, when I was nine, I

KYMBERLEY

started my period. My mom's first words to me when she found out was "Congratulations, you're a woman now!" Eww! The thought of that scares me. I truly hated it and I made up my mind that I wanted to be a boy. I had always done boy-like things. I guess I thought I was a boy from age 1– 4 because everyone told me I was a tom-boy. Well, my name wasn't Tom but I felt like a boy. . . . To be honest, it feels horrible not to know exactly what sex you are. Your brain is one gender and your body is another. You feel out of place, like you've been deceived by nature. Like nature has cheated you out of being normal or ever having a normal life.

AJ told his mother at age fourteen that he didn't want to be a girl and at sixteen said that he wanted to transition.

Patric's early experience as a male in a female body was humiliating:

I never felt female, I mean, never. I remember when I was 6 and went into kindergarten and there was this 3-ring circus and I was chosen to be a ballerina. And I mean, that was just like humiliating beyond words. It was just a horrible experience, and I wanted to be the lion tamer or tiger or something. But to have to be a ballerina was horrible.

In fact, many of the discovery stories I heard were stories of pain. Nicholas (FtM) "cried for a month solid" when he got his first period. . . . "My first depressive episode." Ashley (MtF) knew at age three she was a girl and cried herself to sleep, "asking God to make it go away so I could just fit in like everyone else." Jessica (MtF) was confused at age four by resistance to her being female. At puberty, "I felt disembodied, hyper-aware of my genitalia and progressively irritated by any part of me that appeared masculine." And Karen (MtF) tells a story that speaks to feelings no child should have to experience:

I think the first time dysphoria seized me was when I was seven, in Grade 2, when my best friend at that time told me I couldn't come over to play at her house because I was a boy. I was stunned and speechless as I hung on to the chain link fence. I was sure if I let go of the fence I'd collapse. My throat was in spasm, my chest was burning, and I was gasping. She tried to comfort me for a while, and after she left I tried to compose myself wondering what hit me. It would hit me often over time.

Mixed Gender Feelings

An unsupportive culture exacerbates years of conflicted gender feelings. "Conflicted" might be the wrong word, however, since it implies that the individual is responsible for the conflict. The individual embodies the conflict of society—something that could change, if and when we find ways to celebrate gender self-awareness and authenticity. Many people mentioned being in a mixed gender state for years, or even permanently.

Casey (butch lesbian) never identified as female. "As I was growing up I thought there were boys, girls, and people like me. I never felt isolated or alone, but I could not understand why people wanted to call me a girl when I did not feel like one. I was never confused, and I never thought that I should have been male, but I never thought I should have been female either." Max (transgender stone butch) also did not feel quite female or male:

When I was beginning to go through puberty I realized how much I felt like I had male parts that in reality I didn't have. When I was 16 I realized to what extent I felt masculine and decided to fully project that in the world. A lot of this stuff was inextricably linked to my coming out as a lesbian at 12—lesbian to me meant someone whose gender wasn't totally "woman." Later I changed my views about that, but at that point it was linked to my masculinity. It was scary and isolating to feel so different.

Joy (MtF) called coming to terms with her being not quite male or female "disorienting," whereas to Simon (tranny boy), "It feels a lot better to feel not quite female or male than to try to feel the one 'right' way." Keven (two-spirit) said, "I knew I was a boy/girl when I was very young. I didn't accept it until around five years ago though. I thought I could overcome it. I never felt right as a female or as a lesbian. I didn't like people to see me naked because then they would think I was female and would not know me." Being neither boy nor girl is also how cj (transgendered) explains trans status:

In elementary school I didn't know what to attribute to my being different. I figured the existence of loners was inevitable and didn't question why me. I wasn't compelled to be part of any group. I emanated both "boy germs" and "girl cooties" depending on who you asked. I kinda liked not being a boy or a girl to my classmates. I didn't befriend anybody then; I hung out with girls if they were doing something I wanted to do, and hung out with boys when they were doing something I wanted, forming allegiances to neither side. Boys and girls were frequently put in competition with each other by teachers; this confused me and I didn't like it, but went along having little choice in the matter. It was around 6th grade I thought I might be gay, but I didn't know anyone gay and no one talked about it. I was under the impression that being gay was really rare, so me being gay seemed unlikely. I thought that might make sense of my boy-girl status somehow. . . . I don't know what triggered it, probably something I read online, but I was laying in my room thinking about stuff and out of nowhere I thought, wow, maybe I'm trans. . . . For a month I went back and forth until I decided I was neither male- nor female-identified and started explaining it to a few friends.

Such anecdotes suggest that socialization as one gender but identification with another produces a sense of not being *fully* one or the other, at least for some people. This status is perceived quite differently depending on the person. Dana, an intersex person identifying as MtF, has this perspective: "Being intersexed I suppose I don't feel quite female either, but I've never felt male—never. Now I accept that I feel like myself, which is very liberating." Julian (male-bodied, ungendered) says that, as a child, "[I] must have thought of myself as a boy to some extent. . . . but I've honestly never felt more like a man than a woman (stereotypically speaking), or less like one than the other, nor like a combination of the two."

Cross-dressing in Childhood and at Puberty

Many male cross-dressers recognize early that they desire to wear feminine clothes. That we are supposed to wear the "appropriate" clothing and accessories related to our birth gender is, however, made obvious by the culture. Children observe what others say and do. The confusion and conflict that emerge when a child is attracted to the "other" clothing is so great that, early on, children learn to keep this attraction—and their acting on it—secret. Cross-dressing will be one of the first, most accessible gender transgressions, usually before the young person even understands gender identity.

Some cross-dressers begin quite young, such as at age five or six, especially if they have access to the clothing of older sisters or their mother. Lydia (MtF), for example, started with her mother's stockings: "Mom had these little flat boxes with her stockings folded up in them. And they were on this shelf in her room, and I would go into her room, you know, and put these stockings on."

Mary (male cross-dresser) shares, "When I was about four years old I enjoyed wearing my sister's dresses. My mother found out and was displeased." Another male cross-dresser, Asia, has a story with an amusing twist:

When I was a child, I was probably 11 or 12 when this happened, [another kid and I] started playing this little game where we would take our mother's underwear. And it got to the point where we took so many things, underwear, panties, stockings, girdles, it got to the point that we took so much that my mother was afraid that someone was breaking into the house. So out of guilt, I fessed up to what we were doing.

The issue of the erotic or sexual component of cross-dressing is contentious. The link of cross-dressing with sexual activity clearly stigmatizes it and places it in the category of fetish. It is unfortunate that the fetishizing of clothing is viewed as a sexual *perversion* because, in truth, all people of all sexual orientations eroticize other people, objects, clothing, and so forth.

Sometimes dressing is done for sexual purposes and sometimes it is not—it could be for nonsexual relaxation or fun. But cross-dressing for masturbation is the typical stereotype. Among the male cross-dressers I spoke with and some of the MtFs, this was most common when they were teenagers. Jamie (male cross-dresser), for example, would "go to parties and look in hampers and steal panties and stuff like that. And that was almost totally for masturbation." Joney (MtF) said, "[I] discovered masturbation when I was able to do that, when I was 13 years old, and when it happened I was in my sister's panties or bra or whatever like that, and I would sleep in it because I felt more comfortable doing that. And then I discovered through sheer accident if I do certain things a certain way, I would get orgasm."

This is a normal and natural act. Dana (MtF) points out:

I think the problem most people have with [cross-dressing for masturbation] is that's all they focus on. And they don't take into account the context and if they were to look at typical heterosexual teenage males they would recognize, and I'm sure they all do, especially if they have teenage boys as kids or were teenage boys, that sex was the only thing they ever thought about. So, why would it be strange if a teenage transsexual would think about sex and might masturbate occasionally dressed as the sex that they imagine themselves to be. I have never had sex fantasizing that I was a male or appreciating that I was a male or enjoying that I was a male. I always imagined myself to be female.

Mainstream representations of cross-dressers portray this boyhood fantasizing as something negative. Although what cross-dressers do is quite similar to what others do, it is cross-dressers who are stigmatized for it.

For transsexuals (people who feel that their gender identity does not match their body), cross-dressing is not about expressing a part of themselves for a short period of time. It is about feeling more complete, more comfortable, and conveying an aspect of who they are. Unlike male cross-dressers, transsexuals do want to alter their bodies (to varying degrees) and do want to live in a gender different from the one they were assigned at birth. Cross-dressing may be part of the process toward discovery of what their discomfort and feelings of not fitting in, feelings they have had for many years, have been about. Within the trans category, most transsexual or transgender people cross-dress before they gain a clear sense of their gender identity; afterward it cannot accurately be called cross-dressing, for they are dressing as the society defines how a person of their identity should be dressing.

Several male-to-female transsexuals who participated in this study started to cross-dress quite young. This makes sense—dressing is what is most often available to the very young to express their sense of self. Devin (MtF) told me:

I think the first time I wore a skirt, a little skirt, I was five. And that's when I discovered that this was not acceptable behavior. . . . [The mother of the girl I played with] had put some of her clothes and stuff in a box for the Goodwill or something and we were standing around and there was a skirt, and I said something like, "Oh, let's try them on." And she looked at me kind of funny and laughed and she said, "I'll only do it if you'll put it on and walk down the street with me." A dare. And something about that, I realized that I don't want to do that. I just sensed that no, this is not something I want anyone to know about. That's when I learned to start hiding.

Kymberley (MtF) started at about the same age:

I started wearing [my mother's] clothing when I was about six, um, between about six and nine my mother and I were the same size. So it was really convenient. It was even more convenient that she kept her summer dresses in my closet. So, I was able to cross-dress at will. Mostly when we'd have babysitters I'd go to bed early and I'd cross-dress. Or my parents were gone, or when I was eight I was old enough to be trusted home alone. I would cross-dress during those times. Unfortunately, one night I kind of was exhausted and I fell asleep on a bed with one of my mother's dresses on. Oh, well, so much for that outfit. So much for all of her clothing. It was pulled out by the next morning. And then in junior high I would find articles of clothing laying around at school and I would be a bad person and kind of commandeer them. And it got easier actually when I turned 16. I got my own job 'cause I was able to afford my own clothing and better places to hide them and things like that. And every time the stress got to be too much for me, I would dress for a little while and it would go away. It would subside and I wouldn't be stressed anymore.

Arianna (MtF) started to paint her nails and cross-dress at age four. "But then I was discovered and that kind of took all of that out of me [not] wanting to do that and go through that humiliation." NiseyLynn (MtF) would steal clothes off her neighbor's clothesline as a youngster. By the time she was in high school, she says, "I failed gym because I refused to get dressed in front of the guys. I felt uncomfortable getting undressed in front of them." Tim (FtM), on the other hand, experienced the high school years in a more satisfying style: "[I] used to dress in my dad's suits and cruise around town."

We turn now to adulthood, when individuals have greater ability and resources to construct the true self.

3

Constructing the Self: Options and Challenges

I have to have supervised visitation with my children for now, and the supervisor asked me, "Why do you feel you have to dress?" and I said, "Well"—and she's a very feminine woman—and I said, "Look, what if I told you you had to dress with a crew cut, a t-shirt, and jeans only. How would you feel?" "Well, I'd be stressed out." "Really? That's how I feel." I said, "Right now, I feel stressed out because I'm dressed as a guy, and it doesn't feel natural. It feels natural when I'm dressed as Joney. It doesn't feel natural when I'm dressed as John." So, it's, I think she's finally, it's finally clicking. (Joney, MtF)

I facilitate this group for transpeople, and I look through the New Yorker magazine every week to see if there's an appropriate cartoon in there, and there almost always is, and I'll bring it in for the group. And a month ago or so I saw one that is absolutely perfect for transition. It's this picture of these people standing around in a big bookstore and there's this big shelf of books that's labeled self-improvement, and right next to it is this big shelf of books labeled self-involvement. And for awhile you have to be completely self-involved because you're re-inventing yourself. (Reid, FtM)

Internal/External Consistency

How one feels internally is one aspect of gender identity. What gender others attribute to us and then how they respond to us is another. There is potential dissonance with each aspect, and for most transpeople there will be an attempt to align the external presentation with the internal sense of self. In this way they hope not only to have a satisfying experience of the self but also for others to treat them as how they identify. In this sense, gender is *being* and *doing*. This is where I feel that there is an aspect of performance to gender; however, unless it is in the context of entertainment, it is the true reflection of internal gender. Wilchins refers to this as a "performance of internal visualization" (1997, p. 155). She continues: "The images we form of ourselves and see in our heads constitute a kind of internal dialogue. They are conversations we hold with ourselves about what our bodies mean, an imaginary construction we undertake over and over again. In time, these images stabilize and become what we identify as 'our selves.'"

Thinking back to the Thomases' quote, "If men [and women] define situations as real, they are real in their consequences," we can see that the expression of an identity does have major implications for interaction, and therefore consequences. Living in a highly gendered culture means that we are treated based on our social gender—males and females are treated differently. Not surprisingly, most people I spoke with felt that it was very important to have internal and external alignment, both for their personal integrity and for the ability to interact with the world as the gender with which they identified.

Many transpeople take steps of physical transition (hormones, surgeries, presentation) both for personal reasons and for how that will transform their social relationships, whether among family, with partners and friends, at work, or in public interactions. However, a few study participants felt that consistency between one's identity and presentation was not necessary. For example, Dylan (FtM) did not see an "inside/outside division. How I move through the world, how I interact and communicate with others, that is both my inside and my outside. To me, changing physically [chest reconstruction] is about more clear communication and comfort for me. It's not about making the outside fit the inside." Holly (MtF), who has no intention of having surgery, said:

I do embrace the notion of expressing outwardly what is within. ("As above, so below.") But because I am so openly gender-variant and fluid, I reserve the right to express the truth of that "in the moment." Surgery might limit this kind of expression. I believe in "shape-shifting" with truth. . . . Is the goal to get from A to B or is the goal to remain open to fluidity? That's the key. So, it's not so much that surgery will necessarily limit your expression, it's the mindset that goes with your need for surgery. Because most folks who want surgery think they're only going from A to B, and that is a limiting mindset. They are ruling out the kind of fluidity I think would make surgery unnecessary. Because you could have any body configuration and if you bought the notion of fluidity, you can shape-shift to anywhere with any body.

Social Pressure

The majority of comments about internal/external consistency fell into three categories: pressure from society, the desire to have others see the real person, and a strong personal sense of needing internal/external consistency. Max (transgender stone butch) raises the question of what "consistency" means:

I feel like there's tremendous pressure to have an external appearance and body that are consistent with the internal identity. What does consistent mean, though? Is everyone who's having SRS [sex reassignment surgery] having it because it's consistent with their internal identity, or are some people doing it because the only images they've been shown of what a woman is are of female women with vaginas and breasts? Or tall men with penises and flat chests? I have spent much of my life desperately wishing I had a male body. But I'm starting to feel comfortable with the apparent contradictions between my female body and my male presentation. This contradiction is part of my strength and my identity, as well as part of what is hot to my lover! It's part of what makes me unique.

Ian (male cross-dresser) also challenges these ideas: "Consistent in whose eyes? I have always believed that it is better to transcend gender norms and expectations than to tamper with one's body. We are all *consistent* as we are. It is cultural expectations that cause all the problems."

Society "demands that we be consistent," says Jamie (male cross-dresser). "The public evaluates one's gender based on both facial and breast appearance," according to Audrey (MtF). Sae (FtM) had trouble accepting that people always assumed he was a girl. He wondered, "If our society [had] embraced me as I was, I probably would have felt differently and maybe not changed, I don't know." The pressure to fit in influenced Gwyneth (MtF), who does not believe women *have* to be a certain way but is "weary of being set apart by something so basic, and having to always explain myself or put up barriers."

The Desire to Be Seen

Others wanted to be seen for who they were. Jeremy (FtM), for example, wanted recognition of his male identity: "I want people to interact with me as a man rather than a woman or a child, and physical transition with hormones and top surgery seems to be the way to go for me." Ashley

(MtF) "felt like a liar and [that] I deceived people 'cause they saw a male and I had to mark things male as my identity." And KT (transgendered, butch lesbian) wrote, "Based on my own experience, when my external identity is not consistent with my internal identity I am left feeling fake, in drag, and definitely not being true to myself."

Wanting to be seen as genuine came up for Beverly (MtF), who asked, "How can you live as a woman if people will be constantly questioning if you are one or not?" Tristan (FtM) felt that without consistency his identity was "invisible to others." And Keven (two-spirit) had stopped short of setting dates for breast reduction surgery and hormones, trying to decide what to do: "How can I look who I am—male and female at the same time?"

Body-Mind Harmony

The personal need for consistency was strong. Lucy (MtF) talked about her need for self-identification and wholeness. Kerwin (FtM) said, "Only after I had transitioned to the point where most people perceived me as male did I begin to feel at all comfortable with my body." Shannon (genderqueer), however, did not feel that there has to be a consistency: "I think the fact of the matter is that, for most folks, any sort of disconnect is very uncomfortable—and *no one* should have to live with that." As a genderqueer tranny boy, Simon was more fortunate: "My internal identity is non-op, no-ho [no hormones], tranny gender freaky pervert punk. Luckily I can express that through dress, conversation, sex, etc."

Angela (MtF) represents other MtFs who feel that SRS is essential to their identity—but *not* because they want to have sex with men. Jennifer (MtF), on the other hand, does "desire to be desired by a man I love and for that man to find pleasure in me. I desire to please someone I love who loves me. I cannot have these until surgery is completed and healed." Sandie (MtF) referred to her SRS, nose job, and silicone breast implants as "the only way for me to survive."

Several male cross-dressers have had electrolysis to "reduce the problems of shaving and hiding the beard shadow" (Joanna), and took steps to stay slim, keep nails and eyebrows trimmed, wear earrings, and feminize as much as they can (Caroline, Rene). For Dawn (hermaphrodite), "hovering between male and female" is comfortable, though now Dawn dresses in masculine clothes and hairstyle. Phillip (metagendered) believes individuals should be congruent, but how, exactly, depends purely on how each person defines that. Phillip remarks, "When someone asks me about 'the opposite sex,' I ask 'which one?'"

Some transpeople do not achieve the consistency they would prefer. Because of his family, BJ (male cross-dresser) has not altered his body. "I won't," he explains, "because I won't make the people I love go through the struggle to accept me as a woman. I have children and grandchildren. There's an intricate network of family that I'm a part of. In that network I'm male and will remain so." For Donivan (male cross-dresser), a diagnosis of muscular dystrophy sidetracked thoughts of taking hormones: "My muscles are degenerating and I have no idea if I can take hormones or what would happen if I did."

Of course, consistency is in the eye of the beholder. For some pregnant butch lesbians, the butch image "is shot" (Epstein 2002). A few male-to-female transsexuals expressed the desire to become pregnant and give birth, and Jennifer (MtF) had explored information on uterus transplants. In 1999, FtM Matt Rice stopped taking testosterone and gave birth to a son, whom he is raising with his FtM partner. Because "men do not have babies," the couple received criticism and even threats for daring to break down expectations of what it meant to be male. Was Matt female-bodied or male-bodied, a man or a woman? He was a man who birthed a baby (Green 2004).

Transitioning

The concept of transition is not the same for everyone. If it is envisioned as a path, one person's beginning may be another person's endpoint. Yet the term "transition" is the best, most widely understood term being used currently to mean a process of gender change. This no longer means only an endpoint of sex reassignment surgery; it may mean no surgery but a process of gender change from one's birth gender. In fact, the word transition seems to me to be used incorrectly. Most people use it to mean going from one identity to another, such as with surgery or the use of hormones. I understand it to mean that the person has the other identity *already* and the transition involves the perceptions of society aligning with that identity. In this "word flip" it is not the person who is transitioning but society, which is transitioning its perceptions of that person. This may occur because the person is giving different gender cues or because society has redefined what gender cues mean.

One of the tragedies of the struggle to be an authentic self when you do not fit into the gender binary or resonate with the gender assigned to you at birth is that history is full of unacknowledged examples of gender variance. This lack of recognition deprives transpeople of valuable role models and denies everyone true knowledge of gender variance. For example, silence about widespread alternative gender roles in North American Indian societies is the result of ethnocentric enthographies, according to Roscoe (1998), who writes about third and fourth genders in those societies. Hijra and sadhin in India, kathoey and bakla in Thailand and the Philippines, and other not-men, hermaphrodites, and feminine men live as gender variants in Polynesia and Brazil, as recognized by Nanda (2000). Feinberg (1996) documents a rich history of gender crossers in telling the stories of two-spirit people, Joan of Arc, and other masculine women; in discussing figures in Greek mythology such as the transgender god Dionysus and the Amazons; and in describing pagan cross-dressing rituals, transgender bands of people protesting social class inequalities, and cultural festivals, carnivals, theater, and literature featuring gender variance found all over the world and throughout history.

There are many aspects of the authentic self—who we are mentally, emotionally, physically, and spiritually. What congruence means to each person can differ on a personal level. It can also differ on a political level. That's because anyone's attempt to achieve personal congruence, however one understands it, raises a key cultural-political question: Does undergoing surgery, electrolysis, taking hormones, wearing the gender-appropriate clothing, and so forth reinforce the gender binary of the culture? On this point, Califia states, "there will probably continue to be conflict between transsexuals who see the sex-reassignment process as confirming their true gender, and transgendered people who believe that their only hope for liberation lies in dismantling biological sex itself" (1997, pp. 274–275).

Glen (human) feels that "without binary maintenance, the TG community could not supposedly 'cross' and 'trans' to become the 'other.'" Trans people "are the ONLY ones that can change society to accept the freedom of gender . . . and the overcoming of sexual oppression." Glen is not convinced that a transsexual becomes the "'other sex' or the 'other gender.' It is its OWN sex." Why not work toward acceptance of that, rather than try to fit into a false binary? Mark (FtM) agrees:

I think when you're born one and cross over to the other side, so to speak, you're really neither. You're really neither one extreme nor the other because you've already lived on the one side. You know how that process goes, politically, socially, culturally. And when you take that over to the other side, that's an experience that your peers on that side don't have. So you cannot solely call yourself that gender either because you're not. And I think a lot of us feel like we're lying, and then we're forced to lie, and ugh. It's like they get you coming and going and there's no way you can in good conscience mark M or F, 'cause neither applies. Or both apply.

Not everyone wants to be a gender warrior, however, or wants to struggle daily with ridicule or isolation, or worse. But some trans individuals simply disagree with Mark and Glen. They see no reason why they can't fully be the man or the woman they feel that they are. I do believe that transition supports the gender binary; however, rather than finding fault with the individuals who choose transition, I want to work toward that as one acceptable choice out of many. If other socially accepted options existed, it is possible that fewer people would feel it necessary to spend the time, money, and energy on surgeries, facial reconstruction, electrolysis, and so forth—unless for health reasons or as a freer choice compared with the only way to be accepted that exists at present.

The Wonders of Hormones

Changing one's hormonal balance probably has a more profound impact than surgery on one's physical body and emotional state. Hormones affect secondary sex characteristics and emotional well-being. Introducing hormones is a very common step for a transsexual to take, less so for a male cross-dresser, genderqueer, or masculine woman. People obtain hormones in many different ways: they find them illegally on the street or in the underground market, take them from family members, obtain a doctor's prescription, purchase them on the Internet from countries other than the United States, and buy herbal combinations.

Hormone levels change dramatically, and cause dramatic changes in the body, at three times in the life cycle. During the first few months after birth, males and females experience their first surge of hormones, which stimulates release of sex hormones. At puberty, males produce great amounts of testosterone, ten to thirty times more than during their childhood, compared with females' approximate doubling of estrogen, though both males and females experience increases of estrogen and testosterone. And in old age, estrogen decreases and testosterone increases in women, while estrogen increases and testosterone decreases in men (Devor 1989).

FtM Changes with Testosterone

Transmen reported fairly similar impacts from being on testosterone (often called T for short), along with discomfort or agitation when levels run low and it is time for the next shot. JT (transman) experienced "upper body muscle growth, fat redistribution (from butt to gut), voice dropped, face squaring, some facial hair, dick growth, 'breast' shrinking, male pattern body hair and hairline, hair texture has thickened." After six months on T, FtM A. J. felt that "it's almost like I'm a young male going through puberty. I'm getting hair almost all over my body, my voice is much deeper than it was before, and my clitoris is growing (it looks like a small penis). My aggressiveness has got worse but not worse in a bad way." And Patric (FtM) found these changes: "Bald, facial and body hair, deep voice, fat redistribution, increased muscle density, calm and more confident mood. I am much more aggressive driven now."

Dustin (FtM), who had been on T for two and a half years, found it brought the validation for his masculinity or his feeling not-female that he was craving. However, he also said, "I feel like by taking hormones, it's just so powerful and almost, I don't know, it's too strong a word, but almost violent in how vastly it changed my body, even my behavior, my metabolism." Nicholas (FtM) found his changes wide ranging, from rage and having trouble crying to acne, "huge appetite, higher sex drive, increased clit size, some hair growth, voice change, muscle mass change, lost my waist, boobs shrank." He lowered his T dose and then stopped altogether after eight months, with the intention of resuming. "I'm very willing to experiment with testosterone."

Jon (intersex) was treated with testosterone and experienced his voice lowering, increased body hair, and an increase in aggression. His personality changed, and his sex drive increased so much that he felt like "a raving lunatic." He got off T to bring peace to his family relationships. Dawn (hermaphrodite) gets "extreme mood swings when testosterone is too low." He says that is when estrogen seems to "poison my body." He is on testosterone to keep its levels higher than his levels of estrogen, his body's own unique equilibrium.

MtF Changes with Estrogen

Once on estrogen, male-to-female transsexuals experienced two major types of changes—emotional and physical. Some examples of the emotional changes included "peace of mind" (Jessylynn), "a feeling of peace within myself" (Beverly), "more relaxed" (Tina), "sense of comfort" (Dana), "more peaceful within" (Susan), and "happier, more positive" (Laura). The physical changes were wide ranging. For example, Lonny said: "What little body hair I had is gone. My facial features have softened.

I've grown breasts to nearly a B cup. I've been taking hormones for one year and I am very happy with the results." Karlette had been on hormones for one year. "To date these are my changes: My aggression level has dropped in half. My hair on my head has stopped falling out. I am growing breasts. My body hair and beard growth has diminished greatly. I feel wonderful and happy most of the time. And I don't 'need' sex any more. I feel like I am becoming more feminine with each passing day." Rachel found "increased breast size (A-cup), softening of skin, dramatic decrease of muscle mass, thickening of hair on head, lightening of hair on arms and chest." She was also "more emotional and able to relate to other people's feelings but generally happier and less susceptible to depression."

Softer skin, breast development, weight redistribution to the hips, less body hair, and loss of muscle mass were common. Also, sex drive commonly decreased and the penis and testicles atrophied. Many MtFs welcomed the change in sex drive. "Estrogen makes my desire for sex diminish (but I don't miss it)," commented TeriSue. "Lack of spontaneous erections is a blessing," added Dana. Jessylynn saw her "greatly reduced

LONNY

sexual desire" as a "welcome blessing." "Sex," said Susan, "is not as important. Relationships are more important."

The emotional and physical changes that hormones bring about for MtFs and FtMs make a dramatic difference in their lives. They begin to look and feel more like the societally defined gender they identify with, and certain characteristics they abhor start to diminish or disappear. Many transsexuals find that hormones are the only measure they can afford to take, are willing to take, or are medically able to take. Transition for most transsexuals involves cross-living while taking hormones.

FtMs masculinize dramatically with the addition of testosterone, and can be seen as men within months. The changes for MtFs are slower. The voice is not affected by estrogen, but many softening features occur that feminize the face and body. To be seen as women, MtFs need to block or eliminate the production of testosterone in the body. This can be accomplished by taking anti-androgen drugs or by surgically removing the testicles.

Spironolactone

Anti-androgen drugs such as spironolactone suppress the body's production of testosterone. Since these drugs are hard on the liver, some transsexuals opt to have an orchiectomy, a surgery that reduces the production of testosterone by removing the testicles. With the reduction of testosterone, introduced estrogen is able to work more effectively in the body. Several participants in this study mentioned their experience with spironolactone. Jayne (gender variant) had been on estrogen for a year but had to stop because of cancer and high blood pressure. On spironolactone, she finds that her excessive hair growth has slowed. Mary (male cross-dresser) has been taking an anti-androgen in her prostate cancer treatment. "My wife says that I have changed, and I do have enlarged breasts, loss of body hair, and hot flashes. I am impotent, but I love cross-dressing even more."

Intersex individuals, too, have found that anti-androgens can help with their hormone imbalances. Dalelynn (intersex, MtF) wrote:

I've been off and on hormones for quite awhile, 15 years or more now. The current set that I'm on I've only been on about two years ago. Yeah, it's an on-going thing for me as my body doesn't produce the right things and I'm still producing some of the wrong stuff (testosterone). . . . if I take my spironolactone it seems to do that for me better than dex and some other stuff.

Herbal Combinations

A few individuals I spoke with were buying over-the-counter herbal combinations. These are not known for strong effects, but some individuals do feel minimal impacts. Kara (male cross-dresser), for instance, feels that his breasts have enlarged. Dakota Lynn (MtF) has experienced "some breast growth and my skin is a lot softer and my hips are a little fuller. . . . And my mind has calmed down." Ace (FtM) is using herbal combinations until he can afford a hormone prescription:

Testrone SX has orchic substance. I don't know if that helps or not. I don't have a bottle here, but it has other substances that I felt were very helpful. It kind of evens me out. I take it also with DHEA, it kind of evens me out, makes me feel more solid, more concrete. It's hard to put it into words. I can feel the difference. I experimented with herbs for years and years and years, masculine-enhancing herbs or tinctures to see how they would work. Not all of them worked too well.

Stopped Hormones/No Hormones

Of course not every trans-identified person is willing to take hormones, especially if he or she is not transsexual. KT (transgendered, butch lesbian) feels this way: "While I do like to reduce my being seen as feminine, I don't know that I want to go so far into masculine either, which would happen were I to take hormones. For me, this is why I am not transsexual; I don't want to become a man. I'm just not comfortable as a woman either. I am a butch!" Somewhat similarly, T.I. (naturally bearded dyke) does not view being bearded as a masculine characteristic. Since she does not find anything about males attractive, she has no interest in taking hormones and joining the ranks of masculine women who take T.

Max (transgender stone butch) was on hormones for six months, "and there were changes to my musculature and an increase in sex drive as well as permanent results of a deepened voice and masculinized genitals. I am also a little hairier than I was, though not much! I've never once regretted my choice to go on hormones, nor my choice to get off them." Ted (masculine woman) took testosterone for about five months, but stopped three years ago. "[My] voice got deeper. Got bad acne across shoulders, libido went thru the roof! Some clitoral enlargement. World became much more visual. Found myself looking at other people's bodies. Found it more difficult to cry."

Glen (human) represents a different view about gender. He did not want to take hormones once he realized that this would mean trading one role for another role:

I was always going to take hormones but only after I understood why I had this need to wear dresses. Once I figured it out that it was a need to be "human" then the need to take hormones simply meant that I would be changing my body to go from one oppressional role to another. Being either "a man" or "a woman" is still being only half a human being as far as I'm concerned. Changing one's body to rationalize "the role" of one versus the other is to still NOT *have solved the problem and to yet understand that either of society's gender roles if adhered to only, are oppressional.*

Several male cross-dressers I spoke to were interested in taking estrogen for breast development—if only it would be a temporary change. For example, Rene (male cross-dresser) told me: "I'd like to take hormones to feminize my body some more but that's a kind of irreversible thing. I can't transition back and forth. Hormones would stimulate a little breast development that just wouldn't go away when I wanted to be my guy self most of the time." And K. (male cross-dresser) made a conscious choice to not take hormones, "because I do not want to tamper in any way with my natural male sex drive."

Simon (tranny boy) hasn't taken testosterone yet:

It's something that I definitely think about all the time. But, the process isn't so much of coming to think about it, it's rather coming to the fact that it's something I'd rather not have to do. And I've definitely talked about and thought about the fact that, quote unquote, I am my mother's daughter. And, my body pattern will fit hers, and it totally freaks me out. The idea of becoming an older woman in my body really scares me. I think that would be the point where I'm no longer able to see, to conceptualize my body as masculine. And a lot of it has to do with good old fat-phobia, and misogyny. But hopefully, the other thing is, I can conceptualize my body now as masculine, but who's to say that in 15 years I won't be able to do the same thing? So, I really don't know.

Voice

At puberty the surge of testosterone in males enlarges the larynx, an impact that cannot be undone, resulting in a deepening of the voice. This is why FtMs on testosterone have a voice change but MtFs on estrogen do not. The difference in pitch between men's and women's voices is almost a full octave on average. There are other differences as well: women often end statements with a question-mark inflection, they keep conversations going, and they use a different vocabulary (Brownmiller 1984). Nora (MtF), the only person I spoke with who had undergone voice surgery, described the results:

They measure it [pitch] in hertz, and the normal range for a genetic female is anywhere from 180 hertz to 250 hertz. I mean a female can get a lot higher than that, but that's just normal speaking range. When I first began my normal speaking was 130 hertz. I was told to expect 215 hertz after my surgery. Well, about a month or so after my surgery, [it was 315 hertz but] supposedly it was gonna come down. Seven months later my normal speaking voice was still 315 hertz. And it was extremely high. I could etch crystal with it. I flew all the way back to Portland and I was going to get the surgery reversed. I was really, really, really dissatisfied with it, especially for $7,000. So they talked me into doing voice therapy, and I did a week's worth of that and then came home. And I went and went and went and it still never came down. So finally I just got depressed and I said, I'll just abuse the heck out of it and see what it does. So I just started, I'd cough and I'd do anything to stress it. And after six or eight months of that it started, it started coming down. And now, when I'm hydrated and things it's not real squeaky like it is tonight. I like it fairly well. It's in the 200, somewhere between 220–225, something like that I guess now.

Others tried to change their voice without resorting to surgery. Dana (MtF, intersex) was taking voice lessons. "It's hard for me to maintain a female voice for any extended period of time. Those are muscles, again, it just takes exercise." And Amy (MtF) "went [to voice lessons] for about two months, but with electrolysis it was just too expensive." She "just couldn't continue." As Dee (MtF) commented, "It is possible to buy tapes and books on what to do but in the overall like everything else in transition it depends a lot on how motivated and dedicated you are as to how successful you will be."

Voice was an issue many MtFs commented to me about. They were discouraged by how their voice "gave them away." It was very hard to hold a feminine-sounding voice for any length of time. "When I'm in certain situations I talk softer," Joney (MtF) explained. "You know the problem is, I tell people, then I sound like a phone sex operator . . . and I don't want to sound like, I know some drag queens and they all have this voice and it just sounds so contrived." Erin (MtF) agreed: "you can do it [speak at a higher pitch], but it sounds so fake. It's a bigger giveaway than just trying to talk low [low-volume, softer] and be low key."

While some individuals felt that they had improved their voices somewhat, others just had to accept their lower, deeper voices. Devin (MtF) never took voice lessons.

DEVIN

I have always felt my voice should be better than it is, but, you know, it's like, I seem to get by ok with it. I don't pass. I don't get ma'amed on the phone very much. Occasionally I do. But for the most part, if I'm on the phone, who cares? Usually when you're on the phone, if it's a social call the person on the phone knows and it doesn't matter. If it's a business call and they think you're a guy, you get a bit more respect, you know. And you get better results.

Laura (MtF) felt that people took in her voice as one of many gender cues. "If someone sees me presenting as a female [my voice] is accepted as female. When someone sees me as male, they accept it as male."

The Meaning of Surgery

The common term for genital surgery for transsexuals is sex reassignment surgery (SRS). To take the emphasis off sex and keep it on gender, Green (2004) proposes using the phrase "gender confirmation surgery," and Cromwell (1999) offers "sex and/or gender congruence surgery." While the presence or absence of certain types of genitals does not magically confer masculinity or femininity, some trans individuals feel strongly about conforming to the social definitions they have incorporated into their understanding of gender—strongly enough to change their body in order to confirm those social expectations.

A minority of transsexuals actually undergo surgery, yet reference to surgery status has become a widely used shorthand descriptor of an individual's experience. MtFs may undergo orchiectomy, vaginoplasty, tracheal shave, facial feminization (including brow lift, chin reconstruction, rhinoplasty, scalp advancement, face-lift, etc.), electrolysis and laser resurfacing, voice surgery (crico thyroid approximation, or CTA), breast enhancement, and hair implants. FtMs may have chest reconstruction or double mastectomy, phalloplasty or metoidioplasty (types of bottom surgery), hysterectomy, salpingectomy/oophorectomy (removal of fallopian tubes and ovaries, usually if there are concerns about cancer), and possibly hair transplants. These types of surgeries are not comparable in terms of cost, result, or what is done. Is an FtM pre-op or post-op if he undergoes chest reconstruction only? Would a hysterectomy make a transman post-op?

The terms used to describe surgery status are inadequate, indicating a mismatch between the terms and what is really meant—a gender transition from a person's assigned gender, of which surgery is only one small part. Yet, legally, surgical status is the definitive measure of gender change, much to the disadvantage of those who transition without surgery. Denny (1997) suggests minimizing the emphasis on surgical procedures when the trans experience is primarily about individual authenticity and identity—not merely body parts.

There is, naturally, a range of feelings about surgery. Most of the transsexuals I spoke to wanted SRS (especially chest reconstruction for the FtMs and vaginoplasty for the MtFs). Jennifer (MtF, female) felt that her pre-op body "is a matter of anatomical and legal contradiction to my gender and the dysphoria is—for me—so severe and is not resolvable by any means other than surgical. Even if society became totally tolerant, I could not have the fulfilling relationship that meets my desires and my needs without surgery."

Gail (MtF) felt that SRS "is a sort of cosmetic completion, 'cause everything else is there." And Lydia (MtF) felt similarly, since "when I do have the surgery, my appearance and my demeanor really isn't going to change. So for a lot of transsexuals or transgendered people, the surgery becomes less and less of an issue . . . in fact the big changing point is when you begin to live full-time. And the surgery sort of becomes an anti-climax, in many ways." None of this is to say that surgery is unimportant; my intention is to point out that surgery is, perhaps, overemphasized in the mainstream understanding of gender transition and occupies an inordinate amount of Internet and support group conversation time. This is attributable, most likely, to the fact that SRS is commonly understood to mean *genital* surgery. There are numerous types of body modifications such as nose jobs, face-lifts, liposuction, tattooing, piercing, electrolysis, circumcision, breast implants, and so on, but none of them elicit the responses that genital surgery does in the West.

Some folks I spoke with mentioned that surgery was an expectation. For instance, Andrea (MtF, transgenderist) was asked many times at her support group about when she was going to have surgery. "If you say you're not or you don't know, you're a heretic," she explained. Robert (FtM) also felt pressure from his support group members: "even though they were well meaning, were very condescending, this made me very hesitant. And I didn't want to conform to them either. I finally decided that I should just ignore everyone in the entire world and I should be exactly what I wanted." Tasha (MtF), who lived many years in Southeast Asia, commented:

I do think the trans sub-culture in the West puts too much emphasis on SRS, ignoring the fact that not everyone wants the same things. Ironically, in this respect I think that the trans community, from the surgeons downwards is still VERY much binary-minded. You are that, or that, ts [transsexual] or not, and just as in the male-female binary, a lot of people don't actually fit into that! Fortunately for me, I pretty much do, but for those who don't they get just as much discrimination from the trans community as they do from everyone else.

FtM Experience with Surgery

A major issue for masculine-identified transpeople is breasts, especially large breasts, which are one of the most important gender markers in our society. More than half of the FtMs I interviewed had already had top surgery. Dan (FtM) had a breast reduction in his early twenties before he started thinking of himself as a transperson, although even then he had begged the doctor for a full mastectomy. Now he would like to have the mastectomy: "I need my chest, I need it. The penis thing I can almost deal with, but the chest, not having your own chest is really hard." KT (transgender, butch lesbian) was considering breast reduction. "It's often called the 'butch curse' and I don't know why but butches seem to have big breasts. It's kind of, I don't know, it's God's joke on us or what. But I wonder if I wouldn't be more comfortable if my chest wasn't quite so obvious. And to just reduce it doesn't feel like I would be denying my female body." Patric (FtM, male, intersex) explained the discomfort well:

After chest surgery, it was kind of neat to not be stared at all the time. I would always, I mean, having a flat top and a 4 couple D chest, looking pretty butch, I would always kind of get attention no matter where I went. So it was kind of nice after my transition all of a sudden, this white noise went away, it just got quiet and calm and it was just kind of cool. . . . My chest was so big I really couldn't bind. So I felt real awkward because my voice dropped down and I had the facial hair, some body changes, but I still had this humongous chest.

Kyl (FtM, genderqueer), with 36C breasts, would have liked chest surgery but didn't have the money. "I don't like the fact that they give me away all the time." AJ (FtM), also with 36C breasts, was glad to have top surgery shortly after we spoke, while Tim (FtM) had to delay the surgery because of finances. "I feel booby, you know, that's my big thing. And if I could go tomorrow and do that surgery I would do it." Al (FtM) was delaying hormones and name change until he could afford top surgery because he wanted these changes to be "associated with a guy with no boobs." Only Dustin (FtM) mentioned a problem with surgery. "My top surgery got botched, so that I really don't look male or female."

The unlikelihood of successful penis functioning kept most FtMs from pursuing bottom surgery; only a small number had had this surgery. Jeff's (FtM) concerns after his surgery included "keeping the dick in straight and not falling out of my underpants that annoys me, [and] having to come out [as trans], because surgery is not good enough like the MtF lower surgery."

Keven (two-spirit) had a hysterectomy, a double mastectomy, and had started low-dose testosterone. "Now about 60 percent of the time people think I am male and 40 female. . . . I am looking forward to increased male features so that ambiguity decreases although internally I like the androgyny—just not socially." Mark (FtM) had his uterus, ovaries, and fallopian tubes removed, as well as a double mastectomy. Testosterone had enlarged his clitoris and created folds in the labia majora to create a scrotal look. "I have enough of it for the locker room. I don't worry about it too much."

MtF Experience with Surgery

Male-bodied female-identified individuals have a wider range of surgeries to consider because estrogen does not affect secondary sex characteristics as completely. The most common choices are electrolysis (a must to eliminate beard growth or shadow, and sometimes also done on arms, chest, and back), breast implants, orchiectomy (especially if SRS is out of the question, since orchiectomy lowers the production of testosterone owing to removal of the testicles), and SRS.

About half of the male-to-female transsexuals I interviewed had had SRS by the time I talked with them or have had it since. (Others may have, but have not been in touch with me.) Some of these individuals went to Canada for surgery, some to Thailand, and some stayed in the United States. Regardless of where the surgery was done, Angela's (MtF) story is typical:

ANGELA

My surgery was wonderful. I went to Brassard in Canada, because of the price, but primarily because he has such good aftercare. He puts you in like a hospice. It's actually a converted house to which he's added bedrooms and he has nurses there on duty 24 hours a day, in case there's a problem. They serve you all three meals so you never have to leave the place, and it's just wonderful. The atmosphere is great. You get to talk to other people like you. And meet people from around the world. It's just a wonderful healing environment.

Sandie (MtF, female) had her surgery earlier than anyone else I spoke with, in 1982. Sandie began to live as a female when she was nineteen. She moved to New Orleans and had a nose job, silicone injections in her face, and breast implants in the early 1970s. After years of drug abuse and time in drag bars, she moved to Kansas City, where she became a prostitute and her addiction continued. A boyfriend borrowed money from his wealthy parents to help finance her surgery, which was completed in Youngstown, Ohio. After hitting rock bottom three years later, Sandie moved back to her family and became a caretaker for her relatives. Today, she writes: "I am a wonderful aunt, helping raise a niece from birth. Involved in the community, doing theatre and winning many awards. I am involved with supporting the mentally challenged, a job which I love. . . . I am very fortunate to have lived, to have had this amazing journey. At 48, I deal with my transsexuality with tenderness instead of shame."

Bonnie (MtF) had been doing electrolysis for over a year when she went to Thailand for surgery. It pains her to still have to shave. "The stress of having to shave (as I sometimes shave three times a day) has brought me to such a low point at times I have contemplated suicide. I do have a therapist and she tells me lots of women have to shave and deal with facial hair but it has been a terrible issue for me." Making a point similar to Al's (FtM, quoted above, who does not want to proceed with transition until he has top surgery), Bonnie wishes she had started electrolysis earlier.

Amy (MtF) also went to Thailand, although she had originally hoped to stay closer to home. In her case, diabetes complicated her surgery.

Diabetes [has had an effect] on my journey. It has been slowing down my progress. First with the reduced hormone dose. Then getting turned down twice for surgery in Montreal. Then getting higher rates for surgery from Dr. Shrang in Wisconsin because he would have to bring in another doctor to manage my diabetes for surgery and follow up while in the hospital after surgery. This was all going to be extra of course. This doctor is a lot higher priced to begin with. Nor [has it been easy to deal] with re-regulating my insulin pump after going back off the female hormones for pre and post surgery purposes. Then going the other way again when I start them up again after surgery. I have had to get a lot more documentation for my flight to Thailand, as I have to take my insulin pump supplies with me. This includes needles, lancets, infusion sets, and a pair of surgical scissors, too!

MtF Audrey's transition changed course because of a diagnosis of prostate cancer. She had completed electrolysis and had her letter for hor-

AMY

mone therapy; then she was diagnosed and had a prostatectomy. "I remember waking up in the recovery room, and shocking a nurse by telling her that I wished that I was waking up from sex-change surgery instead of prostate surgery. . . . I am of the opinion that eliminating testosterone, replacing this with estrogen, and undergoing a sex-change will improve both my physical and mental health."

Is Male Privilege Automatic?

Some MtFs hear comments about their downward mobility living as women. On the other hand, one might think, FtMs must experience upward mobility. But FtMs don't necessarily gain status as men. Male privilege involves a sense of one's entitlement to space, rewards, and status, a sense that is absent when one is brought up as female. Bornstein makes the point that "male privilege is not something that's given to men in this culture; it's something that men take" (1994, pp. 107–108). Apparently, some FtMs acquire this attitude. Emery (FtM) felt that he saw other FtMs "see themselves as superior and in charge." And Simon (tranny boy) was shocked by other young white FtMs who needed to "check their shit" and take anti-misogyny training because of the privilege they now experienced. Simon felt that this training should go along with the psychologist's letter stating Gender Identity Disorder diagnosis. Even downward mobility had its competetive side: some male cross-dressers, like Marlene, observed displays of male competition regarding who passed better as a female!

Mark (FtM) experienced what he felt was "heaps of male privilege." One example of this occurred when his wife had health problems and wanted to have a hysterectomy. "The doctor would not do that until I went in with her. I said 'She's a big girl and she can make that decision herself, and whatever she decides is ok by me.' But I can walk in and say 'I'll have an order of hysterectomy with oopherectomy on the side.' And they'll say, 'Sure, would you like fries with that?'"

Not everyone assumed, however, that female-to-male transsexuals automatically gain access to male privilege just because of the social and political consequences of being male (Halberstam 1998). For example, Raven (transgendered FtM intersexual) challenged the notion that male privilege is automatic for all males:

The longer I've lived as male, the more I realize that male privilege is only what your class, ethnicity, and social grouping allow it to be. A white woman in a suit has a bet-

ter chance of being hired in a corporation full of suits than a black male with long dreads wearing tie-dye, even with the same resume, penis or no penis. You only get into the old-boy network if you are the right kind of old boy. I've got long hair to my butt (hippie!); feminine mannerisms (faggot!); no college degree (ignorant!); work a physical labor job (low-class!); live below the poverty level (redneck!); wear big boots and a leather jacket (thug!); and I'm an out FTM intersexual with a female history (freak!). If there's a male privilege club around, they haven't come knocking on my door. (Kaldera 2001, emphasis in the original)

Green (2004) is also highly critical of the notion of automatic male privilege. FtMs often experience unemployment and career crises because of transition. Before transition, living as females, they may have been undereducated and underpaid, working in jobs without high-powered career paths that could lead them to a powerful position after transition. Furthermore, different management styles based on gender socialization do not automatically change because of SRS. And some of the privileges of being male (how salespeople address you, being handed the check at a restaurant, and so forth) are balanced by losses, such as women crossing the street to avoid you, people assuming you do not like "feminine" things, and the ever-present challenges and dangers of macho posturing. Ironically, for some FtMs, the message they received as little girls—that they could "do anything"—changes to a disempowering "tone it down" after transition.

The Cross-dresser's Self-Construction

Visiting a boys' or men's clothing department is quite different from visiting the girls' or women's department. The clothing styles, colors, fabrics, and accessories create two distinct looks. A female-bodied person who wants to present a male image often wears a white undershirt and a front-buttoned or polo shirt over that, both of which are staple items in a men's department and bestow a "male" look that women do not tend to wear. The women's department, on the other hand, would offer a wider range of types of tops to wear (blouses, jerseys, tank tops, halter tops, sleeveless, short sleeves, three-quarter-length sleeves, long sleeves, etc.) in a wider range of fabrics and colors.

We could not have the concept of cross-dressing if our ideas of what clothing goes with what gender were not so firmly entrenched and intractable. Yes, it's been acceptable since the 1920s for women to wear pants, but it is a rare woman who wears only pants or slacks. Women's clothing, jewelry, scarves, hair styles, and makeup are distinctly feminine. These items do not contribute to an androgynous look, which usually includes short hair, plain pants, plain tops, and minimal accessories. Male-bodied entertainers who are androgynous or gender benders, like David Bowie or RuPaul, are feminine-looking males who do not generally wear skirts. It seems that what really pushes a male into the category of cross-dresser is daring to wear skirts or dresses, makeup, jewelry, and other feminine items and wanting to be seen as feminine—not androgynous. A female who wears clothes from the men's department and seeks to be seen as masculine in looks, behavior, and mannerisms is rarely called a cross-dresser. The fact that the clothes are "men's" may not even be noticeable.

Cross-dressers are not the same as drag queens (males in women's clothing) or drag kings (females in men's clothing), who cross-dress for performance. Cross-dressers are also not the same as employees who cross-dress while on the job because of a need to follow a dress code (everyone must wear a tie). Nor are they the same as people who follow fashions (females wearing boxer shorts) or actors who costume themselves in cross-dress because of a role they are playing. Cross-dressers are following inner desires that relate to gender expression, comfort, or eroticism.

According to Tri-Ess, the Society for the Second Self, Inc. (an international nonprofit volunteer organization that provides information, support, and activities for and about cross-dressers), cross-dressing is about the expression of gender identity and has nothing at all to do with sexual orientation, sexual identity, or sexual deviation. It is the outward expression of inner feminine feelings; cross-dressers seek to emulate femininity. Males who cross-dress do not want to stop being males and being masculine, but they do want to be able to express their feminine side occasionally or often. Tri-Ess literature explains this as a natural trait, similar to being right- or left-handed. Marlene (male cross-dresser) viewed it as an "obsessive-compulsive behavior," and Dave (male cross-dresser) experienced it as a "form of addiction." Virtually everyone I spoke with said it was an impulsive behavior that could be put off only for so long. It is typically not a desire that goes away with counseling, getting married, purging one's clothing, or willpower.

Purging

It is very common for male cross-dressers and MtF transsexuals who start with cross-dressing to go through cycles of "purging"—stashing women's clothing, dressing, throwing everything away, and repeating the cycle. Fear of discovery, a desire to stop, guilt over dressing, or an unhappy partner are motivations for purging. Jamie (male cross-dresser) said, "I used to buy myself things and hide them, but always felt guilty and threw them away." Cris (male cross-dresser) "purged due to fear." Caroline (male cross-dresser) threw everything away when he moved from Puerto Rico, "but then it all came back."

Melissa (male cross-dresser) was more practical. When "[Melissa's] stuff starts to take up more than half the closet, when I can't get John's work shirts on his side because Melissa's got too many of her skirts on her side, that's when I say, what haven't I worn in the last six months?" Devin (MtF), on the other hand, would "put it [the women's clothing] all in the trash and put the trash on the curb when it was trash day. Then I would go out to the trash and bring it back into the house. I couldn't even do [without] it for a few hours."

Erin (MtF) had convinced herself she was only a cross-dresser. She tried purging, but the compulsion to cross-dress "never went away. It always came back, and it [purging] got harder each time it came back." Lauren (MtF) also purged her clothing, was drinking heavily, and was failing classes at school, "'cause if you don't go to classes, you don't pass. And if you drink too much, you don't go to classes. But I blamed it on the clothing. I blamed it on this thing that was wrong with me instead of the alcohol."

Purging has a different dynamic for males who cross-dress than for MtF transsexuals who purge their closets of the clothing of their assigned birth gender. The former are attempting to deny their compulsion to dress in feminine attire, or attempting to conform to society's disapproval of such desires. The latter are "symbolically coming out of the closet as women" (Bolin 1988, pp. 147–148). Transsexuals, when they can finally live full-time in the gender they identify as, will keep only one type of clothing. Androgynous individuals and genderqueers may have masculine and feminine clothing that they blend in their own style or wear to express their gender identity for that particular day, depending on their mood. However, it is the male cross-dresser who hides and purges, revealing the extent of society's misunderstanding of (and disdain for) them in particular.

Cross-dressing in the Military

Males who want to express their feminine side might seem incompatible with the macho image of the military enlistee. And, in fact, it is illegal to cross-dress while in the military. Still, the military has many closeted cross-dressers and transsexuals in its various branches who haven't yet transitioned. Even though a common reaction might be surprise, the reality of "macho" men wearing dresses is not so odd if you think through the reasons why trans-identified people may be attracted to the military. One reason is to prove their masculinity against the contrary evidence of their internal feminine feelings. As Gail (MtF), who joined the Navy, said, "It was a way to prove my manhood. Hey, I'm a man, aren't I?" Second, an individual may actually hope to die as a way to be free from painful gender questioning. Denise (MtF) confirms: "And I joined the military. I even volunteered to go to Viet Nam to get killed to put me out of my misery." Another reason is the thrill of adventure. Barbara (male cross-dresser) felt that the adrenaline rush of her tasks in the army matched the first time she "was in public dressed as a woman."

Obviously, gender-variant people who enlist face challenges. DaleLynn (hermaphrodite) found it difficult to feel secure in the military. "You know, it wasn't uncommon for me to get up at 2:00 in the morning, take a shower. Well, nobody else was in there, right?" Lonny's (MtF) eight years in the Marine Corps were tough because of the "rough and tumble image of men. I don't like that. I want to be seen as a female." Gabriel (intergendered), by contrast, enlisted in the Coast Guard as a female-bodied person and did not have any problems, even as the only "woman" with thirty-two men.

Mary (male cross-dresser) has cross-dressed for decades except when he was in the armed forces, from 1949 to 1954. In those years he dressed only when home on leave. Marlene (male cross-dresser) was in the Army in the 1950s, serving as a mail clerk and storing his dresses in the mail room:

> If they'd caught me at that in 1953, they probably would have shot me. . . . I had a big stash of dresses in the mailroom and I would go in there after midnight because I had a key and nobody else had a key except the company commander. And I would dress, watch television, this sort of stuff. Almost got caught a couple of times. And I finally transferred my stash to my car, which was at least a little safer.

Joanna (male cross-dresser), who was in the military for twenty-four years, only risked under-dressing, that is, wearing lingerie or nylons underneath his clothes. Rita (MtF) cross-dressed in the military "when you could get in jail for it at that point in time" but did not cross-dress while in Vietnam, because she was too busy and there was no privacy. Joney (MtF), who served fourteen years in the military, was court-martialed for being seen in a state of cross-dress. The charge was "indecent liberties by cross-dressing with a minor," meaning that a minor (her daughter's friend) had seen her cross-dressed and told her mother. Viewed as a sexual pervert, Joney was sentenced to two years in military prison, served one year, and now must register as a sex offender.

Tri-Ess and Support

For many trans-identified people, including cross-dressers, the Internet provides a revelation: it is the way they learn they are not the "only one." They use it to gather information and to network with other people. But scores of support groups across the country provide personal, face-to-face social contact. Tri-Ess, a prominent example, was founded in 1976. In 2002, there were thirty chapters nationally with a membership of over 1,100 male cross-dressers and 320 wives (Bloom 2002). According to Tri-Ess, a cross-dresser is defined as

> an individual, typically a heterosexual male, who occasionally chooses to make a social role presentation considered appropriate for persons of the opposite genetic sex, *for the purpose of personal expression*, without the intention of entering a program leading to sex reassignment surgery, and without attempting to attract a partner of the same genetic sex. (membership application, emphasis in the original)

In other words, Tri-Ess is closed to gay males and to transsexuals.

Further, Prince states that individuals involved in "other behavior patterns as bondage, punishment, fetishism for rubber, leather, or other, or domination and humiliation" are also excluded (1976, p. 41). The reason given for this, Prince continues, is the safety and comfort of Tri-Ess members who are overwhelmingly married heterosexual men with children, with "reputations, community responsibilities and professional standings that need protection." Excluding gay men, Garber (1992) suggests, is a way to reduce the connection in the public's mind between cross-dressing and eroticism. If gay men were members, the public would be more likely to think about the sexual connection; furthermore, wives might fear that their husbands would form gay relationships through contact at the meetings.

For many cross-dressers Tri-Ess opens up a world of socializing, parties, and trips—all to be done while cross-dressed with others. Marlene (male cross-dresser) said that in one year he went to "four three-day weekends at Santa Cruz with two dozen gender folks; a one week stay at Lake Tahoe with 30 gender friends. I love to gamble en femme in Reno! Holiday en femme in Chicago, four days; nine ALPHA chapter meetings in Burbank; a dozen meetings in Fresno; frequent house parties with Visalia gender friends." Halloween parties are also big events. Rene (male cross-dresser) found Tri-Ess more comfortable than mixed transgender groups because "there were quite a number of genetic females that attended with their spouses. And the cross-dressers seemed to put forth a greater effort to present feminine appearance than in some of the more open groups that I met."

But Tri-Ess does not work for everyone. Before Rita (MtF) came out as transsexual, she identified as a cross-dresser. When Rita was en femme, she did not talk about her male-oriented pursuits, such as work, hobbies, or sports. To her surprise she found her cross-dressed sisters at chapter meetings "talking about trains, motorcycles, fixing the roof, etc. . . . A typical greeting of two cross-dressers at a Tri-Ess meeting: 'Why, hello, Jane, got your Corvette on the road yet?' 'Delightful to see you again, Mary! No the carburetor is still running too lean. Hey, how 'bout those Phillies?'"

Of course, not everyone has a Tri-Ess chapter within driving distance, and not everyone can make the meeting times. Some may join an open transgender support group, or no group at all. Some may attend a gender conference such as the annual Southern Comfort, held in Atlanta, Georgia. But as Lynn (male cross-dresser) said in praise of support groups, "[My group] is the only place I can go dressed where they're actually genuinely glad to see me."

Transsexuals and Cross-dressers: Reflections of the Binary

Where is the boundary between cross-dresser and transsexual, the difference between cross-dresser and transgender, or even between cross-dresser and genderqueer? These categories are not distinct or neat. Although many transsexuals go through phases or spend years cross-dressing either before realizing they are transsexual or before transition, they generally do reach a time when they know "cross-dresser" is not the label that captures their identity. But the timing of when that point is reached varies greatly by individual.

As a social construct, the gender binary attempts to force people to appear and behave in feminine or masculine ways—not both or neither, or bits of one today and parts of another tomorrow. Whether because of socialization and incorporating the gender binary into one's worldview, or because of negative sanctions around social acceptability and fitting in, most transsexuals try to be masculine or feminine in public, and most male cross-dressers hide their femininity. Tri-Ess establishes rules to keep its members heterosexual and sexually conservative while advocating for their display of femininity. Since this advocacy has been only minimally successful, most male cross-dressers know they live on the outer margins of acceptable gender behavior.

I heard from a number of people who were male-to-female transsexuals about their discomfort around cross-dressers. In spite of the fact that both groups conform in different ways to the gender binary, the general perspective was that the groups, though not completely distinct, have very different issues. Gail (MtF) said, "their issue is so far from mine, it's kind of difficult to connect. And I kind of find it absurd for men wanting to wear dresses, if that makes any sense." Jessylynn (MtF) told me: "I have to admit, someone who is living full-time [having transitioned] has to put up with a lot of things that the occasional closet fetish cross-dresser does not. They know they can jump back on their side of the fence and it will be safe in there." Part of the dislike of "closet" cross-dressers that Jessylynn admitted to stems from being lumped in with a "fetish" category by the public. Dee (MtF) continued this line of thinking: "When people think of transvestites they think of somebody having some type of sexual deviance. So then you basically get hung with them." Maryann (MtF) couldn't understand that either: "I don't have any time for casual guys, casual dressers who will part with their boxer shorts for a couple of hours and then change back into them."

Tristan (FtM) found it unfortunate that this division exists:

You both have to deal with your families and your kids and your friends, there's a lot of things that can join people together emotionally, rather than looking at the differences. And I think part of the problem is that some transsexuals see cross-dressers as not legitimate. It's like if you're gonna cross-dress you should be one of us kind of thing. Some people go through that progression where they start off that way and then they realize they're transsexuals and other people just come to the conclusion that they're just cross-dressers and they always are. It's like the attitude of some transsexuals is if people are cross-dressing, they're just transsexuals who haven't figured it out. It's kind of like gay people saying bisexuals are gay people who haven't figured it out yet. Stupid.

Of course not all transsexuals feel negatively toward male cross-dressers, but tensions often surface at mixed support groups when medical information about transitioning dominates meetings week after week. People who are not transitioning feel that their needs are being ignored. Many cross-dressers are reluctant to go out in public, such as to a restaurant, while many transgender people are eager to go out. The stereotyped matronly cross-dresser or, in contrast, those in miniskirts and fishnet stockings, embarrass some transsexuals. Possibly the horizontal hostility that generally exists within marginalized groups is responsible for the internal tensions, complaints, comparisons, and disparagement (Clare 1999).

Food for Thought

Constructing the self in such a dramatic way that the body is altered to fit what is in the mind is surely an enormous step. And taking this step is often seen not as a choice but as a necessity. Yet the journey is not all of a piece. There is a physical transition and a social transition. For the social transition to be successful, some would argue that the elements of the physical need to be in place. To be taken seriously as a man, they would say, it's important for a female to have top surgery; to be viewed as a woman, one should not be balding or have beard growth.

There are countless stories of how individuals go about their transition, some with starts and stops, others as if in the express lane. Lucy (MtF) went slowly, first occasionally cross-dressing by herself, then joining a church where she could go alone as Lucy, then telling her family, seeing a therapist and starting hormones, coming out at work, and starting to live as Lucy full-time. Her painstaking process took more than two years. It seemed that her family would accept her, but by the time she had SRS she and her wife had separated, and she had also lost her job.

We cannot know what the concept of gender would mean for someone like Lucy if our culture was more open to gender variability. Would she define masculinity and femininity the same way and still want to transition physically from male to female? Possibly, yes. Perhaps constructing the self in a more open society would mean only that more ways of construction would be available, not that construction would occur less often. What I would most like to see is, at minimum, an end to the binary choice—and, at maximum, a new conceptualization in which masculinity and femininity are not so rigidly tied to certain body features. Could we see breasts, for example, as appropriate on a man?

Mark (FtM) raised this issue when he told me of a time he and trans friends went skinny-dipping:

What occurred [was after my] transition [and] 10 years without meeting another of my kind, and I got in that river—and I don't know what the hell my expectations were about what I was gonna see—but there was a male-identified male and a female-identified male, and about everything that ran in between. There were breasts and penises, and hair on the shore, and breast [forms] on the shore, and all these naked configurations, and I'm going, gee, "Mark, what the hell did you expect?" And it's like, I had my own feelings in the community, all these concepts, about who people are by what they wear, by how they portray themselves, and so putting people into boxes. And when I became aware that I was just as guilty of this [as non-trans people] then I could let it go. I could go, "Oh, they're just people. They're just people." They've got all these different configurations. And they're just people. I could see who they are, I could treat them as who they are rather than as [bodies], and I think if we were all blind to the appearance of people and get to expectations, then we could truly begin to treat each other as human beings and not as objects.

I ask again: Could we see breasts, for example, as appropriate on a man? Could he be one type of man? I believe so. I believe it isn't the lack of breasts that makes the man—it's his internal sense of masculinity. Hence, I believe that a man is a man with breasts or not—if that's what his gender identity is.

One's identity is one's own—one's own to recognize, embrace, change, express, and communicate to others—and we need to allow that. What we lack is the imaginative framework to capture that. We need more than two acceptable body categories and more than two corresponding gender categories. Clearly we don't have enough labels, but more than that, the broadened framework needs legitimacy. Gender variance needs to be encoded in a vocabulary we already have (though this needs to be expanded), but even more important, the gender schema needs to be seen as valid—not deviant, not other, not abnormal.

4

Coming Out to Community, Family, and Work

I can assure you that not one of us who has transitioned hasn't considered that we may be signing our own death warrant, just by saying the truth of who we are. (Lynnea, MtF)

Another thing is that everybody has their little secrets, their little behind closed door secrets, but when you come out as transgender or transsexual or cross-dresser or whatever, it's like there's nothing else. Everybody knows all of your secrets. They know all of your personal life, and it's like, there's nothing, you're like bare, stripped. I don't think the people you try to tell appreciate that. They don't understand that and appreciate that fact. (Devin, MtF)

How does a person reveal a secret he or she is ashamed of? How do people tell others something they fear will lead to rejection by people they love? How does someone explain an aspect of the self others may not understand? If the secret is gender variance, words and concepts fail; society's grasp of this issue is limited. Not everyone wants to be a pioneer or martyr for social change. Yet personal authenticity is at stake. Honesty to oneself and in relationships drives the need to tell. Not being honest means that the individual could be discovered and discredited, and being discredited is all the more serious if it is done by people you care about—family, spouses, children, or close friends (Goffman 1963, p. 65). Secrecy itself carries risks.

For many trans-identified people, coming out is not the same as it is for gay men, lesbians, or bisexuals. Gender variance and homosexual orientation are both personal secrets, and people may respond similarly to both, with aversion or surprise. But a different sexual orientation does not challenge people in the same ways as gender variance. Some individuals who are trans-identified will probably continue to look the same and may take on the same gender role as a gay man or a lesbian, but a transsexual will dramatically change his or her appearance, body, and gender role. A genderqueer may vigorously confront others' ideas of what a man or a woman looks like or acts like. A male cross-dresser challenges notions of what a "real man" is. These revelations, changes, and confrontations defy people's strongly held ideas of gender and human nature (Brown and Rounsley 1996, pp. 119–120). Kand's (transgendered) comment touches on all these points:

I typically find myself wishing everyone knew about my gender stuff. It gets hard carrying around a big secret. On the other hand, it is an ordeal to sit people down for "the talk." . . . And I look back to when I was coming out as gay 20 years ago, and compare the two, and it was easier because you could say, look I'm gay and people knew exactly what you were talking about. This requires explanation, processing.

Telling

Because telling others about one's gender variance entails risk and vulnerability, it is a significant decision. When to tell, what to tell, and whom to tell are all weighty factors. Sherri Lynn (MtF) acknowledged that people she had known for a long time seemed the most confused, "because they thought you were just being you all those years and when you finally have to tell them, 'No, I was pretending' . . . they don't understand when you tell them that was not the real me. I couldn't show the real me." For Dave (male cross-dresser) as well, deception was too limiting:

[I]t's worse to not disclose that kind of thing because then I'm hiding. Then I'm secretive, which then leads itself to other kinds of secrets and not telling full truths and not being totally present with the person you're with. I don't want to do that. I want a real relationship this time, and it's gonna involve being, disclosing who I am completely.

Some people I spoke with felt that acknowledging their past was important. Jeremy (FtM) said he would "tell close friends simply because living as a girl and then a woman has been a significant part of my life experience." Abe (FtM) agreed. "I feel it is a very important part of me and my history."

Some struggle more than others with their decision. Kymberley (MtF) found that the stress before coming out "was starting to manifest itself physically in that I was having chest pains consistently every day, headaches would occur at least once if not two or three times a day . . . when I began cross-living, the headaches and the chest pains were gone within a week." Others have less trouble wanting to be seen for who they are. Shannon (genderqueer) talks to new friends about both sexual orientation and gender identity.

If I don't say something, they're just going to see me as a "regular old dyke," which I don't want—about as much as dykes don't want to be seen as straight. I don't want my gender identity to be invisible. And if they're going to be my friends, they need to know about—and be okay with—my genderqueerness. If not, they're out the door.

Max (transgender stone butch) keeps her gender journey a little more private. "I'll often let people think I'm a butch dyke or a man without feeling like I have to tell them about the intricacies of my journey. But when I get close to someone, I want to tell them more." And Kyl (genderqueer) sometimes tells, sometimes doesn't. "It depends a lot on their level of experience and maturity. I don't usually 'clarify' for people who are confused—better to keep them guessing . . . and thinking."

How people told others about their gender identity often went beyond the usual "I have something to tell you" conversation, or the explaining that is usually done in a more casual, private conversation. Sometimes way beyond. Joney (MtF) was outed in her court-martial, "so it is impossible to hide it now." Melissa (male cross-dresser) was on an MSNBC investigative show called *The Secret Wardrobe*. He said, "I had heard that they were doing it and looking for heterosexual male cross-dressers. So I contacted the producer and said, 'Hey, I'm a heterosexual cross-dresser.' And they said, 'Will you go on camera?' Can we ask you questions? Can we put you in a dress?' 'Sure.'"

Becky (male cross-dresser) told his wife the way Tri-Ess recommends: "know what the answers to the three major questions are going to be. Are you gay? Where's this going to end? And what else have you hidden from me?"

Robert (FtM) viewed outing like a sport and was enjoying it. "I never sit anyone down and say, 'There's something you should know. . . .' Instead I either purposefully bring it up casually ('When I got my period . . .') or just let it come out as it inevitably would ('I can't hang with you tonight, I'm going to a transsexual function.')."

Lauren (MtF) did not want to give up an aspect of her female privilege so didn't tell many others: "I mean, people talk to me about some very intimate things. I wouldn't be able to sponsor other women in AA if I wasn't seen as a genetic female, they wouldn't open up to me. Some would, a lot wouldn't." And Dawn (hermaphrodite) felt that he was mostly on a private journey but told select friends. "I find Native Americans seem particularly open to IS [intersex]. So, I tell my Native friends. They have been OK with it. I avoid telling lesbian (non-Native) friends because they have been repulsed by the idea I am half-male."

Pronouns

The pronouns "he" and "she" are used in the English language to refer, simultaneously, to both a person's birth sex and the gender expression of the person—obviously a dilemma for trans-identified individuals, intersex, and genderqueers. Although not in common use today, he-she and she-male refer to a person's gender expression with the first pronoun and

SHANNON

the person's birth sex with the second. This hyphenation "signals a crisis of language," since birth sex and gender identity are supposed to match (Feinberg 1996, p. 97).

What we do not have in the English language is a gender-neutral pronoun. "It" refers to inanimate objects, not people. Some alternatives have surfaced, but they are in limited use. Websites, some books on gender, and some trans-identified people use *sie* (pronounced see) or *ze* (pronounced zee) instead of he or she, and *hir* (pronounced here) instead of him or her. S/he or the phrase "she or he" can be used to suggest an either/or or both identification. Rothblatt suggests replacing his and her with *hers*, he and she with *heesh*, and him and her with *hirm*, but I believe we are a long way from adopting any of these pronoun variations (1995, p. 127). The addition of Ms. to Miss and Mrs. as a manner of address does set a precedent. The use of Ms. challenged the idea of using a title to indicate whether a woman was the property of some man, but attempts to change pronouns are a more extensive and fundamental confrontation of the binary sex/gender scheme.

How does one assert his/her authentic identity in such a limited framework? First, the identity has to be acknowledged and understood—no easy task for the participants in this study. November (genderqueer, trans) pointed out:

ROBERT

The "wrong" pronoun depends on the situation for me . . . if I'm with friends, or in a group of queers, then "she" is the wrong pronoun. Usually I (or someone who knows me) will correct the person, which often leads to some uncomfortableness. Often in public places (the grocery store, for example), the clerk will call me "he" or "sir," and then think they were wrong and correct themselves . . . more uncomfortableness. . . . If I was to use [hir and ze] I just think people would not know what I was talking about. I mean, no one outside of my little queer community would get it, most people would not even register that as a pronoun.

Some individuals felt that no pronoun fit them. Glen (human) noted that there is no pronoun for "human being," since he/she and him/her are binaries. Phillip (metagendered) would like the pronoun e, since there is no metagendered pronoun in use and sie and hir don't appeal to him. Jon (intersex) felt that he was a he/she and not one or the other but said, "I identify as intersexual as much as I can." Matt (genderqueer, androgynous) would also prefer a mix of pronouns, since "I don't consider either of these [he or she] to be correct, and I wish people wouldn't use them and thus decide my gender identity for me."

Genderqueers seem to have the most difficulty operating in the he/she binary, but others have trouble as well. Many butch lesbians or transgender butches prefer a male pronoun, but they might not be offended by a female pronoun. It often depends on setting. Max (transgender stone butch) gives this example:

I've been perceived as a butch dyke, a gay man, a straight man, an asexual young boy, etc. I've been called she when I preferred he, and he when I preferred she. I prefer she, but in situations that are dangerous "he" is much safer for me. People have been shocked by hearing me referred to as she, and it makes it less safe because I'm no longer passing

KT (transgendered butch lesbian) shares:

At this point, my girlfriend uses male pronouns and I'm pretty active on an online butch/femme community and of course there everybody uses either male pronouns or gender-neutral pronouns to refer to the butches. Other than that, in daily life I'm always referred to as she and in terms of female, and while I'm very used to it because that's how I've always been referred to, it doesn't feel quite right.

Male cross-dressers often have the problem of being called "he" when they are presenting as female. Rene (male cross-dresser) told me: "At times when I am cross-dressed, people will 'sir' me either intentionally or not. That is understandable. I am six feet tall, have masculine shoulders that cannot be completely disguised, and even my best feminine voice can betray me."

Transsexuals reported having great difficulty with pronouns—people deliberately calling them the wrong pronoun out of meanness, people being confused or forgetful, and just mix-ups. Dakota Lynn, a male-to-female transsexual, was taken as a female-to-male transsexual in this amusing incident:

Well, just last week I was at K-Mart and a cashier asked if I was a FtM and then told me that she thought that I could pass as a man very well. . . . When she first started, she looked at me, she said, "I don't mean to pry," she said, "but are you taking hormones?" And I kind of puffed my chest up a little bit and I said, "Well, yes I am." "You know," she said, "It is working so good with you." I mean, my head's getting big and everything. And I said, "Thank you very much." I said, "I'm trying." I said, "I have to work a little bit better on the voice." She said, "No, you've got the voice down perfect. Nobody would guess that you're not a guy." And I just went, "Thank you, thank you very much." And I never told her her mistake. I didn't want to embarrass her.

Sexual Orientation

The power to define and label an individual's sexuality is crucial. These labels relate to both psychological needs and political power. Years ago transsexuals who wanted sex reassignment surgery had to claim to be heterosexual or they would be denied surgery. Medical gatekeepers both imposed their own heteronormativity (the assumption that everyone should be heterosexual) and suspected that some individuals might want to transition to avoid their own internalized homophobia (if a man lives as a woman, having sex with a man won't be gay sex). They confused gender identity with sexual orientation.

Engaging in a close examination of gender identity and transgender bodies leads us, once again, to an unavoidable reassessment of sexual orientation. In a heteronormative society, the multifaceted implications of sexual orientation become invisible. Nagel summarizes the scope of their impact:

sexual boundaries can be cultural, involving spectacles, music, literature, art, and all of the paraphernalia of cultural production such as gay pride parades and carnivals, sexual contact or performance clubs, sexual websites, straight and queer erotic art, films, and pornography, legal, involving the regulation of sexual practice such as laws certifying heterosexual marriage and outlawing sodomy, same sex marriage, divorce, *economic*, involving the production and consumption of sexual products and services such as contraceptives, fashions, sex aids, toys, and pharmaceuticals, prostitution, tourism, *political*, such as restrictions on immigration or debates over discrimination based on sexual orientation or accommodating domestic partners, and *racial*, *ethnic*, *or national*, such as sexual stereotypes of particular ethnic groups, the marginalization or exclusion of homosexuals from ethnic communities, nationalist calls for compulsory heterosexuality and sex for procreation—to reproduce the nation. (2003, p. 48, emphasis in original)

The conflation of sex and gender is especially apparent in the assumptions governing the "sexual boundaries" listed above—assumptions that are cracked wide open by trans-identified people. Even though there are contested terrains—of objects and types of sexual desire, choice of partners, types of sexual activity, and purposes of sexual activity—examinations of these issues have been too narrowly defined.

One of my first challenges in this regard was presented by male-to-female transsexuals who were lesbian-identified. I did not resist their lesbian identification; rather, what turned it into a challenge for me was the question, What *makes* them lesbians? Is it that they identify as women and are attracted to women—does that make them lesbians even if they still have a penis? If they had surgery, is it that they have neo-vaginas and are attracted to women—so they are lesbians? What about the lesbian culture I was affiliated with—women's music, literature, artwork, festivals, and so forth? Were we the same kind of lesbians if that cultural connection was absent for them?

The people I spoke with consistently reflected the view that their gender identity, and not their physical body, defined whether they were gay, lesbian, or straight. For example, Johnny (FtM) shared this:

When things become physically sexual, my mind feels like a male with all the male sex organs and the need/urge to strap-on and take care of business in a "heterosexual" way . . . not in a way where two lesbians are just "playing" with penetration. I don't like to be touched in a feminine way. I have never felt homosexual with another female, but I have felt very gay with sex with a male.

Seventeen of the study participants stated they were polyamorous, and four said they were pansexual. Raven (transgendered FtM intersexual) discussed his sexual orientation:

I also had to come to terms with my sexual preference. I call myself pansexual because bisexual implies that there are only two genders. There are at least three; even if you discount my transgendered friends, I'm living proof. I like girls, I like boys—but other androgynes are at the top of my list. It doesn't matter which direction they're going in; if it's gender ambiguous, my head will snap around as they go by.

Thirteen people defined their sexual orientation as queer, reflecting a variety of attractions and behaviors. The FtM gay man without a penis, the female-bodied genderqueer partnering with a man, or the androgyne male attracted to pre-operative MtFs—none of these are "straight." Sexual orientation is about whom you are attracted to (object choice), sexual behaviors engaged in, and your own gender identity. There are multiple combinations for these aspects. As Wilchins comments, "By crossing the lines of gender, you cross the lines of eroticism. You also cross the lines of aesthetics" (1997, p. 120).

Autogynephilia

A brief word about autogynephilia, since it has received much media publicity in the past few years due to psychologist J. Michael Bailey's transphobic book The Man Who Would Be Queen (2003). It is transphobic in the sense that it merges transsexuality with sex—a transsexual is either a homosexual or eroticizes the feminine and is autogynephilic. According to Bailey, men undergo sex reassignment surgery because female genitals sexually turn them on. He does not seem to understand the concept of gender identity and portrays transwomen as sexual deviants.

Bailey's book created an uproar in the LGBTQ community, as well it should have. A storm of protest followed its publication, reflecting fears that his "junk science," as Dr. Lynn Conway called it, would be viewed as scientifically sound. Bailey's work was condemned by virtually every nationally prominent transperson, national advocacy organization, and the Southern Poverty Law Center, which compared his work to "racist science." Bailey also became the subject of an ethics investigation into his research methods by Northwestern University, where he is affiliated. The Lambda Literary Foundation, which first nominated his book to be considered for a Lambda Literary Award, ultimately removed it from the list of finalists after a massive protest campaign.

A few transwomen commented to me about autogynephilia, with one stating that as her sexual orientation. Dana (MtF intersex) had this to say about eroticism:

The autogynephilic, you know, homo-eroticism, that some people say that this is, that this is all a sexual turn-on. And I don't believe that's the case. I believe transgendered people do have sex lives and do have erotic lives and do get excited about themselves as women or men, whatever the case may be. But that's just like everyone else. Lots of good-looking women really get turned on when they're dressed sexily, so why shouldn't we?

Andrea (MtF) had also given thought to the concept:

In modern society an awkward sounding new term [has been introduced] in medical literature to describe transgendered longing—autogynephilia—which literally means to love oneself as a woman, and it is used to characterize transgendered males desiring to change their sex. While pre-modern society understood transgendered longing in spiritual terms, modern society has focused on its sexual, physiological dimension. Many transgendered individuals have justifiably taken issue with this term because it is reductive, defining their experience as primarily sexual. While this focus on the sexual aspect of transgendered experience is important, it cannot fully explain the transgendered individuals who are born male and their identification with women. For example, such identification precedes adolescence when sexual feelings are neither that strong nor central.

It is my position that the transgender experience has some overlap with eroticism, as does every gender identity, and that it is stigmatizing to reduce gender to sexual stimulation.

Passing

My personal view of passing is reflected in what Nathan (FtM) told me: "Never have passed as male. Passed as female for most of my life." And in what Felicia (transgendered) said: she has "to act as a male to match the skin on the outside. . . . I'm kind of like putting on a show that's not necessarily true to myself." In other words, passing is pretending to be something you are not. When Nathan successfully portrayed himself as a woman, his birth gender, he was passing; Felicia passes successfully as a male every day. They both were socialized in a gender they did not identify with and had to learn to be what they were not. Passing is pretending to be what others expect of you, not being who you are.

However, the word passing is more commonly used to mean being accepted as who you really are, without considering that you might be or have been something else. You'd be passing if seen as a woman, not a male dressed as a woman. Transpeople have lived in every historical period, but the concept of passing is a recent development. Passing, according to Feinberg, is "a product of oppression"—hiding a true identity out of fear (1996, p. 89). The word as it is used today generally refers to fitting into the gender binary as a man or a woman. In order to pass in this sense it is not enough to be who you are—you have to alter your gender appearance and behaviors to fit notions of masculinity and femininity. This may be important to gain civil and political rights, employment, safety, and family acceptance. But in so doing, individuals may need to hide their trans history, and keep that stigma invisible (Goffman 1963). In this sense, "Passing becomes silence. Passing becomes invisibility. Passing becomes lies. Passing becomes self-denial" (Bornstein 1994, p. 125).

Repeatedly I heard, "Passing is very important to me." Y. (transgendered butch) told me, "I like when I do pass and get the acknowledgement of my masculinity because I feel they are really seeing ME." Beverly (MtF) asked, "How can I deal with all the issues of being a woman if I am constantly worried about being read?" And Nora (MtF) said, " I just want to be treated as any other woman would be and if people know that I'm TS they tend to treat me differently than a genetic female in most cases." This view of passing is quite common.

JT (transman) touched on an important point—people's discomfort with gender ambiguity. "For the average transperson, passing is a definite goal in order to alleviate discomfort when interacting with others." An example of this is Simon (FtM tranny boy), who was job hunting when we spoke:

And, yes, so when I go to the job interview at the local elementary school, which I'm hoping to do not too long from now, I'm not going to be, "Oh, by the way, I'm trans.". . . I'll just be a masculine woman looking for a job. And, probably everyone will be, like, "Oh, she's a lesbian." I'll be, "Sure, lesbian, great." And I'll totally defend it because that's who I used to be. That's my community, and I'll definitely fight for the right to be a masculine woman as a teacher.

Many male cross-dressers (CDs) would agree with what Melissa (male cross-dresser) said: "Passing is the most important issue for me. As a CD, my goal is to pass when I am en femme." Rene (male cross-dresser) explained further: "I am blessed to be able to pass most of the time. So I never really have difficulty in public. But my definition of passing is not to completely fool everyone I meet. To me passing is presenting an image that is sufficiently feminine so that most people will accept me in the female role."

Glen (human) has a different view. He believes that "the key is if you can go out in society and say I know I don't pass, and you can have the strength to do that for yourself, that everybody that looks at you knows that you're a male when you're wearing a dress and make-up and all the rest of it, that is so liberating, it's unbelievable." Eric (male cross-dresser) concurs:

Passing is not an issue for me because I don't try to disguise myself as a woman. I just enjoy wearing women's clothes—my feminine side feels liberated when I do. . . . I want others to know that a man wearing women's clothes is not bad or wrong. I think if more people were in tune to their masculine and feminine sides all of us and them would be better off.

Gabriel (intergendered) simply says, "there is nothing to pass as."

If an individual passes, then he/she will not be publicly challenging the binary. For this reason and others (such as wanting to feel true to oneself), some, like Shannon (genderqueer), do not want to pass: "Passing really isn't a goal for me. In fact, I'd prefer not to pass (which does, in some ways, still make passing an issue)." November (trans), by contrast, offered this opposing view:

I feel that I'm passing if I get read as "either" gender . . . sometimes I pass as a girl and sometimes I pass as a boy. Sometimes I don't really pass as anything. Sometimes I'm very intentional in trying to pass as a boy (usually not as a girl) but not always. When I pass as a boy or a girl, I think it presents a challenge to the gender binary, since neither of these is the "right" or "true" gender for me.

Going Stealth

One type of passing is called going "stealth," an option that arises if the passing is quite complete. It is not uncommon for MtFs and FtMs who attend support groups and are active in the LGBT community to disappear after their transition. They begin new lives, sometimes in new cities with new jobs, but they leave behind their trans friends, male cross-dressers, and genderqueers. There is nothing wrong with this choice; it is not the choice everyone makes or even has as an option to make. Gwyneth (MtF) talked about going stealth:

For the most part, we are normally socialized individuals, who don't at all like the transgressive frame we're placed in as a result of our condition. Very few people want to be freaks. Those that do have no problems with the fact that society sees them as other. It becomes a statement. For many, it is an unwelcome statement, one that they never chose to make. The "transgressive" aspect is a projection of the culture, as you point out, not of the individual. What then is the proper response? To shout out "Hell, yes, I'm a transgressor!" when all you wanted was to function normally for some part of your life? Or to say "No . . . I am not a transgressor. I am a civilian. Please take that spotlight off me, give me my papers, and let me alone."

Others feel that stealth is not positive for the community as a whole. Patricia (MtF), for example, told me: "I hear people nowadays that their objective is to pass and go totally stealth, and I can understand that feeling, but that's not really being part of the answer. I think we owe a lot to those who have gone before us and that if they had all done the same thing, transitioned and then gone stealth, would our lives have been better today? I don't think so." Tina (MtF) will not go stealth either, because "denying who or what I am, pretending that I did not live as a male for 45 years, would be just as debilitating as forcing myself to live male for the rest of my life."

Concerns about safety make passing an important issue for trans-identified people. For example, Max (transgender stone butch) said:

Passing must be done sometimes, in order to be safe. But I can't imagine living a stealth life where no one knows I'm trans. I think it's important for there to be people who are visibly challenging the gender binary. But I don't think it's every transperson's responsibility to be a gender crusader. Sometimes safety has to come first. But I wish that stealth trannies still supported the important role us visible gender-benders have in achieving gender liberation for everyone instead of distancing themselves from us. As for me, I pass as a man at one job and as an out TG stone butch at another. I never feel safe because I never know how I'm being perceived.

Invisibility

Coming out, telling others, going stealth—these are all issues of visibility. Many trans-identified people feel, and often regret, that their identity is invisible to others. For example, Dylan (FtM) felt trapped in a dilemma between telling people he was a female-to-male transsexual, with the resulting "processing fest," and not bringing it up but then not feeling "totally seen." Stephe (androgyne male) pointed out the consequence of minimal understanding of nonbinary identities when he mentioned

the frustration androgynes feel about being stuck in between all sorts of polarities, like between man and woman, between transvestite and transsexual—and between het-

erosexual and bisexual (since the jury is out on whether sex with a tranny makes one het or bi). Much like the intersexed, androgynes don't have much visibility and don't have a peer group.

Similarly, femmes are often invisible as lesbians, especially in comparison to the more noticeable butches.

I heard from a number of FtMs about invisibility because they were passing so well as men. Reid (FtM), for instance, while wanting to be seen as the male he was, felt that the problem was "the unconscious assumption that I always have been," meaning that there would never truly be a place for him in the culture—a male with a female history. Is there a place for his story to be told and accepted? For Max (transgender stone butch), being seen as male is sometimes fine, but "sometimes I feel invisible even to other queers." And Nathan (FtM) had this experience when he visited Northampton, Massachusetts: "It was odd to be there surrounded by women who looked right through me as they passed me on the street. When I was living as a lesbian there was a certain amount of attention that I was accustomed to. . . . Now I am simply a black man—often either the inspiration of fear or fantasy."

A few years after our interview, Tristan (FtM) wrote me:

I began transitioning by simply wearing "men's" clothes and cutting my hair shorter. I lived with that for a while, asking myself if it would be enough, and found that it wasn't. One thing I did not consciously anticipate was the fact that in attempting to make my male identity more visible, I actually made it less visible. The reason for this was the fact that some lesbians wear "men's" clothes and have short hair; consequently, I went from being perceived as a heterosexual woman to being perceived as a lesbian woman. I have found this extremely frustrating because, while previously observers were getting it half right (I'm not a woman, but I am attracted to men), they are now incorrect about my gender identity as well as my sexual orientation.

Whatever gender identity an individual has, it is important that others confirm it. As Adrienne Rich (1986) says,

Invisibility is a dangerous and painful condition. . . . When those who have the power to name and socially construct reality choose not to see or hear you, whether you are dark-skinned, old, disabled, female or speak with a different accent or dialect than theirs, when the authority of a teacher, say, describes the world and you are not in it, there is a moment of psychic disequilibrium, as if you looked into a mirror and saw nothing.

STEPHE

Lesbian Community

Trans-identified individuals are negotiating not only their belonging to (and identification with) communities of women and men but also their being identified by sexual orientation. This has been especially significant in the lesbian community.

Historically lesbians were considered to be females whose gender was "inverted," in that they were seen to behave like men and were believed to want to be men. Devor (1997) points out that the sexologists' "invert" classification of lesbians in the early twentieth century was very similar to the present-day view of female-to-male transsexuals. This definition of lesbians as "not women" conflicted with the views of lesbian feminists of the 1970s and 1980s who promoted a lesbian identity that had little tolerance for masculine qualities.

For many FtMs, the lesbian community is, during some period of time in their lives, the best associational fit. As lesbians they do not have to look or behave like stereotypical women, they can take on a butch identity allowing for masculine expression, and they come to realize that gender identity is distinct from sexual orientation. But they are not quite at home yet. When participants in a study by Devor discovered they were FtMs, "they embraced it as both an escape and a homecoming" (1997, p. 98).

Likewise, among participants in this study, Reid (FtM) was attracted to women and at first thought he was a lesbian. He ended up not thinking that, and explained why he felt "different":

But the feelings of being very uncomfortable in women's bathrooms, being really self-conscious about my body, those never went away. And in fact, they kept getting stronger over time. And so, it was only true for part of my identity. There was another part of my identity that was very uncomfortable but it didn't have to do with sexuality, it had to do with gender. And I had gender identity and sexual orientation completely conflated in my mind. . . . I kept trying to look at well, what does this mean. I'm a lesbian but why don't I want to call myself one?

Ace (FtM), too, came out as a lesbian but said he "never totally fit in . . . I just feel uncomfortable in any kind of a woman-oriented atmosphere." Ace is comfortable "with the good old boys, with the working on cars, getting nice and dirty, going camping and fishing and all that other good stuff, when I was a kid I wanted a wife and kids so badly."

Kerwin (FtM) married, had a son, divorced, and then thought perhaps the problem was that he (she at the time) did not want to be with men. He

ACE

began living life as a feminist, partnering with women. But "to me it was sort of like, well, this is second best. This is something, at least I can do this, it's better than being a feminine woman and a wife and all this stuff, but I am not really that." So he "tried for many years"—until he came out as transsexual.

Emotional debates over the existence of transsexuals have been divisive in the lesbian community. Female-bodied people living as men belie the idea that women are sisters and allies against male entitlement and male dominance, while male-bodied women who claim to be feminists and lesbians undercut the notion that all men are the enemy (Califia 1997, pp. 91–92). Until the 1980s, female-to-male transsexuals transitioned in isolation; after that, however, lesbian communities around the country experienced several or many transitions at a time (Meyerowitz 2002). Simon (tranny boy) told me the "dykes that I hung out with in '97 were the boys in 2001. . . . The community was in huge transition."

Nathan (FtM), once a butch lesbian with numerous community affiliations and awards, clearly challenged his lesbian friends. "The more clear I became about my gender," he said, "the more freaked out lesbians got. And, so I went through this period where in the beginning it was 'Oh, yeah, sure' to 'Oh, my God' to 'What the fuck?' 'Wow, he did it.' And for gay guys it was like, 'Oh, that's interesting, honey,' and they'd pat me on the head to 'Dang!' to 'Wow' to 'Do you want to go out?'"

Nicholas (FtM) represents another experience: "I work as a guy, but play in dyke community where I am out as trans but not stringent about passing." Nicholas hasn't had top surgery and does not bind when he's in lesbian space. He came out when he was seventeen, eighteen years old and has been in lesbian community for ten years. Since this community has been "fundamental to my surviving my early 20s," he said, "I don't want to give that up. And I resent it when they try to throw me out."

Lesbians who have partnered with men also share this sense of complexity in regard to defining who belongs in lesbian community. Lesbian and heterosexual women sometimes challenge these women's identities and tell them they are not lesbians and cannot claim to be lesbian (Schecter 2005, p. 9). Lesbian partners of transitioning butches have also been attacked. As Loree Cook-Daniels (2004) has written, "This erasure of my history, commitments, experience, achievements, sacrifices, rights, and identity has been devastating, resulting in deep depressions and an inability to continue my work. What may be to some of us an abstract, theoretical discussion may be to someone else a very real personal attack." The lesbian partner of a now-transitioning FtM, has had her own identity caught up in the controversy and put into a tailspin. Politically, psychologically, and spiritually she may not want to be partnered with a man or seen as a heterosexual.

Another issue that aggravates the controversy over who belongs in which community is that many women want to protect their women-only space because of the oppression of women by men. But women-only space is not what makes women safe. If we understand that gender identity is not rigidly bound in binary categories and that sexual orientation can be fluid over a lifetime, we should allow for the complexity of identities, feelings, behaviors, and personal histories. Policing artificially rigid identity boundaries creates a false sense of security. Men are not the only perpetrators of violence against women—women batter and sexually assault other women as well (Girshick 2002).

Coming Out to Parents and Siblings

Parents, siblings, friends, lovers, partners, and children undergo stress when challenged by role changes, name and pronoun changes, or altered gender expression of the trans-identified person in their lives. Parents are routinely viewed as responsible for "shaping the development, character, and adult nature of their off-spring" (Ettner 1996, p. 27). Given the widespread misunderstanding of transsexuals, cross-dressers, and other gender variants, it is not surprising that many parents question "where they went wrong" in raising their trans-identified children. In some cases, parents accept the criminal behavior of a child more easily than a gender transition (Ettner 1996, p. 28).

Jennifer (MtF and female) said her mother "wanted to know what she had done wrong in the way she brought me up and is still very angry with God for letting this happen to her firstborn." Raven (transgendered FtM intersexual) said his dad ignores him, while his mother "feels that my transition is proof of her failure to properly indoctrinate me in femaleness, like you're supposed to do with IS [intersexed] kids." Melissa (male cross-dresser) had this experience with his father: "I really got the feeling that my father thought that everything he'd tried to teach me about being a man was for naught. And I think that really bugged him a lot. I don't think he thought I was gay. I think he just wondered where it went wrong. My son's got lace underwear, where the hell did I fail?"

Not surprisingly, in many families the reactions are mixed to news that a family member is transsexual, genderqueer, a cross-dresser, or transgender. Matt, who identifies as genderqueer and androgynous, encountered both support and nonacceptance:

My sister and brothers teased me a little at first, but now are completely accepting and open-minded. Since they've grown up with me, they understand that I've been this way all my life, so that helps. My parents, on the other hand, were a different story. My dad's okay with my dating men, but he feels ashamed that I act "feminine" and has actually dragged me to his shrink to try and fix me. . . . My mother is a fundamentalist evangelical, so she thinks all of this is caused by the fact that I stopped attending church as a teenager (again, reversing the causal relationship). She probably still prays for me every morning.

Emery (FtM) experienced a mixed reaction from his sons: "My gay son was ecstatic; my older son thought I'd joined a cult." Susan (MtF) had a gay brother who could not empathize with her transition:

My brother accepted the cross-dressing aspects, however when he realized that I actually wanted to live as a woman he was upset. . . . We could relate to each other and be a support system. But he couldn't understand why I would want to be a woman, 'cause his idea was to pump iron and get in real physical shape as a guy.

Lauren (MtF, female) had a rough time during transition, living full-time after alcohol treatment. Her mom, with whom she now has a close relationship, took a few months to come to terms with the changes. She said to Lauren, "I don't totally understand this but I think I've come to the decision that I'd rather have a daughter that was alive than a son that was dead." Erin (MtF) also had a serious drinking problem. When she got sober and transitioned, her brother said to her, "You were going to die when you were drinking." Then he continued, "if this is what your problem was and you're going to stay sober, and I don't have to cry over you no more, I'm happy that you found who you are. That's fine."

Of course, many parents and siblings are not supportive, and some are outright hostile. Holly (MtF), for example, was the oldest sibling. "I went from the highest status to like an untouchable, an unspeakable, because of sexism and fear and all that. It's a powerful twist. Yeah, roles in the family are obliterated." T.I. (naturally bearded dyke) said her family was very intolerant of her appearance. At one point her mother suggested she have a sex change operation—to be female! "I think she was commenting on my appearance and my nascent beard or whatever it was." Patric (FtM, male, intersexed) was written out of his parents' will and told not to attend family gatherings. When he told his mother he had almost killed himself at one point, she replied, "Well maybe you should have." Lynnea (MtF) said her family also responded with hostility. Her brother made death threats over the phone. Her mother "thought I had lost my mind. My wife chose divorce."

Rejection by some family members was dictated by religious beliefs. Farah (MtF) said her brother, a Pentecostal preacher, "told me to stay away from his family and that I was going to Hell." Dustin (FtM) didn't experience complete rejection, but his family was certainly upset: "they think I'm crazy and a failure, I've mutilated my body, will never find love, am going against God." Both of transwoman Joy's brothers are fundamentalist Christians. "I really have no idea," she said, "if either of them will ever be able to hoist themselves far enough out of the religious morass to even see me clearly. Their fear of God, or Hell, or whatever, is so great they can't seem to question anything in the Bible. I'll miss them."

Sadly, many family members react by cutting a trans-identified person out of the family. This was Kymberley's (MtF) experience:

Ninety percent of my family has turned away from me. I do not get birthday or Christmas cards from anyone anymore. Last Thanksgiving I asked if I could attend as a woman (I have just come out) and was promptly told "No, and your invitation is revoked." I then said that if I was invited to Christmas, I would go as a man, but I was never invited.

When JT (transman) told his family, they didn't speak to him for a year. Melanie (MtF) said her family, too, had cut their ties with her. "Both [my brothers] really have not had me up to their homes. I hardly interact with my nieces. In my own immediate family I'm not invited to Passover or things like that, and it's in essence a shunning."

Of course, the other option is not to come out to one's family. Some individuals I spoke with had not told their parents of their trans identity. Some in Eric's family know of his cross-dressing but have never seen him dressed. Julie (male cross-dresser) said his mother discovered his stash of female clothing and "insisted I not tell my father." His sister knows and is very supportive. Arianna (MtF) summed up the experience of not sharing trans identity with family: "After my young attempts to challenge gender roles, my blood family through humiliation and lectures made me hide or even to attempt to vanquish my innermost desires. . . . Since my journey began by changing and hiding due to my blood family, I am totally in the closet as far as they are concerned."

Intimate Relationships: Spouses or Partners

Ashley (MtF, female) told her wife before they married that she was transsexual.

She thought she could change me and I didn't think she could. And that was very difficult for her. She said if it was another woman she could at least fight it, but you are the other woman. So, that was very hard because I know that she loved that person, loved me. I see it as me but she sees it as another person.

Rachel (MtF) said that her girlfriend (now ex-girlfriend) accepted her cross-dressing at first.

However, distance between us grew as she did not want to educate herself or attend meetings. She preferred to pretend it did not exist. When I told her I was a TS and later began using hormones, it was a big problem—she thought I was choosing this path over her. Eventually a wall of secrecy and isolation formed as I kept my feelings to myself and she asked no questions.

Laura (MtF) was married for more than twenty years, cross-dressing privately the entire time and feeling very unhappy in a male role. Finally, she decided to be honest with her wife.

I began going to a support group for cross-dressers, and I began to buy female clothes. I got a job as a female impersonator at a nightclub, and sat down and told her a different version of my life than she knew. And, she thought that the last 20 years were a lie, and so, we went to a marriage counselor, and did that for awhile, and the marriage counselor ended up saying to us, my wife's name is J——, she said, "J—— maybe you don't want to be married to [Laura], and [Laura] maybe you don't want to be married to a woman." And, we went home from that and let that settle in, and a week or so later—I had already come out to my daughters who were teenagers, and they were tremendously upset—and so my wife asked me to leave.

Robyn (MtF) had an even more severe experience. Her wife tried to kill her when Robyn confessed to cross-dressing after more than twenty years of marriage. They went through ups and downs of sleeping in separate bedrooms, debates on whether to tell the children, and whether they would move to another state as had been planned. Her wife went into fits of rage, attacking Robyn on more than one occasion, and Robyn had to flee for her life. After a separation, when Robyn began to live her identity full-time, they agreed to divorce when one of them felt the need. Robyn filed for divorce after her present husband proposed to her.

ROBYN

Cross-dressers and Their Intimate Partners

A problem that causes great anxiety is deciding "how much honesty and when," according to Leslie (male cross-dresser). Fear of rejection by a prospective or current partner keeps many cross-dressers in the closet. As Caroline (male cross-dresser) said,

I have not been able to tell all my girlfriends before now for fear of losing them. I almost told my last girlfriend. We went together to a couple of Halloween parties with me en femme. But she felt uneasy and threatened because I looked better as a woman and I diverted everybody's attention from her.

Although telling has been a challenge, Julie (male cross-dresser) has found that his previous girlfriends and his present wife have all been supportive. Cris (male cross-dresser) has been married thirteen years, and his wife is supportive. His wife "would prefer that I didn't feel the need to dress but accepts it as part of who I am."

BJ (male cross-dresser) told his wife when they first married, and she attended some Tri-Ess functions. His wife has "struggled to understand and has become at least tolerant, somewhat supportive." BJ dresses at home, and they go out three or four times a year. "I'm not interested in

CAROLINE

pushing her beyond her level of comfort" he said. "I believe she does accept my inner womanliness, even if she can't wholly comprehend the outward expression of it." Male cross-dresser Becky's dilemma is to accept the high degree of tolerance by his wife: It's "very hard to put panties, bra, nylons on in front of her as we're dressing for the work day."

Some wives accept their husband's cross-dressing but with stipulations. For example, Joanna (male cross-dresser) and his wife negotiated some ground rules "about some days of the week when I've got to be very masculine," he explained, "and other than that I can do more or less what I want. . . . My wife just says she needs to have some total maleness for a good part of the time."

Kara (male cross-dresser) would like to shave off his body hair, but his wife doesn't want him to so he doesn't. Julie (male cross-dresser) also wants to shave his body hair: "We struck a deal," he explained, that "if I want to do it, I ask first. I shave about one time a year, and during that week, I dress more. I would do it two or three times a year if my wife didn't mind. She likes hairiness."

For some couples the agreement is to keep the cross-dressing out of the bedroom. Jamie (male cross-dresser) has an encouraging wife, but "she will not have sexual relations when I am dressed. She says she wants a man, not a woman, making love to her." Joanna (male cross-dresser) said he "would really like a romantic or sexual role for my female persona,

Joanna. I would like this to be with my wife, but this will never happen. This is disappointing."

Probably more wives are not accepting of their husbands' cross-dressing than are. Melissa (male cross-dresser) said:

I am divorced because I could not stop cross-dressing when I married. My ex-wife went to extremes to enforce her prohibition of CDing, even though she knew that I was a CD when we married. This challenge continues as she now continues to try to have the court make this a condition of child visitation. Fortunately, the court has refused to recognize this as an issue worthy of consideration.

Elayne (male cross-dresser) was married for twelve years. His wife "never really, really wanted to understand it. . . . She never looked it up or read about it or anything. She just kind of thought it was sick."

Since Eric (male cross-dresser) divorced many years ago, he has told every woman he's had strong feelings for about his cross-dressing. "In 95% of the cases, my cross-dressing was an issue. What I've learned is to stop falling for women that will never accept me for who I truly am."

Unwelcomed Lesbian Identity

If a male-bodied person marries a female-bodied and female-identifying person, when the male-bodied person transitions and is post-op, does that mean the other woman is a lesbian? In the cases in this study nearly every wife confronted with a transitioning male-to-female spouse reacted negatively to the idea that she was now a lesbian if she continued to be intimate with her partner. Whether lesbianism is defined as sexual intimacy between two individuals with the same gender identity (as women) or with similar body parts (vaginas), these wives *are* lesbians. Yet they had lived their lives as heterosexual women who married men. This change in identity was thrust upon them without their consent.

I believe it is too simplistic to say that if you love a person it should not matter whether he/she is feminine or masculine or has had surgery that alters the genitals or chest and/or takes hormones that change the body. These are major components of attraction. Such qualities in our intimate partners affect our own self-esteem and our views of who we, ourselves, are. Furthermore, in social interactions people respond to one another based on identity and appearance. It is not surprising—given homophobia, sexism, and heterosexism—that societal baggage complicates the relationship for the partner or spouse that is not transitioning. Negotiating how roles change in the relationship is one part of the challenge. Understanding personal identity changes is another, often insurmountable, part of the challenge—unwanted and possibly rejected.

MtF Rita's sexual intimacy with her wife ceased after Rita came out about her authentic gender. "While very open and tolerant," Rita said, "[my wife] is also very straight, and just couldn't handle it." MtF Jennifer's wife "came to the conclusion that our practice was a lesbian one and she was not a lesbian." Sherri Lynn (MtF), who does not live full-time as a woman, was able to save her marriage because, "Although [my wife] does not want to live with a woman she does not seem to mind seeing me switch back and forth."

In MtF Audrey's case, prostate cancer was one factor affecting her intimate relationship with her wife. But in addition, her wife was "totally against anything that is not conventional." For Nathan (FtM, male) a big challenge occurred when women he was with began to identify as lesbians and wanted their relationship to be more "lesbian." Nathan was moving in a firm male and heterosexual direction, and he no longer identified as a lesbian. Rickey Lynn (MtF) reported: "My wife still has problems with my changes, but is trying to work out her own feelings in this situation. I have shown her that we can still have an intimate relationship, but she is concerned about becoming or being considered a lesbian. As far as I am concerned there are worse things to be in this world."

Degrees of Acceptance

While most marriages of transsexuals and cross-dressing participants in this study ended, some were redefined. Karlette (MtF) and her wife have been married for thirty years. "We had to redefine our relationship," Karlette said. "We are no longer husband and wife. We are now very close friends and business partners." Laura (MtF) similarly said, "The disclosure ended the intimate part of our relationship. After much work, we are now close friends; perhaps closer than before."

Kosse (FtM, male, female) has been fortunate in that he married an exceptional man:

[My spouse] always knew I was different. He enjoyed my lack of conventional femininity. We are best friends and always will be. He's made big sacrifices to help me out, and he understands and respects my identity. I don't use the term husband any more, I use spouse or partner. In public, we look like two men and he is fine with that. He is still affectionate and close. His defining remark about it all has been, "When I think of loving you, gender has nothing to do with it. I just love you."

Lauren (MtF, female) knew she had to tell her fiancé that she was transsexual even though he didn't seem to have any idea she wasn't born in a female body. She told him her story, and he replied, "I want to tell you something, I want to tell you that I mean this, because I wouldn't say it if I didn't, when I met you you were 100% a woman, when I made love to you you were 100% a woman, and you're still 100% a woman."

Jamie (male cross-dresser) worked with his therapist for the courage to tell his wife, and finally he did. "She has accepted me beyond anything I hoped for," Jamie said—including the fact that he likes to dress and use makeup. Patricia (MtF) discovered that her wife went through three emotions after Patricia told her she was transsexual: anger, fear, and relief. "Relief because she had known for years there was something wrong between us. Didn't know if it was me, didn't know if it was her. And it was relief, 'now I know what the problem is.'"

Opening Up to New Relationships

Living as a trans-identified individual leads to challenges in pursuing intimate relationships: Do I have the "right" body parts? Will my new partner respect my identity and be sensitive to my needs? Is the other person ready, as Melanie says, "to look at their own gender identity?"

Several people I spoke with felt that not having the body parts partners expected or wanted was a hindrance to their intimacy or their sense of satisfaction. Kerwin (FtM) had been in sexual relationships with men and women, but, he acknowledged, "I simply do not have the genitals to do what I wish to do, with either a man or a woman." As Alston (FtM, male, intersex) put it, "No parts = no intercourse = no relationship." After Sae (FtM, transgendered) had chest surgery, he said that he "felt immediate relief and now that the incisions are stable, it feels good, actually, to reclaim my nipples and enjoy my chest." But Dawn (hermaphrodite) felt that his biggest challenges in intimate relationships were "being resistant to behaving in [only] one gender role and [hoping] my body parts [are] not offending [a] mate. I don't know if I had infant surgery, parents don't talk about it. I don't see any scars, but my genitals have very little feeling in them. That leads to frustration in my (previous) girlfriends. That creates tension."

Glen (human) has been in relationships with women who thought they would "cure" Glen's dressing in feminine clothing:

In other words, they believed that in having sex with me, this would make my want/ need to wear dresses and makeup, diminish and eventually go away. It was like "they" were a replacement for "me." They couldn't see that my going out in a dress and makeup was a totally and separate activity from finding them attractive. One female said to me, "You don't need a woman, you've got yourself."

Ace (FtM) has been celibate for many years. He felt that partners were putting him into too male a role: "I am a non-hormone FtM so I wish they'd be less prone to compartmentalize me into a man." Y. (transgendered butch) was looking for "someone who provided everything I wanted in a relationship who also wanted a family, a monogamous commitment, who wanted to be my wife and wanted me to be her husband as in a butch-femme marriage."

Those who do not conform to the gender binary sometimes confront the great difficulty in trying to communicate their identity to potential partners. The question then becomes how much they should keep trying. November (genderqueer, trans) puts it this way:

It's usually hard for people to think about gender outside of a binary system, so my friends and people I date generally try to fit me into existing gender categories. Some simply see me as a girl, and refuse to think otherwise. Some respect that I want to be seen as a boy, but they still see me as essentially female. Some are willing to think of me entirely as a boy. Unfortunately, none of these are exactly correct—while the last category is the most respectful, it still has the effect of placing me in a box in which I do not belong. I find that I spend a lot of time and energy in relationships trying to get out of the boxes in which others place me—they think, "Oh, I get it—you're not a girl. Therefore, you must be a boy. I get it!" And then it's hard to convince them otherwise, or to have further discussions about gender with them.

Dan (FtM), like many female-bodied male-identified people, needed to teach partners how and where to touch him:

Here's what you have to do to not make me feel uncomfortable and here's what you need to do for me and here's what I can do for you. This is what has to happen otherwise I will get no enjoyment out of it. That's not really setting us up for a really good sex life. So, that's basically how I do it. There's certain parts of the body like the chest area, actually, the whole pubic area is pretty much hands off from my partners. I do use a prosthesis. I find that's absolutely necessary for me. . . . I need to teach them how to not touch me so I don't feel feminized.

Internalized Homophobia

Dustin (FtM) has found that "even tranny fags are homophobic, particularly when the actual body is trans." Indeed, many male-to-female transsexuals have been conditioned to reject male-male relationships as unnatural. But when they transition, they may be attracted to men or identify as bisexual. Overcoming the internalized homophobia they didn't realize they even had becomes yet another issue for them. Andrea (MtF), for instance, was in a relationship for two years with a gay man. "That was very important for me to break the ice and be with someone who was accepting. It was difficult working through gradually my homophobia." Rickey Lynn (MtF) had this experience:

My biggest challenge was when I was first approached by a male. All the rules of homophobia came flying back to me and I had to run out of the area to get control of myself. Since then I have had several relationships with men and have learned to accept and even enjoy them. Some of them have shown me true kindness and gentleness that I had never known when I was a male. I now consider myself to be bisexual, as I still have an interest in females, but have been developing an interest in males at the same time.

A. J. (FtM, male) experienced his homophobic feelings before transition—identifying as a male when others around him treated him as a female:

I never felt comfortable with a boyfriend because it made me feel gay. I felt like a boy on the inside and I was so embarrassed to be seen in public holding another guy's hand. I hated my body and I was so embarrassed by it I wouldn't let any guy touch it. And it's funny . . . that's how I felt as a girl. But as a guy, it don't bother me. I could hold a guy's or girl's hand and it's cool.

Parents' Relationships with Their Children

Telling your own child you are a cross-dresser or a transsexual causes high anxiety, because no one wants to lose the unconditional love that children have for their parents. Relationships will be altered in significant ways. If a divorce is pending, gender may be used as a weapon against the trans-identified parent.

Younger children want reassurance that their parent isn't leaving them. Ashley (MtF) transitioned when her daughter was two and her son was almost five. "I remember getting a phone call from him when I went the first time dressed as Ashley. The next day he called, he goes, 'Does this mean I don't have a daddy anymore?' And I go, 'No [son], I'll be whatever you want me to be.'" Now, eight years later they are doing quite well with visitation. Ashley's ex-wife has remarried, and the adults are cordial and focus on the well-being of the kids.

Kosse (FtM) has four children (fifteen, eleven, eight, and five). "They are the ones who understand and accept me best of all," he said. "They never give me a minute's stress over it. They see I am happier and still their parent and that is all that matters to them. I wish other people could be as wise."

Laura (MtF) has two sons and two daughters and has had mixed results in their acceptance of her:

I have two young sons and I have simply said nothing to them at all. I've not referenced the subject, though they see that I look a lot different from any of the other dads because I have long hair and no facial hair. And I've got these boobs that stick out when I wear t-shirts. But the other day I was talking to my 9-year-old and he saw a picture of me from years ago, and so I said, "Well, I look a lot different now, don't I?" And he said, "Yeah, you do." I said, "Well, I probably look at lot different than the other dads, don't I?" He said, "That's ok. And I like you just the way you are."

I heard more stories of acceptance by children than not, even if it took some time. Tim (FtM) kept custody of his now twelve-year-old son after his divorce:

We had to work through some pretty unique things that were pretty interesting. About a year and a half ago when I told him I'm not going to be living as mom anymore, I'm going to be dad, I said, "You come up with a name that feels comfortable for you to call me, because I know you can't do the dad thing right away." And he worked his way through and just accepted dad after awhile. But one day I noticed he was really looking sad and I walked up to him and I said, "This is really rough on you, isn't it?" And he said, "It's just confusing." And I was like, "Come here, give me a hug." And he hugged me, and I said, "Who does that feel like." And he said, "My mom." And I said, "And it will always be. I'm both."

But not everyone had a rosy outcome with their children. Robyn (MtF) has one child who was getting married and specifically excluded Robyn from the wedding. MtF Audrey's daughter was somewhat understanding but won't let Audrey see her grandchildren if she completes her transition. MtF Gail said her son tried to kill her when he heard Gail was transsexual: "He came after me with a baseball bat."

Others were not regularly seeing their children. Dana (MtF, intersex) lost her two kids in a custody battle in which her wife used Dana's trans status against her. Joney (MtF) had visitation with her two kids only four hours a month. She filed for a modification of the court order but that has dragged on for three years. Bonnie (MtF) hadn't seen her ten-year-old son for over a year and a half. She is keeping a journal about her life that she intends to give him when the time is right.

In her letter to her daughter, Rachel (MtF) explained what transsexuality was. She shared with her daughter some of what she was experiencing, and she asked for love and time for understanding. Rachel's last paragraph included: "I can find another home. I can find another job. I can find new friends. There are many things in my life that I can replace. But I could never find a way to replace you."

Workplace Issues

Loss of the ability to work—to support oneself or one's family and to engage in authentic expression while at work—is probably the number one type of discrimination against trans-identified people. This is especially a problem for transsexuals who go through visible change in gender expression and through legal measures such as a name change. Unemployment and underemployment are some of the biggest fears for transsexuals. If they haven't had those experiences personally, they know others who have.

Transitioning individuals have a need not only to be authentic in order to fulfill their sense of self; they also need to demonstrate that they can socially and financially function in their gender. The World Professional Association for Transgender Health (WPATH, formerly known as the Harry Benjamin International Gender Dysphoria Association) calls for a year of "Real Life Experience" (RLE, when a person lives full-time in his/her true gender) in preparation for sex reassignment surgery. It can be a huge challenge for a person trying to meet this one-year requirement to keep his/her job or find a new job, owing to many factors that are out of his/her control—especially the views and reactions of employers and coworkers. Furthermore, the transitioning individual will need money for new clothes, hormones, therapy, perhaps electrolysis, and other transition-related expenses for all this to work successfully. At the end of the RLE year the individual may hope for surgery, adding to the need for stable employment so as to have the funds to pay for it.

It can be a long and agonizing decision whether to try to transition on the present job or to apply for a new job somewhere else using a new name and with a new appearance. Staying on a job that one has worked hard for, been successful at, and which is stable seems an obvious choice. Many transitioning people have invested in career training, have accrued benefits, and may feel comfortable on their job. However, it can be difficult for coworkers who know a person as one gender to adapt to that person's new gender presentation. Some coworkers may feel betrayed, confused, or disgusted at the prospect of a transsexual on the job. Transitioning on the job means telling everyone, not only the supervisors. It entails working out the bathroom issues, changing work records, and being under a microscope. Because of sexism and gender norms, the individual—even though he or she remains the same person—is often treated very differently by coworkers. Friendships will most likely change.

To avoid being treated like a man in women's clothing or a woman who doesn't belong in the ladies' bathroom, to eliminate the prospect of being fired or passed over for promotion, or to escape facing the anxiety of how transition might be viewed in a conservative workplace, many transsexuals leave their job and apply for a new position in their true gender. Some even move to a new city. There are many challenges here, since their work history will not reflect their new name and gender, and their résumé may not match up with what they say in an interview. This, of course, defeats part of the purpose of the new job—to start anew without reference to their past gender.

Jessica (MtF) transitioned before beginning her current job. She had witnessed a few transsexuals transition at her old workplace, but they didn't stay there long. She told me:

And these people, they were being ridiculed. And they just couldn't take it and so they left. That has to be such a difficult position to be in. I don't have to worry about that now but at one time, I said, I don't think I could do that. If I'm going to start, I'm going to start one way, not change at some point in the middle. It just seems too difficult on top of everything else that was already difficult enough.

Workplace Protections

According to a 2002 poll commissioned by the Human Rights Campaign (HRC), carried out by Lake Snell Perry & Associates, seven in ten people surveyed were familiar with the term transgender. After they were read a definition of transgender, nine in ten said they had heard of transgender people. Sixty-one percent of Americans believed that there should be laws to protect transgender people from discrimination. However, 57 percent thought federal laws already existed to protect transgender people from being fired, when in fact there is no federal law at this time. Between 2001 and May 2007, the proportion of the national population covered by transgender-inclusive laws increased from 6 percent to 37 percent. As of July 2007, the states of California, Colorado, Connecticut, District of Columbia, Illinois, Iowa, Maine, Minnesota, New Jersey, New Mexico, Oregon, Rhode Island, Vermont, and Washington ban discrimination based on gender identity and expression in employment, housing, and accommodation. In addition, according to the HRC website, state courts, agencies, or the attorney general in four other states (Florida, Hawaii, Massachusetts, and New York) have interpreted existing law to protect transgender individuals against discrimination.

Discrimination based on gender stereotyping was found to be illegal under the Civil Rights Act of 1964 since the *Hopkins v. Price Waterhouse* Supreme Court ruling in 1989. However, there continues to be debate about how broadly this ruling can be applied. Adding gender identity, expression, or characteristics to existing legislation is necessary for consistent and certain protection.

The Human Rights Campaign monitors company benefits for LGBT employees using its Corporate Equality Index. To earn a score of 100, companies must offer transgender wellness benefits (such as coverage for hormones) along with equity in benefits offered to gay and straight partners. In 2006, 133 companies earned a 100 score, up from 101 in 2005 and 13 in 2002 (Henneman 2006).

Living One's Identity Part-Time

Most transsexuals go through some portion of their existence living only part-time in their true gender. This is most likely to happen when they are at home while presenting in their assigned birth gender at work. They maintain the continuity of their career, but they may then find it very difficult to fully transition. Donna (transgendered) was working as a male but wearing female undergarments. She felt that her field was not open to women employees: "The field I'm in has only two women that I know of in it. . . . I would like to work as Donna, but it's hard to do. Now, if I were younger, yes, I would. . . . Donna is always out just not attired." Maryann (MtF) was also working in male mode. She wakes up in her nightgown, she said, and "I'm completely en femme, and I stay that way underneath, and I have to create a [male] costume for the world to see."

Devin (MtF), who was living full-time as the woman she is, went back to passing as male because of her cancer diagnosis. "I need to keep my insurance," she explained, "because I need to keep my treatment, my health care . . . were it not for the fact that I'm dealing with the health issues, I would have asked them to let me transition on the job or quit and found another job as a female." Devin also needed to keep her stress level low. "I just don't want to mess with it, having to explain to people and knowing that people feel uncomfortable because you're there. I don't want that stress."

Forced Out

Some who transition on the job are forced out or find their position eliminated. Such discrimination against transsexuals and transgender people is impossible to document because it is not overt. Rather than understanding the issues and acknowledging the bravery of trans individuals who take steps to be who they are, non-trans people let their ignorance and prejudices come to the forefront. This happened to Tina (MtF), for example, who worked in an administrative job at a college. When she told her college president she planned to transition, the president said she wasn't sure if Tina would keep her job or not. Tina paid $1,000 to have her therapist come to the campus, consult with administrators, and make presentations to staff and faculty. "I was called confused. I was called a wolf in sheep's clothing. Someone said that they were going to have a lawsuit coming, there was bunches of things." Tina transitioned, and her contract was not renewed—under the guise of reorganization. (Although it's impossible to know for sure if people at the college felt that Tina's therapist was biased, bringing in a neutral third party to address them might have been a better choice.)

Susan (MtF) transitioned while working for the U.S. Postal Service. She experienced hostility from both men and women, and coworkers called her "Mr." For a time she was forced to continue using the men's locker room. She was looking for another job because of the stress. Finally, one night a machine malfunctioned. "So I struck the top of the machine like you do the TV sometimes when it's not working. And it broke a little switch inside and the next thing I remember I was being escorted to my car as a violent postal employee. I think they were looking for an excuse to get rid of me. And, that was real traumatic at the time."

Gail (MtF) was vice president of a tribal college. When she first came out to her staff, people were accepting. But as news spread to the tribal council, all Gail's past commendations carried little weight. She was forced to accept a contract buyout. Gail commented:

I really loved my job. It was a job that I could have stuck to. It wasn't so much the money, it was the fun I had at it. And so when I moved to Minnesota I got a job as a chicken sandwich maker, a check-out clerk at a grocery store, a packer of candy at a warehouse, which just about killed me. And I thought things were turning around when I got the job at the computer company that provides help, software issues, and I was there two weeks and one night a lady calls me and says, "Gail, just clean out your desk and leave." They never would tell me why I was laid off. So I haven't been working since last year.

Transitioning on the Job with Positive Outcomes

For many transsexuals, transitioning on the job works well. A large corporation may have policies in place, pull in staff from Human Relations, and hold meetings to answer employee questions and affirm that the trans individual is to be treated respectfully. A smaller workplace may deal with the situation more informally. Erin (MtF) works in a warehouse. She found that going slowly with her changes has been key to acceptance from her coworkers. "Over the course of two years," she said, "I've managed to be accepted wearing nail polish, bras, berets in my hair, etc., and being able to be more feminine in general and being comfortable with them. This has been a milestone in my transition."

Karen (MtF) announced her transition at a meeting that included her spouse, the director of her department, and the CEO of the medical institution. She said:

The staff were generally not surprised. A number stayed and they wished me well and that sort of thing. It went over very well. A number of staff also said I don't understand what it's about, but whatever it is, we'll help you. And since then it's really been a non-event. . . . I just show them very much more of the same only it was apparent from my appearance that I was being mistaken for a woman all the time by my patients. And the staff sort of felt uncomfortable, they felt they had to apologize [to the patients] and cover up. Oh, no Dr. H's a guy, he's married, he has children. They were protesting and protecting my masculinity.

Kymberley's transition also went well, though she feared she might lose her job at a large casino. She spoke first to the Human Resources manager, after researching the company's policies. From there she met with other supervisors. She'd been slowly changing on hormones and had let her hair grow long. When she had her new legal name and the gender designation had been changed on her driver's license, she met with her coworkers:

On a Tuesday I came out to co-workers at one job, and it was the entire graveyard shift, which was my department, which was the money counters for the casino, the security guards, the janitors, anybody who happens to be there on graveyard shift were involved in that meeting. Oh, and all the department supervisors as well. Well, on Wednesday I had an e-mail from a friend I hadn't talked to in two years at a different casino, "I heard something about you."

Still, every person on the verge of a workplace transition is unsure of how the announcement will go. Lydia (MtF) circulated a letter at her workplace. "To my colleagues and business associates: I am writing to inform you of a significant change in my life, and to ask for your understanding and support. . . ."

Coming out as trans is not really a choice if a person wants to live life fully. We are who we are, and living in ways consistent with who we are is key to a satisfying life. No one should have to experience the stress, rejection, expense, or pain of the always challenging transitions described by participants in this and other studies. A more welcoming environment of better-informed and accepting family members and coworkers would alter such stories dramatically.

5

Gender Policing

While transitioning, I go to the bathroom in a movie theater. The female ticket taker objects when I try to go into the ladies' room. The male ticket taker objects when I try to go into the men's room. When I confront them both and ask which I should use, they refuse to come up with an answer, both just desperately reiterating that I can't go in either "for the sake of the other patrons." Rather than call the manager, make a scene, and leave my kid sitting for a long time alone in the theater, I go out back and piss in a dumpster and then went back to the film. (Raven, transgendered FtM intersexual)

I'm frequently made uneasy by offhand comments, jokes made at the expense of cross-dressers or gays. It's not as acceptable as it used to be, at least not in the academic community I live in, but cross-dressers are still fair game, especially in the media, where almost routinely in television commercials they are employed for the sake of a guaranteed laugh. In this way, I'm reminded of the attitudes deemed appropriate by the majority. It's as if a cultural edict has been issued: Thou shalt ridicule those who cross the gender line. (BJ, male cross-dresser)

The gender binary has a little wiggle room. After all, some men are househusbands, some women are astronauts, some men have long hair, and some women sculpt their bodies, muscles bulging, through bodybuilding. David Bowie, Boy George, Dennis Rodman, and Marilyn Manson are hugely popular. But, in general, it is a serious offense to violate gender norms.

One way to understand how dysfunctional the gender binary is for everyone is to see what happens when expectations are transgressed.

Some transgressions that are public—such as when transsexuals transition and face job loss, or when masculine women are harassed in the bathroom—give us clues as to what kinds of departures from the binary norms draw people's ire. Other transgressions that are often private—such as when males cross-dress in secrecy, or when intersex people cannot access their own medical records—indicate their importance by the shame attached.

While women can wear pants, it is not socially acceptable for men to wear a skirt or dress. And many women are working in traditionally male occupations, though still not in top management levels, as they should be. This is not to say that females have an easy time of crossing gender barriers as they are conceived of in the binary system. Max (transgender stone butch) voiced her observation that "[o]nce a female crosses the line from tomboy to 'butch,' from boyish to 'manly,' you are fair game for harassment, violence, etc.," though Raven (transgendered FtM intersexual) points out, "Butch women are punished, but not nearly as much as femmy men. Tomboys are 'cute,' [but] sissy boys are dragged to the shrink or beaten. I've walked down the street as a butch woman and as a femme man. I know which is more likely to get me killed, which gets me more hostile glances, which gets me worse negative comments."

Bathroom Policing

Public bathrooms, with the familiar stick symbols for men and for women on the doors, are, as Dan (FtM) put it, "a perfect crystallization of all the gender norms in place. . . . It's like this amazing literalization of the more abstract binary teachings we get everyday." For Dan, bathrooms have been a "site of terror." He continued: "All it takes is one snotty person to make you feel like you don't deserve to live. I've had security guards remove me because they had quote unquote complaints from other students. And being removed from a public washroom at the University of Oxford isn't the sort of thing you want to tell your parents."

I heard from many genderqueer and butch women that women had reacted negatively to their using the women's restroom. These upset women had challenged the right of androgynous and masculine-looking female-bodied individuals to use the bathroom. But you shouldn't have to be a certain kind of woman to be entitled to use a public space; some women should not be privileged over other women. Why do feminine women feel that they have a greater right to use the bathroom, and furthermore why are they allowed to humiliate or antagonize other women?

KT (transgendered, butch lesbian) has never had problems in the men's room, only the women's room—and she is female-bodied. George (soft butch, queer) says she uses the women's bathroom but gets "looked at and commented to." Laura (MtF) says she gets "into trouble using public restrooms of either sex. Men don't want me in the men's restrooms, likewise for women."

Hostile reactions to gender-nonconforming people using public bathrooms are common. cj (transgendered) had his wrist broken in junior high by two girls he didn't know who told him he "didn't belong" in the girls' bathroom. At that point cj identified as a lesbian. "It made me analyze everything I did in terms of masculinity and femininity ('gayness' and 'straightness')," he recalled. Someone called the guard at a mall, saying there was a man in the women's bathroom—meaning NiseyLynn (MtF). She showed the guard her driver's license, which had an F for female on it. (Later, Nisey-Lynn complained to the head of security at the mall, and she did receive an apology, and the guard was fired.) For A.J. (FtM), "seeing the words 'Men's' and 'Women's' above each door, knowing I wasn't either" created shame. And as Dan (FtM) asked, apropos of finding five security guards outside his washroom stall, "Is our society a little paranoid or am I?"

Entering a public bathroom for the purpose of a necessary biological function should not be a shaming experience or a problem of any sort. Yet Caroline (male cross-dresser) is afraid to use a bathroom. When he drives any distance at all while cross-dressed he brings a bottle to pee in. Lucy (MtF) also has been afraid to "stop at a rest stop for fear of the police being called. So Lucy had a large drink cup in the car. "Yes, I peed in the car." And for Reid (FtM), who was athletic in junior high and high school, "Changing in that locker room was one of the most traumatic things I had to do, and I had to do it every day. It was torturous. . . . And I couldn't begin to tell you where any of the girls' bathrooms were in any of those schools because I never went in one. Never once, I just didn't go to the bathroom." Not going to the bathroom can cause serious health problems, such as bladder and kidney infections, cystitis, urinary stones, and chronic dehydration.

For transitioning employees, use of the bathrooms at work is a contentious point. Oftentimes transpersons are either told they can't use the bathroom of their gender identification or told to use a bathroom on a different floor or in a different building. Lucy (MtF) is able to use a small women's bathroom. But, she says,

I wait until it is empty and affix two, yes two, unisex signs to the door. One over the "Women" sign and the second by the handle. The second sign by the handle is a nau-

seating green color. I had started with just the one sign over the "Women" on the door. Apparently some ladies are visually challenged, so a second sign was incorporated. It is working. And there are women who have taken the plunge and joined me after I went in. When I leave I take the signs with me.

At other workplaces, management has taken a strong stand to support every employee's right to use the bathroom of self-identity. Robyn (MtF) shared:

The problem, of course, was the ladies room. I had already foreseen and I had volunteered to Human Resources I would use the ladies room on a different floor. We have a 12-floor building for my business unit. But two of the younger women objected to my using the ladies room. And HR said, "Well Robyn has already agreed to using the ladies room on another floor until she has her surgery." "But wait a minute, you're going to tell the people on the other floor, right?" "Well, no." "Well, you're going to post someone outside the room or something, aren't you?" "No, that would be sexual harassment against Robyn, you see." "But you can't let people, you have to tell people." "Wait a minute, ladies, Robyn's not the only transsexual." "You mean there might be one using our floor?" And the HR lady said, "Ladies, deal with it!"

Clearly, the issue of who uses what bathroom creates anxiety for many non-trans or non-genderqueer people, and these fears do need to be addressed. Everyone, whether male or female, needs a safe place to go to the bathroom. Some women feel that a sex-segregated bathroom increases their safety, but an unlocked door that anyone can walk through doesn't really make them any safer. The stereotype that only men (and never women) are potentially violent or rapists is factually incorrect (Girshick 2002). A violent male or female can walk through that door. Greater safety would be achieved with either single-user bathrooms or multiple-user bathrooms with locked stall doors that go from the floor to the ceiling. And as Rothblatt points out, "The thought that persons of any sex can enter any restroom at any time should discourage sexual violence in restrooms" (1995, pp. 91–92).

A second concern of some women is that men are messy when they pee standing up. That can be ameliorated by having toilets with push-button plastic sanitary seat covers that change with each use. Businesses and public works can also have bathrooms cleaned more frequently. This may be necessary, as Max Valerio (2006) points out that male pee has a strong odor and males are often sloppy with their toilet bowl aim. Perhaps boys need stronger socialization in bathroom etiquette.

The thought of all-gender or gender-neutral public bathrooms, sometimes proposed as a way to secure everyone's right to equal access, makes many people uncomfortable. This is something they aren't used to. However, after much resistance people got used to race-desegregated public facilities, and people can get used to gender-desegregated facilities. Right now, because of the harassment they encounter, some people are denied safe access to freely use the bathrooms they need and have a right to use in public spaces, at work, or at school.

Since going to the bathroom is not in itself a safety threat, we should work on education to decrease the discomfort of people who feel that sex-segregated spaces are natural and necessary. They are neither. In fact, taking the "Men" and "Women" signs off bathroom doors and calling them "Restrooms" would go a long way toward loosening the idea of the gender binary. It would eliminate the experience of intersex individuals' having to choose which type of bathroom to enter, and of someone, such as a butch woman or male cross-dresser, not fitting in. Everyone of any gender expression fits into a restroom.

The Women's Movement and Who Is a "Woman"

Sadly, feminist politics has its share of controversy around the boundaries of who qualifies as a man and who as a woman. Since women-only events are largely organized and attended by lesbians, lesbians have been in the forefront of debates about whether transwomen qualify as real women. A polarization opened up in 1973 when the lesbian rights organization Daughters of Bilitis splintered on the issue of whether MtF Beth Elliott, who had been the group's vice president, was a woman. She was expelled as not being one. Later that year Elliott, also a musician, was performing at the West Coast Lesbian Conference and was shouted off the stage. There was a huge split among attendees regarding Elliott's status. The next day, feminist leader Robin Morgan denounced Elliott in her keynote speech, accusing male-bodied transsexuals of "leeching off women."

This fracturing around transsexual issues continued among lesbians and feminists. In 1977, some lesbians protested the hiring of MtF Sandy Stone at Olivia Records, a collective that was formed to record and sell women's music. In 1979, the publication of Janice Raymond's book *The Transsexual Empire* added to the bitterness, since it was an anti-transsexual tome written from a feminist separatist perspective.

One of the most contentious efforts in the lesbian community to police who is accepted as a woman is the policy of the Michigan Womyn's Music Festival (MWMF), which is open to "women who were born as women, who have lived their entire experience as women, and who identify as women" (statement by festival owner Lisa Vogel). The policy divides women along lines of "real women" and "fake women." MWMF is the oldest and largest feminist women's music festival in the country, dedicated to creating women-only space for safety, cultural renewal and production, and escape from sexism, misogyny, heterosexism, and homophobia. While it is open to women of a wide range of gender presentation (bearded, butch, androgynous, and femme), transgender and transsexual women have not been welcome. Ian (male cross-dresser) looked at it this way:

I can really see both sides of the argument and I think it's problematic. Because I can understand why, I guess to me a male-to-female transsexual will never be the same thing as a genetically born woman. They've had a very different past experience. Now I'm not saying they're not women. But I can understand the need for some genetically born women to say, well, this isn't what we're about. Yet, I can see how painful that must be to the male-to-female transsexuals because they're someone who's been misjudged all their life. Now they're being rejected by the very group that you hoped would be a little bit more sympathetic.

In 1991, a transsexual woman, Nancy Jean Burkholder, was asked to leave MWMF after another festivalgoer asked her if she was a transsexual and she replied, "Yes." (She had attended the year before without incident.) By policy, MWMF workers will not question an attendee's gender, and they rely on individuals who attend to respect their policy of "womyn-born womyn" only. In other words, they request that transwomen stay away for that week of women-only space. Yet their "don't ask, don't tell" policy means that transwomen, genderqueers, tranny boys, and others who don't mention they are trans or perhaps are male-identified can attend. Nicholas (FtM) had this to say: "The 'T' I took is supposed to erase my memory? Turn me against everything I fought for? I'm not different; I'm just me, deeper. Michiganites try to get me to divide me against myself. They preach that I should hate that I'm complex and profound, that I am a new kind of human being. I hate them for it. It hurts."

An educational and protest group called Camp Trans emerged on national forest land across the road from the MWMF entrance in 1995. This staging site has offered protesters a gathering place for workshops and conversation. In 1999, a pre-op MtF and a post-op FtM entered the festival. After they had been seen in the showers, the festival was in an uproar because there were "penises on the land." This resulted in an additional policy of "no penises allowed" and the requirement that women attendees needed to be legally female (e.g., on driver's licenses). That same year Lesbian Avengers from Chicago, members of Transexual Menace, and other supporters marched, leafleted, and held workshops in the festival. Confrontations over the policy ensued, and four trans individuals were asked to leave (which they did).

A survey conducted at the festival in 1992 showed that 73 percent of attendees had no objection to post-op transwomen attending the festival. The exclusion policy has contributed to fifteen years' worth of Internet debate, protesting against performers who have appeared at MWMF, letters to "Lesbian Connection" and other lesbian and/or feminist forums, and countless conversations between friends. Matt (genderqueer, androgyne) said the "womyn-born womyn" policy is the only genderqueer political issue he makes a point of speaking about: "Most of those I've talked to have been supportive of the policy, and don't seem to understand how hurtful it is to many, which has led me to have some painful conversations with such friends. Hopefully I've at least given them something to think about."

At the August 2006 MWMF an openly transgender woman was allowed to buy a ticket. Camp Trans organizers thought that this meant an end to the fifteen-year exclusionary policy. However, the next day festival owner Lisa Vogel issued a statement reaffirming that the festival was for "womyn-born womyn" and that any transwomen attendees were disrespecting the policy.

Apparently the debate continues as to whether transwomen are real women, and the feminist community has vocal adherents to the different perspectives. To advocate only for acceptance of post-op transwomen only is classist and racist, since surgery is an option only for those with money. It is also exclusionary, since many transwomen don't choose to have surgery. To deny the self-determination of individuals who identify as women regardless of the body they were born in seems contrary to feminism. Genitals are not the only markers of femaleness or maleness—some people are born identifying in ways that do not correspond with the gender binary edict. For feminists to reject those who are marginalized by society because of gender identification is particularly unfeminist gender policing. While there are many strands of feminism, and lesbian separatists in particular may always find transwomen incompatible with their politics, the premise of this book is that genitals do not determine gender identity—nor does socialization, as important as that is in influencing gender expression and gender roles.

Bullying, Hostility, and Hate Crimes

Hate-motivated violence arises from a variety of sources: fear, ignorance, bigotry, misdirected anger, intolerance, and a need for control. Perpetrators of violence can be acquaintances of the victim, peers, family members, or strangers. Often, homophobic and gender identity anxieties are mixed up together, and perpetrators may not even be aware of their motivations. While statistics of harassment of and violence against transgender people are hard to come by, a 1996 survey of 397 MtFs by the San Francisco Department of Public Health gives us one impression. Eighty-three percent suffered verbal abuse; 46 percent faced employment discrimination; 37 percent had suffered abuse within the previous twelve months (and, of those, 44 percent reported it was by a partner); and 59 percent reported a history of rape (Nishioka 2002).

Only a small number of the people I interviewed said they had faced no hostility (e.g., Karen, MtF, who was accepted as a woman at her job and by her family, or Matt, genderqueer and androgyne, who dressed and acted conservatively at work and avoided jock bars and dark alleys); most had experienced bullying, harassment, or violence in their lives. Once, late at night, police stopped Raven (transgendered FtM intersexual) and his daughter (to whom he had given birth). They were, Raven wrote,

on a fishing expedition (I had a loud muffler, which is not illegal, but an excuse for them to stop me). My daughter has no ID. I look male, and not old enough to be her father. They act hostile and ask me to prove that I am her parent. My new name is not on her birth certificate, and anyway I am not her father, so I have no proof. I am totally sure that telling them I am her mom would make things worse. I manage to talk my way out of it, with her help, but it is a close one.

Young males in junior and senior high beat up Casey (butch lesbian): "I had rocks thrown at me. I had my car demolished. I had my locker set afire." Kerwin (FtM) didn't fit in as a girl. He was forced to face the "contempt and mockery" of other students: "I never got used to the stares, whispers, and laughter that greeted me wherever I went." The message of this hostility is, You need to change. And while most individuals stand up to this, they do so at considerable emotional cost.

Bullying of MtFs was common. Nora's (MtF) bullying lasted from when she was twelve until fourteen or fifteen: "I had two or three guys that really just loved to work me over." Julian (ungendered) endured violence for not being "appropriately gendered" during his childhood, though this strengthened his determination to work against sexism, racism, and heterosexism. Felicia (transgendered) talked about her discomfort around men: "When I walk into a room full of men, the intimidation starts at the door. I feel intimidated. I feel I'm being bullied even before I even speak or even before they even speak. There's something about a group of men being together, there's a lot of tension in the air. Men are very intense. Highly competitive, violent, rough, coarse." Since Felicia works as a male in a macho occupation, she has been having a difficult time. She is smaller than the typical firefighter and speaks softly. "I've heard lots of comments, you're a fag, you're a sissy, you're queer."

Being yelled at on the street, or accosted by strangers laughing and asking, "Are you a man or a woman?" are not uncommon experiences. cj (transgendered) has had "strangers freak out and call me perverted and pull young kids farther from me." These insults and shaming comments are forms of gender policing, attempts to keep people who are preceived as gender transgressors in line. Melissa (male cross-dresser) has felt this ridicule whenever a male yells to him: "'Hey, baby, nice legs!' and you know that that's not the tone of admiration. You know that he's saying, 'Hey man, nice dress you're wearing there, buddy!' And he's giving you the full brunt of his masculinity." And once, says BJ (male cross-dresser), when playing dress-up with his sister and cousin, "a handyman was in the house and saw me and teased me, asking if I was a little girl, and I remember feeling deeply embarrassed. This is how the gender police work, of course, making you feel guilty, ashamed."

The verbal taunts, bullying behaviors, and harassments are preludes to the more severe physical violence inflicted on many of them. Dee (MtF) was beaten up and urinated on while in the military and stationed in Germany. A former lover who "couldn't deal with the gender situation" beat up Keven (two-spirit). Jennifer (MtF) was told by her wife before their separation that a man Jennifer's wife had slept with had offered to kill Jennifer. Laura (MtF) has been beaten up several different times by men denigrating her transsexual status.

The ultimate and irreversible gender policing involves the hate crime of murder. Hate crimes are defined as being motivated by hatred or dislike of someone because of that person's identity, perceived identity, or affiliation with a particular group. Police view a crime as bias- or hate-motivated when it involves slurs or name-calling against the particular identity or group, and/or extreme violence. Trans-identified victims of hate crimes are often called fags or queers, or hatred is expressly directed toward transsexuals. Hate crime laws address the violence that is motivated by bias and provide for the tracking of these crimes, the training of law enforcement personnel, and sometimes the mandatory enhancement of penalties at sentencing for those convicted of hate crimes. As of December 31, 2006, ten states (California, Colorado, Connecticut, Hawaii, Maryland, Minnesota, Missouri, New Mexico, Pennsylvania, and Vermont) included bias against gender identity in their hate crime laws. On the national level, the Local Law Enforcement Enhancement Act (LLEEA) passed the House of Representatives in 2005, but wasn't signed into law. It was reintroduced in the House in March 2007, and if enacted it will add the categories of sexual orientation, gender, gender identity, and disability to federal hate crime legislation.

The FBI tracks hate crime statistics but excludes crimes motivated by gender identity or expression. Hence, even though murder based on the victim's gender expression outnumbers every other motivation category tracked by the FBI except race over the last ten years, this category is not officially acknowledged. According to the FBI, there were six hate crime murders in 2005 (three based on race, three on ethnicity/national origin). However, there were six transgender victims of hate not counted (Ashley Nickson, Timothy Blair, Donathyn Rodgers, Christina Smith, Delilah Corrales, and Sidney Wright). Internationally, the numbers of transgender and transsexual murders have been consistently steady at one every month for the past decade. The FBI needs to acknowledge this form of hate murder, for it reflects broader sentiments of how serious it is to step (or fall) outside gender norms.

A report by the Gender Public Advocacy Coalition (Wilchins and Taylor 2006) titled 50 under 30 examines the murders of fifty people aged thirty and under who were targeted because of their gender presentation or identity in the previous ten years. The findings are significant: most victims were people of color (85 percent Black and Latino), most victims were poor (often unemployed and/or homeless), 88 percent of the victims were from the LGBT communities (4 percent were heterosexual, and 8 percent of identities were unknown), 92 percent of the victims were biologically male but presenting some degree of femininity, and most cases were ignored by the media even though assailants used extreme violence and the murders typically took place in major cities. Only 46 percent of these cases have been solved (compared with 69 percent of all homicides nationally).

In spite of the category's lack of official recognition, some murders of transgender individuals in recent years have received important media attention and are raising awareness. The killing of Brandon Teena in 1995 was a turning point for trans activism, marking the first visible demonstration against hate murders of transpeople when activists vigiled outside the courthouse in Falls City, Nebraska. Vigils followed for Tyra Hunter, Chanel Picket, Deborah Forte, and Christian Paige. In 2002, the convicted killer of sixteen-year-old Fred Martinez (who was murdered on June 21, 2001) was sentenced to forty years in prison. In August of 2002, two transgender teens, Ukea Davis and Stephanie Thomas, were murdered while they sat in their car in Washington, D.C. They each had ten bullets pumped into them. And in another case that made national headlines, two of the three young men arrested for the 2002 murder of Gwen Araujo were found guilty of second-degree murder and received sentences of fifteen years to life in prison in September 2005.

Such hate crimes have an importance beyond the loss of precious life. They are also message crimes committed against an entire group. When any transgender person is attacked, verbally and physically, because of being transgender, the message is that something is terribly wrong with all transgender identities and behaviors. Continue to be this way, the message goes, and all of you face this type of punishment—humiliation, pain, or death. It is clearly an extreme form of gender policing. I found that most participants in this study were aware of the risks they were taking just to be themselves. Because of the fears and ignorance of other people, they risked their very lives.

Medical Gatekeeping

Trans-identified individuals face many barriers in accessing medical care. Although the hormones, procedures, and surgeries that many seek are medically necessary and essential for confirming their sense of self, all too often doctors, therapists, and insurance companies view these treatments as cosmetic or elective. Health care providers may not be well informed about transgender issues, and their low level of cultural competence may result in stigmatizing behaviors, insensitivity, or denial of needed services. Dustin (FtM), for instance, says, "I have a huge fear of transphobic doctors and that fear prevents me from getting GYN exams, getting physically examined, getting health insurance, and even getting T refills and post-op care."

An FtM may have difficulty accessing gynecological care, whether for a pap smear or a hysterectomy. An MtF may need tests for prostate cancer. Non-trans men who have gynecomastia (excessive breast tissue) can have breast tissue removed and the procedure covered by insurance, but a female-bodied transman who wants his excessive breast tissue removed through double mastectomy is not covered. Hormonal imbalances are not uncommon, and people who are non-trans routinely have insurance coverage for their thyroid medication, estrogen replacement, or T prescriptions for low testosterone levels. But a transsexual's medical need for hormone replacement therapy is not generally covered by insurance. These double standards are linked to judgments of acceptable medical conditions and the view that gender is determined at birth (see also Green 2004).

Perhaps the most significant gender-policing mechanisms our society employs for transsexuals are the diagnoses of gender identity disorder (GID) and transvestic fetishism (TF) found in the current *Diagnostic and Statistical Manual of Mental Disorders* (DSM) of the American Psychiatric Association. The label "gender identity disorder" suggests that to have a gender identity different from the category a doctor assigned to one's body at birth is disordered, confused, illegitimate, or perverted. Such an individual is dysphoric, perhaps neurotic, bipolar, autogynephilic, or has a dissociative personality. The TF diagnosis labels cross-dressing by heterosexual males as a sexual fetish. Application of these diagnostic labels unnecessarily pathologizes transgender and gender-variant people.

When the DSM was updated in 1994, GID replaced the diagnosis of gender dysphoria, which referred to an intense, persistent distress with one's physical sex characteristics or their associated social role. But transsexuality should be seen as the medical condition it is and not a mental illness, since there is no illness or disease to cure. The real medical issue is more with the person's physical body than it is with the person's gender identity, but the GID label focuses on cross-gender identity as a problem, a "disorder," rather than on what can be done to alleviate the distress of the mismatch. The fact is antianxiety medications, antipsychotic medications, and electroshock do not relieve gender dysphoria. The only measure that "works" is living in the gender the person identifies as.

The university-affiliated gender identity clinics that opened in the mid-1960s were highly experimental and research-oriented. The treatment they offered was quite limited (serving a tiny fraction of the people who contacted them), and those individuals who were successful in obtaining what was then called sex change surgery told the therapists and doctors what they wanted to hear. At that time, based on little actual knowledge, therapists believed that the drag queen was the ideal model of the MtF. Those male-bodied people with exaggerated feminine looks and mannerisms, who were highly sexualized and who expressed sexual interest in men, were considered to be transsexual. Well-adjusted people who were not homeless, unemployed, or on the brink of suicide or drug addiction were not believed to be transsexual. Such individuals were denied not only surgery but also access to hormones (Denny 2002). The concept of GID is both sexist and heterosexist in its application and its gendered expectations.

In the heyday of the gender clinics in the United States (1966–1990), transsexuals were sent away in droves without help. The clinics were not staffed to handle the numbers of people looking for treatment, and in any case the research and knowledge that would have been needed did not exist. Clinics often demanded that patients agree to research interviews and years of therapy, that they divorce spouses, or that they change jobs. Many of these demands would be seen today as unethical (Denny 2002).

Although this "illness" of GID had no cure, therapists did become the primary gatekeepers for transsexuals who were seeking to gain access to their medical needs. This role was solidified when the Harry Benjamin International Gender Dysphoria Association (HBIGDA, now renamed WPATH: the World Professional Association for Transgender Health) was founded in 1979 and put the Standards of Care (SOC) into effect.

Today, the SOC is the protocol used by most doctors in the United States for providing medical care to transsexuals. It calls for a therapist's diagnosis and consequent letter that can be presented to an endocrinologist for hormones and/or a surgeon for sex reassignment or chest reconstruction surgery. A surgeon will usually require letters from two therapists. The SOC also calls for a transitioning individual to live full-time for one year in true gender identity (called the Real Life Experience, RLE) before having surgery. As discussed in chapter 4, the yearlong RLE is supposed to show the patient's ability to adjust. Many see this year as a very dangerous time: the transitioning individual, now living full-time as what will often seem to others the "wrong" gender, is at higher risk for hate crimes, hostility, job loss, and family rejection because the measures (such as hormones or chest reconstruction) that might help that person be better accepted as the gender he or she is are the very measures being denied. Still, it is wrong to blame the SOC for these risks, which reside in social attitudes and practices. The latest revisions of the SOC in 2001 are a huge improvement over earlier versions, since they clearly state that the standards are guidelines and that individual cases and needs might vary. They are pro-patient, and clearly state that gender identity disorder is not something to be "cured."

A group known as GID Reform Advocates is calling for removal of the GID diagnosis from the *Diagnostic and Statistical Manual*, which will be due for revision around 2010. These advocates argue, first, that a psychiatric diagnosis is unnecessarily stigmatizing for transsexuals, who in fact have a physical (body) problem, and, second, that calling it an "identity disorder" suggests that cross-gender identity is not legitimate. The *Manual* does not acknowledge that it is the *distress* of gender dysphoria that is the problem, and that medical steps that make cross-living easier alleviate this distress. While there are some fears in the trans community that without GID being available as a diagnosis there would be no access to health care such as hormone therapy, a different way—without stigma—must be found to provide access to needed medical services. These should be available just as prescriptions and procedures are provided for other medical conditions.

Legal Documents

Medical gatekeeping influences far more than just access to medical care. It also influences legal status, since the "letters" that are written by therapists and surgeons provide access to legal change of one's gender status. This in itself is problematic. Most transgender people do not have surgery, because they either do not want it, cannot afford it, or it is medically contraindicated. Furthermore, many transgender people, including transsexuals, do not have surgery or therapy or take hormones, yet they live in their true gender. Therefore, the requirement that they need proof of such medical interventions to validate their authentic gender clearly impedes their ability to function in society. Since they are no longer living as their birth sex, they cannot freely access services (employment, housing, health care, travel, etc.) dependent on identification that indicates one's sex (passports, driver's licenses, social security cards, etc.).

One's legal status as a male or a female matters. It matters for marriage, divorce, adoption, child custody, inheritance, immigration status, employment; for access to services such as shelters, clinics and centers, health benefits; and for identity papers and personal records (name, driver's license, passport, birth certificate, school transcript, work history). For trans individuals, even those who are not transitioning (e.g., genderqueers or male cross-dressers), being stopped by police or showing a driver's license to cash a check can be stressful. The M or F on a driver's license may not jibe with what people see (or how the person identifies). Some transsexuals carry their therapist's letter in case they find themselves in precisely this kind of situation, needing to "justify" who they are. The anxiety this causes, and the ridicule or embarrassment that may follow, originate from a personal medical matter that should be no one else's business. As a medical issue (since being able to fully live one's true gender is therapeutic), trans-identified people should have an easier time getting the legal documents they need to complete their transition or live in their preferred gender—they should not have to deal with the complexity and roadblocks they now encounter.

Identity documents may seem completely reasonable documents to have, but for trans-identified people they become a form of gender policing. Required procedures for changing names and/or sex designations are time-consuming and costly, with rules varying from state to state. Most states require documentation of surgery before issuing a new birth certificate, and the birth certificate is needed, in turn, for changing other forms of identification. Individuals who are adhering to the Standards of Care (SOC) find themselves in the precarious situation of needing to work for one year in their authentic gender but are denied their sex designation change from Social Security because they haven't had surgery yet.

When I started the research for this book, people could change the sex indicators within their Social Security records without having proof of completed surgery. That changed in October 2002. Since Social Security numbers must be given to employers and everyone needs a Social Security number to work, this is where inconsistencies are caught. The Social Security Administration runs audits of company records, and sex gender markers will not match up if the trans individual has not changed his or her records, outing the trans individual when employers are notified. New laws initiated since 9/11 are also more stringent regarding sex and gender documentation, and have the potential to out transsexuals to employers (and hence subject them to firing or other forms of prejudicial treatment).

Documentation becomes equally problematic outside the workplace. If a new birth certificate or letter of GID diagnosis is needed for a change on a driver's license, and a driver's license is needed as an ID for everything from doing business at a bank to buying alcohol, a trans individual often does not have the proper legal documentation he or she needs for daily life. It is not uncommon for transpeople to look one gender and have a mix of sex indicators on their identity documents depending on where they are in their transition, whether they have access to financial resources for surgery, which state they live in, and other variables.

Leslie Feinberg talks about these labels:

> Why am I forced to check off an F or an M on these documents in the first place? For identification? Both a driver's license and a passport include photographs! Most cops and passport agents would feel insulted to think they needed an M or an F to determine if a person is a man or a woman. It's only those of us who cross the boundaries of sex or gender, or live ambiguously between those borders, who are harassed by this legal requirement. (1996, pp. 61–62, emphasis in original)

In fact one could argue that these designations are so often incorrect as to render them meaningless—or at least to reduce their usefulness to the point that we should not depend on them as part of a true identification.

After all, intersex individuals may later realize they are not the sex and/or gender the birth certificate states, and transsexual individuals undergo surgical changes to align their identity. The records were wrong originally and need to be corrected.

Legal name change is supposed to be available to anyone as long as that person is not seeking to defraud. Tim (FtM) was nervous in court but elated afterward: "When I was walking out of the courtroom there was this song, 'Walk Like a Man' in my head." While laws vary, usually the individual fills out a petition, pays a fee, publishes an intention to change name in the local paper or posts it on a board in the court building, perhaps submits letters of character reference, and the name change is granted after a designated waiting period. However, I personally know of a judge who would deny any name change he thought was for a transsexual—a clear violation, based on personal prejudice, of the law. To get around that judge, individuals had to file in a different county after establishing residence through a post office box. People should not have to resort to that or any sort of subterfuge, for any reason. Kosse (FtM), for example, did not want the change to be public:

Well, the usual course one follows for a name change is to make out an application at Probate Court, submit a fee, and agree to publish the intention in a local newspaper of the court's choosing. And the record of the name change remains open to anyone who might want to look it up later. I did not want that because of the nature of my name change. I wanted the intention unpublished and the record impounded. To do that, I had to go before a justice and explain what I wanted, and why (this happened on National Coming Out Day, in a crowded courtroom, of all things!). The justice would not agree to it unless I made out a detailed financial statement and also signed that I was not attempting to defraud any creditors, which is absurd since I'm still married and intend to stay that way. So it was stressful to be questioned about my motives and have to wait to hear by mail, about a week post-courtroom appearance. But I might have been the first candid transsexual to appear in the H——court, so that was a good thing in my estimation.

After name change, the driver's license is often the next item to change. Some manage to change it without documentation of completed surgery but with a letter from a therapist. Procedures vary depending on the state and where you go in the state. Some male cross-dressers have managed to get licenses for their female persona and continue to use the original license as well. Rules have become tighter since 9/11, but some people before that managed to get changes, or a new license in a new state after moving, based only on their appearance. Lauren (MtF) changed her docu-

TIM

ments before stricter rules were in place (including those at Social Security). Here is what happened when she went to change her driver's license:

I wore nice short shorts and a really tight top because I knew it was mostly males over there. And he put his hand on the small of my back and helped me across the room and said, "Ma'am just sit down here." And, I was renewing my license as well, so we did that part first. And then I said, "And I need to get a name change." "Oh, no problem. If you got married we can get your married name and if you've gotten divorced we can get your maiden name." And I said, "It's a little more complicated than that." "Oh, what is it?" "Well, let me just put it this way," and I put the name change document there. "This is what my name used to be, and this is what my name is now." And his mouth dropped, because he'd been kind of looking at me. He stopped looking, and before he could even think—'cause if I gave him a chance to think he probably would not do it—I handed him two forms of ID that had female on it and said "And this is my current gender." And he quickly did everything, gave me my driver's license with female. Of course he had to do the name, that was legal.

Birth certificates are another key item that needs to be changed. Three states—Ohio, Tennessee, and Idaho—do not allow a change of sex designation on birth certificates. Other states will change the M or F after receiving a letter from a surgeon stating that the individual has gone through irreversible sex change surgery. While this has generally been interpreted to mean genital surgery, some FtMs have succeeded in getting their birth certificate changed after having only chest reconstruction and being on testosterone. A court order showing the name change is also needed.

Some states amend the birth certificate; others issue a completely new document. NiseyLynn (MtF) had her new name on her birth certificate but hadn't yet changed the sex designation at the time we last spoke. She was not pleased to have an amended, as opposed to a new, version:

My birth certificate, I actually have the original one which has all the information, it has a line going through it, old name, with the new name above it with name changed by M——Probate Court—they didn't even cross it out that good. Anybody can see the old name. They could put two and two together when they see a male name and all of a sudden you see a female name. People aren't stupid; they're going to know it's a sex change.

Lauren (MtF) changed her birth certificate in North Carolina, which issues a new one upon receiving a letter from a doctor stating you've had surgery. But even a new certificate may indicate that changes have been made. County records are sent to the state capitol and sealed, Lauren explained. "They then have the county of origin issue a new birth certificate as if that's the way I came out of my mother. So, even though it's issued in 1997, it still says birth date 1959."

New York City had been unique in issuing new birth certificates without a sex designation altogether. This in itself was embarrassing. It made the certificates less useful as identification, and because only transsexuals had this type of birth certificate, they were outed. In September 2006, the New York City Department of Health and Mental Hygiene proposed liberalizing the rules so that birth certificates could be changed even if individuals did not have surgery. However, in December of 2006 city officials slowed the rule-changing process in order to consider whether this proposal might conflict with new federal rules that are being developed. The Department of Health did, however, change its policy of eliminating gender on the certificate. Now the birth sex will be listed until a letter confirming irreversible sex change surgery has been performed.

On the federal level, the most recent ID legislation of concern for trans individuals is the Real ID Act (HR 418) passed in 2005. This law requires states to have or develop identity documents and procedures that meet national standards. States will have uniform requirements that applicants must satisfy in order to obtain identity documents, and driver's licenses will all contain information in a magnetic strip on the back. States will also be required to keep electronic copies of all documents used to support ID applications, including name changes and gender markers. All this information will be stored in a national database. If states are out of compliance with the law's requirements, IDs from those states will not be accepted as valid at airports or federal facilities, or by federal benefit suppliers. The Departments of Homeland Security and Justice are still creating the policies and rules needed to implement the Real ID Act. It remains to be seen how this law will affect transgender and transsexual people, but it most likely will create even more hardship for people without access to surgery, for people without adequate finances for application fees and related costs, and for those who transition over many years.

Marriage is another area where trans-identified people encounter roadblocks and risks in their pursuit of happiness. Legally, marriage is a union between a man and a woman, except for same-sex marriages in Massachusetts (since May 2004) and civil unions in Vermont (since 2001), Connecticut (since 2005), New Jersey (since 2005), and New Hampshire (as of 2008). If a birth certificate establishes the legal sex of an individual, then a heterosexual transsexual who wants to be married needs to have that document changed. However, even in cases where the birth certificate has been changed, marriages involving transsexuals have been successfully challenged.

In 2002, the Kansas Supreme Court invalidated the marriage between J'Noel Gardiner (MtF) and Marshall Gardiner. After Mr. Gardiner's death, his son contested Mrs. Gardiner's inheritance, and the court ruled in his favor by refusing to recognize Mrs. Gardiner's birth certificate and what the court deemed to be a same-sex marriage.

In 2004, Sandy Gast (MtF), also in Kansas, was arrested on charges of swearing falsely in an application for marriage. Ms. Gast had a driver's license, Social Security card, an amended birth certificate, and a letter from her therapist stating she was treated for transgender issues. Gast was charged with a misdemeanor, bond was set at five times the maximum fine, and she was subjected to a strip search by a male officer.

On the positive side, a ruling by the Board of Immigration Appeals in 2005 allowed the male spouse of a transwoman from North Carolina to immigrate. The board ruled that the marriage was legal in North Carolina, and the marriage was recognized as one between opposite-sex partners.

There has been some concern as to whether marriages continue to be legal after one partner transitions and changes his or her birth certificate. Does this become a same-sex marriage, which is illegal in most states? It would be best if there were no restrictions on marriage—individuals who commit to each other should be able to marry regardless of how they identify. But for now, marriage laws are not trans-friendly. Transsexuals remain at the mercy of the state they were born in, and the gender-policing beliefs and prejudices of individual judges and the court process.

Gender Policing and Legal Protection

Overcoming discrimination is a long and painful process. When someone such as Lauren (MtF) is told that the gynecologist with whom she made a new-patient appointment will not treat her ("The assistant said off the record that what the gynecologist had said was she didn't want it to hurt her practice"), or when someone such as DaleLynn (intersex, MtF) has an insurance claim denied because her type of medical care doesn't match up with her gender, we have proof of a gender system that does not work. There is an urgent need for nondiscrimination policies and laws in government jurisdictions, at workplaces, and in schools and colleges to prevent discrimination against trans-identified people.

In the workplace, 307 employers have nondiscrimination policies that include gender identity as of April 2006. This includes 162 private-sector companies (81 of which are Fortune 500), 8 state governments, 79 city and county governments, and 38 colleges and universities (Human Rights Campaign 2006). As of November 2006, 31 percent of the U.S. population lived in a jurisdiction where transgender people were explicitly covered by antidiscrimination laws. Some of the jurisdictions had laws pertaining only to employment; others had laws that also pertained to public accommodations, housing, education, and/or the right to sue. As a comparison, at that same point in time 48 percent of the U.S. population lived in an area where laws prohibited discrimination based on sexual orientation (National Gay and Lesbian Task Force 2006).

Although such legal coverage is spreading (at the end of 2000, only 5 percent of the population was covered by transgender-inclusive laws), countless individuals still lack the protection they need against discrimination based on gender identity or sexual orientation. Peter Oiler, for example, found this out when he was fired by Winn-Dixie in 2003 after working there for twenty years. The reason? Oiler had mentioned to a supervisor that he was an occasional cross-dresser. Darlene Jespersen was fired by Harrah's Reno casino after eighteen years of employment for refusing to wear makeup, hence not following the new dress code for female employees. The Ninth Circuit U.S. Court of Appeals ruled in December 2004 that Harrah's policy was not a form of sex discrimination.

There have been victories, such as the 2005 Supreme Court decision that found Philecia Barnes had been a victim of discrimination when demoted while transitioning from male to female as a Cincinnati police officer. However, access to this kind of protection must be extended to everyone. As of July 2007, only thirteen states and the District of Columbia had antidiscrimination laws that covered transgender individuals statewide. What is needed is a federal law that specifically includes gender identity and sexual orientation among the kinds of discrimination it covers. The version of the Employment Non-Discrimination Act (ENDA) that was re-introduced into the House and Senate in 2007 includes both gender identity/expression and sexual orientation. When Republicans controlled both houses of Congress, previous versions of ENDA (which only covered sexual orientation) never made it to the floor for a vote. Now, with Democrats in control, there is a possibility that this version will pass. Whether President Bush will sign it into law is another matter.

Gender policing has complicated the lives of trans-identified individuals because of the barriers it has created, the personal stress it has produced, and the physical and emotional risks it has exposed them to through reinforcement of their presumed abnormality. Medical and legal gatekeeping, lack of legal protection, and other forms of gender policing facilitate the ongoing harassment of, and discrimination against, trans-identified people. In the next chapter we look at the negative personal toll this takes as well as creative responses.

Inner Turmoil and Moving toward Acceptance

I always just felt wrong, like something wasn't right and I hadn't a clue as to what that was. I gradually figured more out as I became interested in girls, because I knew that I wasn't attracted to lesbian girls, just the straight ones. So after a while, being strange became the norm, until I got to college and was more suicidal than ever. I started looking for answers, and found them, because I had to. I'd never heard of problems with gender before. Nobody talks about this stuff because they don't want it to exist. Well, news flash (especially you fundamentalists out there) it does exist. And it's not a choice. Not many people feel like they are in the wrong body for the fun of it. (Alex, FtM)

I feel absolutely no shame in being transgendered, but I have felt shame at being seen as female. It's an anger that my male side is invisible, as well as an embarrassment that another's view of me is so limited. There is also, undoubtedly, some internalized misogyny, which can be directly related to the culture. (Tristan, FtM)

It would not be accurate to say that every trans-identified person is suicidal, mutilates his or her genitals, or has an eating disorder. However, a significant number of them do experience a range of emotional problems as a consequence of being stigmatized for not fitting in with cultural expectations: confusion and shame for being different, and anguish over losing community ties, relationships with family members, and friends. These personal crises can occur at any age and last briefly or for a lifetime.

Having an authentic self is essential for positive mental health and nourishing, mutual relationships. According to Miller and Stiver (1997), individuals will use "strategies of disconnection" in order to maintain their relationships by denying parts of themselves that others may find objectionable or unacceptable. In other words, trans-identified people often have to abandon their true selves or hide parts of themselves in order to stay connected to people they care about. They are forced to silence themselves to avoid the pain of losing relationships. Jean Baker Miller (1988) calls this "condemned isolation"—being locked out of authentic human connection.

Members of marginalized groups often are silenced and isolated as a result of dominant groups defining what is acceptable. In the case of trans-identified individuals, the policing of dominant gender norms force those who are variant to hide their authentic self and try to make their gender nonconformity invisible; their feelings of shame lead to self-doubts and a sense of unworthiness (Jordan 1989). If they internalize the culture's transphobia, these individuals may also go through periods of self-loathing and even self-inflicted punishment for their supposed perversion or abnormality.

Stigma of Difference

The experience of being different very much defines the notion of "abnormal." One's status as someone abnormal manifests itself in how others treat you and also in how you feel about yourself. Transman JT touched on both of these issues:

Well, according to the dominant culture I don't even exist. There isn't even a transman stereotype (yet). So for years I thought I was simply "sick," a failed person. . . . The issue of gender in social interaction is so large (at least in my experience) that if you aren't "properly gendered" or don't adhere to the rules accordingly every single interaction from conversations to eating to simply walking down the street can become negative or create insecurity. For example, throughout school many other students wouldn't interact with me or were rude to be because I was very masculine (by US standards) and they thought that was weird. People wouldn't eat lunch with me in jr. high and high school because I was "that weird girl" or "that lesbian," and of course they would say mean things about my appearance behind my back. And from grade school until the start of my transition, every other time I walked somewhere people would comment—"What are you? Are you a boy or a girl?" or simply stare.

Many people I talked with spoke about not fitting in and being "unusual." Dawn (hermaphrodite) said: "I've always felt like a freak. Being made fun of by other kids. My mother telling me how much she was ashamed of me. The fact that there is very, very rarely any discussion or recognition that hermaphrodites exist." Such "freak" observations were not uncommon. "Our society definitely has portrayed those who transgress gender as being sick freaks," Abe (FtM) commented. And Ted, a masculine woman, shared that when she goes swimming, her short hair, unshaved legs, and broad shoulders attract attention: "Sometimes people just stare at my body like I'm some sort of freak." Dustin (FtM) points out that "if you're not gendernormal you are crazy, which means you are unstable, undesirable, and a failure."

Dislike of Body

Not all genderqueer people or transsexuals are uncomfortable with their body or parts of their body, while others feel intense discomfort. Differences in these feelings may relate to how individuals associate genitals, breasts, height, and other physical aspects with their sense of gender. Transgenderists, for example, do not alter their body yet live their life in a gender different from the one they were socialized to be. A transgenderist living as a woman might have a penis; a genderqueer or ungendered individual might have a vagina. These seeming contradictions are a function of our socialized gender binary associations; in fact there needn't be any connection between genitals or body parts and our inner sense of gender. And, as Wilchins points out, many people are unhappy with their body—not only trans folks:

> Some are differently abled, some are unhappily fat, some are differently colored, and some are differently gendered. Look, if my mom hates her wrinkles and gets an age-lift—face, boobs, lipo, the works—and is as happy as the proverbial clam feeling young again, no one is going to say she's crazy. But if I want a cunt, even lesbians think I must be some kind of mental case. You figure it out. (1997, p. 193)

Because we *are* socialized to the gender binary associations, many trans-identified people pluck, tape, tuck, bind, or pack. Some have great ambivalence about their body. "I never wanted breasts and hid them, it was awkward and depressing . . . I felt that I could not accept breasts, or menstruation, or people always assuming I was a girl," said Sae (FtM). Transgendered Kand said: "I feel male on a molecular level; my undeniable female parts feel foreign. For example, my breasts feel foreign, like they don't belong; menses, menopausal stuff, it all feels strange and alien."

Jane (MtF) said she "always felt I was a girl and hated my genitals." And Laura (MtF) "always wanted it [her penis] off my body. Always." Jennifer, also MtF, tortured her genitals with extreme cold and hot water and even used a rubber band to cut off circulation and inhibit erections. Patricia (MtF) tried to castrate herself at eighteen; luckily she did not cause herself extreme harm. When Emery (FtM) had his breasts removed, he felt "free of self-hatred (of my body) to a great degree." For Jon (intersex), life has been hard: "I hate being in between sexually. Society says you need to be thin, have six-packs as a guy, big pecs and be very sexually endowed. I fit none of this. Ofttimes, I have thought about how nice [it would be] to be rid of my male parts."

Birth Defect

Some transsexuals talk about their anatomy as a birth defect that they desire to correct—as Dana (MtF, intersex) said, "a congenital anomaly" to fix. This would not be a "mutilation" of her genitals. Most people feel that it is entirely acceptable to correct a birth defect through surgical means. Lauren (MtF) called her male genitals her "sixth toe."

If you had a baby in your church that had six toes, you'd probably raise money to have that sixth toe removed so that baby could lead a normal life. Well, that's my sixth toe. It's a birth defect. I was born a woman. I just happen to have genitalia that the doctors held me up by my feet and said, "You've got a boy."

Having a birth defect, Jennifer (MtF, female) took the logical next step and questioned the label "transsexual":

The term itself does not acknowledge that I am and always have been a woman with surgically correctable anomalies. The term clearly states a change in sex and that is not my reality. I'm not having a sex change, I'm simply having a surgical procedure to correct an anomaly so that the sex that I have been born with as I know it can be recognized by the law and any human who would have access to my private area—my doctor and my spouse.

Suzi, who calls herself a woman born transsexual, added a nuance by using the metaphor of a computer operating system (OS) to describe her birth defect. She had sex reassignment surgery "to correct the birth defect of transsexualism. . . . I consider it a birth defect because I was born with a brain hard-wired to run a female OS and the body which was supposed to run a male OS."

On the other hand, Reid (FtM) questioned the use of birth defect terminology, since defect is closely linked to disability. He feels that he is "gender gifted" and a disability model is contrary to "an expanded world view." Felicia (transgendered) agreed, saying "it's not necessarily a birth defect, no, it's also kind of a blessing. People say, 'Well, it's a curse.' No, it's not a curse because I can see beyond being just a man."

Whether birth defect or not, being different is often something people wish to change. As children, some trans-identified people prayed at night to wake up changed in the morning. For instance, Tina (MtF) recalled:

[I got the constant message] from everyone and every angle, that I was bad, wrong, immoral, and evil. I understood that, and constantly tried to portray that I was good. Being good meant hiding feminine traits at any cost. It meant praying at night that God would turn you into a girl, so that you would no longer be a freak, and waking up the next morning without an answer to your prayer.

Jennifer (MtF, female) looks back at her similar times of praying from a different perspective:

When I was 6 I can remember praying in my prayer when I went to bed asking God to make me a girl. A very fervent prayer. Woke up the next morning and there was no difference. So that night I asked God to make me a magician so I could make myself into a girl. . . . Little did I know that my prayer had been answered. I was a girl. It just took me an awful long time to find out.

Puberty

If prayers aren't answered, perhaps the body will do what gender-variant people want it to do at puberty. But no. Tomboys find this a very difficult time. Their acceptable boyish body and behavior gives way to a feminizing body and expectations of womanly behaviors. At adolescence there is more pressure for girls to respond to boys in a sexualized way and for them to dress and act differently. Those who are tomboys often have to repress that part of their self.

Transsexual teens "typically feel shame, despair, and anger because they are developing the adult body of the wrong sex. Puberty, to them, feels like the 'end of the line' because it provides the indisputable evi-

THERESA

dence that their bodies are never going to match their gender identity"
(Brown and Rounsley 1996, p. 50). Male-bodied females are not happy
with facial hair or intense sexual desires; female-bodied males feel betrayed by breast development and periods. Theresa (MtF) put it this way:

*How did it feel to be a femme self in a butch body going through puberty? Testosterone
is weird, powerful, toxic. Have you ever been raped or otherwise sexually assaulted?
Have you ever acted out an urge to rape or assault? What I experienced felt like both at
the same time; the pain, shame and humiliation of the victim synchronized with the
savage pleasure of the victimizer. And that was merely masturbation.*

Puberty was also difficult for Lucy (MtF): "When I was 15 the aloneness
had become unbearable. I had no one to talk over my gender dysphoria,
my being a lesbian, in addition to the problems most teenagers are faced
with at that age. I lost hope and the will to continue."

Shame

Shame is a very painful emotion that can result from feelings of guilt, unworthiness, a sense of being wrong, and embarrassment. Chronic shame often results in internalized transphobia—the belief that to be trans is wrong, sick, and perverted. Even after people transition, they may spend years dealing with internalized transphobia. As Tina (MtF) mentioned, "Feeling ashamed of who you are is incredibly difficult to overcome, and yet, most of us do. That is the amazing part."

FtMs and transmen are often viewed as failed heterosexuals or failed butch lesbians (Cromwell 1999). They failed because they didn't "make it" as women, since they were too masculine either to be seen as women or to attract men. Even as lesbians they may be "too masculine." Sadly, every identity category adds to shaming when people within that category claim others are "not trans enough," "not really a lesbian," or "too feminine to be a man."

Max (transgender stone butch), for example, stated: "I spent my childhood and teenage years feeling ashamed about how butch I was, because everything and everyone (in the lesbian and straight worlds) told me that was bad, that I was a sellout, a self-hating woman, a pervert. But, I've gotten over that for the most part." Other people's reactions can undermine even fairly secure people. November (genderqueer) said, "I occasionally feel ashamed when I am stared at on the street, or given looks of disgust for holding hands in public, or glared at in a public bathroom."

Because of societal shaming, trans-identified people often feel isolated and confused. Lydia (MtF) had no information on gender dysphoria so thought she must be gay—meaning that she was "perverted, a probable child-molester, insane, going to hell, going to jail, going to a mental institution." Raven (transgendered FtM intersexual) felt shame: "[Intersex] children are taught never to talk about their conditions, because it's freakish and shameful. Now I know that I am not just a freak, I'm a sacred being."

Jeremy (FtM) brought up a different issue, that of the need to legitimize himself as a transperson: "I feel shame sometimes, and it usually manifests in either self-loathing or the intense and irrational need to explain and justify my existence." Jeremy also is sight-impaired and finds overlap between how people treat those with disabilities and how they treat trans-identified people. For instance, when people assume that Jeremy's dog is leading him, they conclude that Jeremy is impaired to the point where he doesn't know where he is going. He has to explain what the dog actually does. When people assume that Jeremy is confused about his gender and question his desire to transition, he feels that he needs to justify himself and explain it isn't all about his genitals. Sometimes, he said, "I just don't have the energy to do all that [and] that's when the self-loathing comes in." This is compounded by the fact that people don't tend to think of those with disabilities as even having gender identities or sexual orientations to begin with.

Males who want to express their feminine side are particularly likely to suffer from the judgment and scorn of others. "The collective messages about what was generally understood that a man is and that I was not and about what a woman is and that I was," Jennifer (MtF) recalled—"it was very clear that to feel and want what I did was a shameful thing for a man but normal for a woman." Leslie (male cross-dresser) felt shame for decades "for taking some pleasure in being seen as 'like a girl' and then shame for feeling that way. My mother and my aunt 'shamed' me verbally, 'Look at the little girl!' when they saw how much I was attracted to my mother's clothes and they were trying to get me to stop dressing up (about 5 or 6 years old)."

Many people I spoke with came from a religious upbringing, and this was mentioned quite often as a shaming influence, particularly if it was in the Catholic Church. "Catholic guilt," Marlene (male cross-dresser) wrote—"I didn't believe the doctrine, but the culture smothers you." Theresa (MtF) stated:

Until my mid-life crisis, I cannot remember a time when I did NOT feel great shame about being queerly gendered. For me, the focal point of my shame was religious. I had strongly internalized the conservative Christian values that ranked male higher than female and implicitly blamed female-ness for Original Sin and most moral errors since. After all God was a male and He valued first-born sons over daughters. Females were clearly subordinate and inherently shameful.

For others, messages of disgust that came from family members, peers, and friends had a profound, shame-inducing impact. Lynnea (MtF) said she "grew up with shame and my father was ashamed of me when he died. I was called 'pansy' and 'faggot,' and beaten, bound and tortured before I knew what those names meant. Parents and teachers said I deserved it. I did not recover for many years." Julian (ungendered) recalled being "systematically shamed and ridiculed in my childhood. I felt shamed by the ridiculers. I was also hit, and due to all that, and other abuse, I am prone to feeling unsafe, and conflicted about my own ambivalent gender presentation." And Denise (MtF) shared, "My brother's a convicted felon, but I'm an embarrassment to my family."

Depression

While there is no way to measure whether gender-variant individuals are subject to higher rates of depression than non-gender-variant people, it seems likely. Being at odds with cultural expectations, having a body that is not in line with one's self-image, needing to hide true feelings and desires, and feeling shame about who you are—all these situations and feelings commonly experienced by gender-variant people suggest that depression and anxiety would also be common. Some individuals I interviewed did make this connection. Dustin (FtM), for example, commented, "My problems with gender are inseparable from my long term depression." This was echoed by Patric (FtM), who said he had "depression and anxiety related to being transgender." And Bonnie (MtF) attributed her lifelong depression to "a very dysfunctional family" and gender issues.

Many people I spoke with had been clinically diagnosed as suffering from depression or bipolar disorder and were on medications and in therapy. Dee (MtF) had had electroshock therapy. She said: "I just wanted to be one person. It did not work. The girl was refusing to die even after they stopped my heart twice during the procedures."

Matt (genderqueer, androgyne) was one who did not succumb to depression, although he was taken to a psychiatrist by his father after his father saw him in drag. Matt recalled:

Fortunately, by then I had pretty much come to terms with my gender identity, and was sufficiently self-secure that I didn't really care what the shrink said. Besides, I'd read some excerpts from the Diagnostic and Statistical Manual of Mental Disorders entries on "Gender Identity Disorder" and "Transvestic Fetishism," so I had a low opinion of his profession's ability to understand me anyway. I went solely as a favor to my father.

Jill (male cross-dresser), on the other hand, had a nervous breakdown and clinical depression. He remembered a particularly difficult time in his life:

And if you've ever heard the term police-assisted suicide, well, I tried that. I went out and tried to get myself shot in the back. It made me realize that anyone who says, "Depression, everyone gets depressed," well, sometimes it's worse than that. . . . [I attempted a robbery] and I was dressed, so I got caught and arrested, and I guess I have a touch of post-traumatic stress syndrome from it sometimes because I still have flashbacks. I think it was a case of, a lot of guys dealing with depression won't ask for help.

It's ingrained. We're taught, "shake it off, hide it. You're not supposed to show your emotions. Cover it up and keep going."

Jill was sentenced to prison for eight to ten years, though released early and placed on probation for two years.

Suicidal Feelings and Attempts

Most individuals did not speak of depression specifically but spoke of suicidal feelings and suicide attempts. Their pain and anger were so great that suicide seemed to offer a welcome release. Carla (MtF) felt that way after she was forced out of the ministry: "I will forever bear the scars of it. There isn't any undoing that. And I will forever believe myself to be always suicidal. I stay in therapy. And I really work on those kinds of ideations from time to time because my life really has been a train wreck and what's left of the train is just limping along now the best it can." Laura (MtF) has struggled for years with similar feelings:

I lost my job, my family and my will to live. Eventually, I could not eat, sleep, work or even think. I did not bathe or change my clothes for weeks at a time. I could not perform the simplest of tasks. All I could do was breathe; in and out, over and over, all day, every day. It took much effort to even perform that. I would look outside; another season had changed; another year had gone. The pain was so intolerable that I wanted to die. My psychiatrist brought me back. I'm still recovering, rebuilding, renewing, growing, getting stronger, learning and re-learning, in essence—living.

For some, thoughts of ending their lives were halted because of family members they loved. Nora (MtF) said:

Shame and guilt over being a transsexual almost caused me to take my life before I came to grips with who I am. . . . I was so ashamed, so guilt-ridden I came close to suicide before I decided to transition. As a matter of fact, I had the pistol to my head and the hammer pulled back trying to think of some reason why not to pull the trigger. And the only thing I could come up with was what it would do to [my wife] and my daughter and my mom and dad. It wasn't long after that that I came out to [my wife]."

Ashley (MtF) almost hanged herself but thought better of it. She didn't want her children to find her and live with the uncertainty and guilt over why she might have done this and what they might have done to prevent it.

NORA

Thoughts of suicide pushed many to accept their authentic self. For Rita (MtF), who had been on the verge of suicide on at least four occasions, transition became "something I have to do. The alternative is my funeral." Jessica (MtF) married, hoping that might "be the answer. We divorced four years later after a crushing depression and near suicide led me to make a commitment to gender transition." And Karen (MtF) considered staging an accidental drowning at age forty. But at this low point in her despondency "I didn't go into the water," she said. "I turned around instead and I came back as Karen."

Many others actually attempted suicide. Puberty launched Rickey Lynn (MtF) into turmoil:

My first [suicide] attempt was when I was about 13 years old. I had no understanding about what was happening to me and my body, and I wanted it to stop. I didn't want to have to shave, and I didn't like the way I smelled. . . . My second attempt was during my freshman year at my first college. I just didn't fit in with anyone or anything. At that time it was unheard of for a person of one sex to transfer to another sex. . . . After my second suicide attempt I finally went to therapy to try to find out what was bothering me and why.

Tina (MtF) also struggled with the physical changes of facial and body hair. She became suicidal in her senior year of high school. "I felt as if there were nothing to live for. I couldn't tell anyone about my gender dilemma." JT (FtM, transman) "started to really think about how I didn't want to/couldn't live as a woman after my 19th birthday, which was also the day I tried to kill myself. . . . A friend talked me out of it and drove me to the hospital to get my stomach pumped." A year later he came out as trans/not woman.

Amy (MtF) "didn't know that I even could change and I felt trapped and suffocating in my male body until I made my first suicide attempt to try to escape all the battles and turmoil going on in my head." She made two suicide attempts at age thirty-four, followed by hospitalization. Sandie (MtF) felt desperate and also made multiple attempts. "I wore bandages on my wrists as if they were a part of my outfit."

After our interview, Dee (MtF) wrote me a long response to the question about whether her depression was related to her being transsexual. Here is part of her eloquent comment:

You think to yourself. I cannot go forward, I cannot go back. I am trapped in a body I hate. I don't want to have sex; I just want to be loved for the person I am. Yet I cannot find it. I am too afraid of rejection to look for it and I am too poor to buy it. So why am I here? Why do I continue to hit my head on the wall? No one is going to miss me. I am a freak, the best thing I can do is just end it now and maybe in the next life if there is one, things will be better. Crying uncontrollably you decide what you want to do. If only you had a gun, if you can only cut yourself bad enough to bleed to death. Maybe I should just take all my medication in the house and go to sleep. Wish I had a rope. I just don't want to be here anymore. Now if you're lucky you will cry it out. If you're lucky you will call a friend or relative to say good-bye and they will take you to a hospital. Then there is that nasty waking up during an OD attempt while they pump your stomach or give you something to make you throw it all up. Believe me it is not a happy feeling. When you want to die so bad that you are angry at those that are trying to save you. There are times I think that the really lucky ones are the ones that make it. They just end the pain. On their terms in their own way. Now I know a sane person is not supposed to think that way. But I think of the greatest hurt and pain you have ever felt. The greatest loss you have ever had and multiply it by hundreds. That is how it feels sometime. . . . So you try to control it. You take the medications you get for depression. You find it makes you tired and lethargic so you stop. Then you get depressed again and it all starts over. If you're lucky, you will get a few years of peace at best. If you're like me, maybe a week or two. You see you not only have to live with the stigma of being Transgendered. You have to live with the stigma of being chronically depressed and suicidal.

Another subculture to deal with. Well, I hope that you will explore the suicidal side of being TS. It is out there. We do lose people that way. Sad part is when someone does commit suicide they write it off to being depressed. No one ever says suicidal depression due to gender dysphoria.

Self-harm

Tim (FtM) was suicidal for many years, as well as self-mutilating. He said:

I wasn't supposed to want to wear a tie. I wasn't supposed to want to be "boyish," I was supposed to be a good Christian girl, etc. I felt very ashamed of me. Still do sometimes. . . . I started to cut myself when I was in high school and it was blatantly obvious that I was doing this. I didn't do it a little, I did it a lot. It was just overlooked. My family never did anything. I didn't even cover up my wounds. It was out there in the open, "Hey, I'm hurting." And it was way overlooked. Of course, it went from bad to worse, and I started to become very very violent with myself. And, yeah, that was really very bad. And I struggled with that for a very very long time because I used to dissociate and that was a way of bringing me back. . . . Once I became who I am it wasn't a need. There was no need to cut anymore.

No one would say that self-mutilation is a positive coping technique, but it would be dangerous to ignore that some people, especially young people, feel a release of tension or some need being filled when they cut. And for trans-identified youth, there are few options for relief. A.J. (FtM) compared the relief he felt when hurting himself to a pain-relieving drug:

I did have a self-mutilation problem which was like a drug to me. I hurt myself any way I could just as long as I was in pain because I hated my body. That started when I was about 11 or so. Right when my body started going through puberty is when I started hurting myself. . . . I have been injury free since I started testosterone.

Like Tim and A.J., cj (transgendered) also stopped cutting when he felt more comfortable with his gender identity: "When I've felt stressed, confused, and misunderstood in the past, I used to slit my wrists to calm myself down. I don't know why it was calming, but it was. I haven't cut for nearly eight months, as I've become more sure of who I am and become less confused."

Lonny (MtF) told her wife about being transsexual, and for a year her wife refused to touch her or be intimate. "I became depressed by a severe sense of being neglected and isolated. It resulted in me cutting myself twice." Max (transgender stone butch) shared that she "used various coping strategies including self-injury, drinking, and drugs. Especially when I was a young teenager."

Another kind of body control—connected with eating—was also mentioned. For some, such as Nicholas (FtM) and Karen, (MtF) it took the form of anorexia. Tina (MtF) was bulimic:

I have gone through frequent bingeing and purging, in some kind of perverse desire to rid myself of this "demon." "Knowing" that what I was doing was wrong, I would congratulate myself with each purge, and promise that I would never do it again. Each time my purge was followed by an even tougher time in dealing with the gender that my birth certificate says I am.

Eating disorders were also shared by Dustin (FtM), Julian (ungendered), and Gunner (gender queer boy). In a hostile culture, these responses to gender variance cannot be surprising.

Domestic Violence and Sexual Abuse

Seeking support services as a survivor of domestic or sexual violence is difficult for anyone, but additional barriers exist for trans-identified individuals. Because of the ignorance and prejudices that are so prevalent in society, service providers, police, or medical personnel may not be sensitive to a gender-variant person who needs help. Examples exist that confirm this possibility at its worst extreme: police who did not protect Brandon Teena when he reported his rape by two men who then returned and killed him and two friends; paramedics who let Tyra Hunter bleed to death after an accident when they discovered her trans status. Other examples are all too common. Intersex individuals who have been objectified and traumatized by medical service providers in the past are unlikely to come forward after an assault. Female-bodied male-identified individuals may not want others to know they have a vagina, so may avoid medical exams or therapy groups.

Nationwide, agencies that deal with domestic violence and sexual assault often do not have staff with adequate training on gay and lesbian interpersonal violence, though they may serve some same-sex survivors of these assaults. Transgender, transsexual, and intersex people are much further from their awareness than gays and lesbians. The educational programs and outreach materials of these agencies often do not mention the LGBT communities, further alienating survivors who need their services. Research by the Transgender Sexual Violence Project of For Ourselves: Reworking Gender Expression (FORGE) revealed that many of the 265 survey respondents felt that they would never heal from their assaults and that service providers doubted their experiences and would not help them (Munson 2004). An individual who seeks counseling for post-traumatic stress symptoms after an assault risks having the therapist confound the assault dynamics with the person's gender dysphoria. Additionally, trans-identified people seeking a therapist's letter for hormones or surgery may be reluctant to admit to being survivors of sexual or domestic abuse.

The current silence about the domestic and sexual violence that happens within the LGBT communities adds to the denial and shame the survivors feel. Too many individuals feel the abuse they endure is deserved or inevitable because they are "freaks." As a mental illness diagnosis, gender identity disorder may add to the perception that they are ill—and perhaps lucky to have a partner at all, even an abusive partner.

Another barrier to getting help is that most shelters and many programs are gender-segregated. Will a transsexual man or woman be allowed in the shelter for battered women? Will the support group for male survivors of sexual assault allow a genderqueer or transgender person? Also, trans-identified people do not want to be outed by agency staff, since this might expose them to job, housing, or other discrimination. Many are concerned that they will not be believed by the legal system, so their abuse goes unreported as well as untreated.

Only a few participants in this study mentioned physical abuse. George (soft butch), Robyn (MtF), and Keven (two-spirit) had been battered by former female partners. Nicholas (FtM) and Ace (FtM) both mentioned being physically abused in the homes they grew up in. Others talked about incest, past rapes, and recent sexual assaults. Riki Anne Wilchins, in *Read My Lips*, points out that

> genderqueer kids present an ideal profile for sexual predators. We are often emotionally transparent, hungry for adult attention and approval, out of touch with our own bodies, socially isolated, lacking in any sense of boundaries, confused about what is "normal," and used to keeping secrets about our bodies. If there are sharks in the water, the social thrashing of genderqueer kids is bound to attract them. (1997, p. 130)

Most of the sexual assaults I heard about had occurred during adolescence. Perpetrators were a male cousin (Dave, male cross-dresser), male boarder (Julian, ungendered), family members and a neighbor (Tim, FtM), other teens and a doctor (Dana, MtF, intersex), an aunt, uncles, and a brother (Dakota Lynn, MtF), male classmates in junior high (Jon, intersex), a group of boys on a camping trip (Gail, MtF), a drug dealer (Kyl, FtM, genderqueer), women in a mental hospital (D, MtF), and unspecified (Dustin, FtM, and Ted, masculine woman). What impact these assaults had on the victims' gender identification is impossible to say, though Max (transgender stone butch) shared:

I was physically and sexually assaulted, and threatened, all through my life including at a really young age which made me try harder at one point to be a more feminine, acceptable girl. But it didn't work, and instead has helped cement my identity as a masculine person and as a survivor, a strong female person, and a gender outsider.

Several individuals were raped as adults. Jessica (MtF, female) was sexually assaulted three months into her yearlong Real Life Experience. Amy (MtF) was raped a month after her sex reassignment surgery, when a seemingly nice man she had agreed to see at her home forced himself on her. She was able to say she'd recently had pelvic surgery and get him to agree to oral sex, an offer she made to avoid penetration. Nicholas (FtM), who was raped before his transition, felt that he was lucky to meet a man who was in the men's rape survivor movement. "That was crucial. I could be a guy and still be out about being a survivor. I didn't have to give up any of the ground I'd fought so hard for. I don't think I could have transitioned at all without that piece in place." He continued:

I wouldn't have to go underground about that. I would still be able to speak about that and still be able to kind of verbally honor and acknowledge what happened. . . . When I became a guy, that was a real stumbling block to feel [that I had to answer the question] do you only want to do this [transition] because this [rape] happened to you? It was also a stumbling block because [being a survivor] is a powerful part of my life and I don't want to go back in the closet about this.

Coping Strategies

Participants in this study had used a variety of coping strategies during difficult times, including alcohol, meditation, therapy, cross-dressing, writing, fantasy, drugs, and isolation. Alcohol was mentioned most often, and many were in recovery from excessive use. Not surprisingly, alcohol had helped them forget about gender issues, helped to lessen feelings of shame and guilt. As Dave (male cross-dresser) told me,

[drinking] started out more as a recreational thing, but when I reached adulthood and eventually married this is when the real confusion and shame hit and I didn't want to or know how to deal with it. [The] thought just hit me, I think I may have sabotaged relationships before they could go too far because I "knew" I could not share who I was completely.

Binge drinking had been a problem for Andrea (MtF), who was reacting to the "great shame, rage, [and] anger I felt that had had a few years to build up by age 17 . . . set off like a wild hungry fire in a dry forest by alcohol." Gail (MtF) had used alcohol and drugs for seventeen years, thinking she "could drug and drink [her feelings of guilt and unhappiness] away." Gail has been in recovery for sixteen years. Rita (MtF) would drink excessively "to try to avoid the pain of having to go back to a male world I detested when I was cross-dressed." Erin (MtF) lived a wild biker life:

By the time I was 13 years old I overdosed twice on drugs and alcohol. I then entered rehab for 21 days. Afterwards I continued this lifestyle. From 28–30 I spent more time in detox units and psychiatric units for alcoholism, losing everything I'd ever worked for, including jobs, spent 18 days in jail. If that's not enough, my mind was shot, my internal organs were shutting down from alcohol, and suicide became an answer. All because I was afraid to be who I am. First I sobered up. After a year I realized that I still felt the same so I started researching and going to groups dealing with transgendered issues. When I found that wasn't enough, I started going to transsexual meetings. I found where I belonged.

Drugs besides alcohol were also used to cope with emotional pain. Marijuana, for example, helped some to relax. Many individuals were in recovery from hard drugs; Dustin (FtM) is one who bears the scars:

I was addicted to coke then heroin by 16, tried everything under the sun, and alcohol has been and still is a major feature. Use is coping/escape. I am clean and sober for now but drugs have already affected my life permanently. I left school at 17 so I'm poor and have few skills, and I have hepatitis C. So societal gender norms definitely make me feel angry and screwed.

RITA

Several individuals talked about isolation as a means of coping. Phillip (metagendered) disengages and socially isolates himself, "preferring not to deal with others and face further misunderstanding and rejection." Matt (genderqueer, androgyne) stated: "My usual coping strategy for stress is to hide in my room, read literature, and not talk to anyone for a long time. It's not particularly productive, but at least it's less self-destructive."

Denial was a strategy used by Kand (transgendered): "I just didn't admit what was going on for a long time," whereas Jeremy (FtM) said he would "fix an image of myself as physically male (cute little sideburns, a lower voice, and a flat chest) in my mind and tell myself with as much pride as possible, 'This is where I'm coming from, even if it isn't obvious yet.'"

Eric (male cross-dresser) used cross-dressing as a coping strategy for loneliness and frustration. Dressing can actually provide tremendous relief to the pressure caused by just thinking about it. BJ (male cross-dresser) found relief in "not letting too much time pass without dressing as a woman." Patricia (MtF) also cross-dressed to cope with her gender tensions, and Jeff (FtM) said that, before age seventeen, "clothes, binding, packing helped in the beginning."

Many people mentioned therapy as helpful (and a few as decidedly harmful). Those who had therapists who were accepting and knowledgeable benefited greatly—Lucy (MtF), for example. Antidepressants prescribed by therapists alleviated gender-related depression. There were also comments about meditation, exercise, close friends, humor, workaholism, writing, dreamwork, and self-awareness as ways of working out stress. Leslie (male cross-dresser) commented: "I ran as far away from my authentic self as possible, to the point of learning Spanish (formal and slang) and becoming a 'white Mexican.' This was a good survival skill in the Southern California public school system, and ultimately has doubly enriched my life—two cultures to draw from and enjoy." Amy (MtF) turned to her pets, raising show poultry and showing them on the national level. "No one ever knew it," she explained, "but the whole reason I did the poultry thing was to serve as a substitute for giving birth to my own baby, motherhood."

After considerable rough times, some were led to spiritual programs or spiritual recovery programs. Leslie (male cross-dresser) has investigated past lives "and gained worthwhile insights because of this." Beth (MtF) spoke for many when she said:

the whole beginning of my journey was started by absolutely knowing my own soul and who I am. And so at that point there is a wonderful comfort with knowing who I am, no matter what the outside physical appearance. Because it is a spiritual thing. I have been on a spiritual path. In fact, my transition over the last six or seven years has had to do more with that really or as much anyway, as the gender, by continuing to peel the onion and looking at myself. And so, on the one level even though there might be times that I am anxious about things and have some anxiety physically, inwardly there is none at all.

For Johnny (FtM), prayer and belief in God helped:

I always played out the hand I was dealt with God's help, believing He wouldn't give me more than I can handle. I never believed I would go to Hell just for being the person God made me. And each step of the journey led me closer to the person I am now. And I've got to believe that He had his reasons for it taking so long for me to get here, where I am now . . . or I couldn't cope with the fact that I waited so long to "come out."

Jennifer (MtF) tried to change her gender feelings through prayer, Bible study and church activities, and even exorcism. But, as she said, "there was nothing to exorcise."

Dawn (hermaphrodite) told me she concentrates on her "Native American religion." When I spoke to Gail (MtF), a Lakota, she was about to take part in a hunka ceremony—a naming ceremony. Gail had been forced to leave the reservation (for being trans), but before this happened another Lakota woman had a dream about her, in which Gail's name was Good Earth Woman. This dream had occurred before anyone knew that Gail was transsexual, so it seemed especially auspicious. Gail decided to take that name in the ceremony.

Role Models

Role models who can provide examples of strength when facing adversity, advice on transitioning or how to live as genderqueer, and how to live authentically, are important in a society unfriendly to gender variants. While most people I spoke with could name actors, musicians, other transpeople, friends, family members, support group members, or authors, a few said there were no role models for them. Dawn (hermaphrodite), for example, said: "What role models? There are no famous hermaphrodites; there is never any recognition that we are real and not a myth." And Holly (MtF) responded, "Not really. Christine Jorgensen and all the early TV talk shows did not provide a model for a gender-free 'faery' like myself. So, after three years in my local gay bar, I forged my own path and started a support group for T-people." Holly was a role model for others. Several other people mentioned that they didn't have role models until after they became more involved in their transition, in support groups, or in the trans community.

Most mentioned other trans-identified people who were in the news or activists in trans issues. These include Christine Jorgensen, Tamara Reed, Renee Richards, Jamison Green, Leslie Feinberg, Marsha Botzer, Kate Bornstein, Riki Ann Wilchins, Judith Halberstam, Virginia Prince, Phyllis Frye, Jan Morris, Deirdre McCloskey, Louis Sullivan, Howard Devore, Billy Tipton, and Harvey Feirstein. Most individuals did not know these people personally but had read their works or knew their personal stories and were inspired by them. Actors and entertainment celebrities, many said, had helped open the door toward accepting their true self by showing degrees of androgyny, such as David Bowie, Steven Tyler of Aerosmith, Annie Lenox, Mick Jaggar, and RuPaul.

Many could name trans friends as role models, or people they had met at gender conferences such as Southern Comfort or True Spirit. Rita (MtF) was quite specific:

My most helpful role model and mentor was a M to F post-op who had transitioned in 1993–94 while remaining on her job as a Captain in the Los Angeles City Fire Department. This was Michelle Kammerer who, with her partner Janis, operates the Center for Gender Sanity, an LA-based consultant group [now located near Bellingham, Washington] specializing in workplace transition issues. Since we both worked in the fire service, Michelle's perspectives and advice on transitioning in a conservative, male-oriented profession were invaluable.

Some had benefited from examples set by family members, such as masculine mothers or grandmothers who were unconventional, from counselors who supported and believed in them, or from coworkers, gay sons, Internet site moderators, and others who were role models in style, attitude, and behaviors. The Ingersoll Gender Center, the Phoenix support group in North Carolina, and the Elder TG and TS Vets Yahoo groups were some of the groups that provided needed support and acceptance. In every instance, the courage and determination displayed by others helped these trans individuals keep on going.

Self-acceptance

Self-acceptance involves coming to terms with femininity and masculinity, decisions about the body, and ways of dressing and presenting. Finding one's own sense of self, as opposed to the judgments of others, means finding and accepting a center that will hold in spite of what others think. It takes courage and a strong sense of self-esteem. Karen (MtF) referred to gender as a type of cement: "If our gender isn't right, the bricks keep falling apart." She felt that her life had been a house of cards that kept falling down—until she accepted herself and transitioned.

Self-acceptance was mentioned as a coping mechanism, but it usually came through a process of searching, naming, and understanding. Tristan (FtM) described how his feelings about himself were evolving:

Since I've been divorced, and I've been very much a part of my organization, I just find that I'm automatically more me in my personality, and less shy, and I behave very differently than I used to. I'm much more vocal, and if I think of something funny to say, I say it. I can make people laugh. I used to be too shy and inhibited, and I would think of things to say but I didn't have the nerve to say them. The more I am me, the more nerve I have.

Bonnie (MtF) has had a similar experience: "My self-esteem has shot way up. I'm so much more confident. I do a lot of things by myself now which I could never do before." Keven (two-spirit) commented, "the more I am myself the more that people in general are healed and happier because they're hanging around someone who is healed and happier." And Holly (MtF) added: "[M]y gender quest is about so much more than just switching and passing. I truly yearn to transcend the bounds of gender, to become the human being I am capable of becoming."

The happiness with one's body and grounded sense of self that come with self-acceptance are transformative. Melanie (MtF) was going to have a rhinoplasty. However, "I was constantly questioning the need for it," she said, "'cause I also saw the ads and I saw how transpeople tend to gravitate and want to look like someone. Well, you know what, I'm happy being me." T.I., a naturally bearded dyke, accepted her atypical facial hair:

I mean I just let my beard grow in at 19. That would have been '73 or '74. And so I didn't shave it because it would be unthinkable. I don't know, to me it would have been unthinkable to shave my beard, my hair, just because that's what women do to hide, to make themselves beautiful to men. You know, pluck their eyebrows. I wasn't shaving my legs.

Jeff (FtM) said he felt "pride in my body," and Kerwin (FtM) was "more pleased with my body than I've ever been. I'm proud to stand up straight and look like what I do look. I'm not ashamed of anything I've done but I am very aware of how other people would feel about it." Raven (transgendered MtF intersexual) stated, "I'm home in my body for the first time in my life" (Kaldera 2001). Nathan (FtM) wanted to be seen as a male and have it known that he has a transsexual history. And Robert (FtM) had just got a T-shirt reading, "This is what a transsexual looks like." Jon (intersex) shared:

When I am cross-dressing or when I, you go through these fantasies, and it's like, here I am, I'm 6'2" and 375 pounds and that ain't pretty. But when I'm in that mode, or in that mood, fuck that concept. I am a beautiful person. I'm sexy. I'm hot.

Creating Alternatives

Any effort to change how we look at gender, if it has any hope of succeeding, will necessarily involve education. False premises resting on a "natural" binary will have to be discarded and replaced in textbooks, schools of graduate study, religious sermons, and family discussions. This in itself will be revolutionary. It entails not only understanding that the gender binary is too narrow to encompass the true, wide range of natural gender forms; the fundamental premises of science, morality, and common sense will need to reflect this truth. I don't merely want to add a kinder view of diversity to our system of gender; I want the gender binary replaced.

Although this might be seen as a social or political movement for gender rights in which the rigidity attached to masculinity and femininity will be dissolved, and in which gender ambiguity will be accepted, it is more than that. Individuals will no longer be attacked for being trans or gay, and no one will be devalued because of gender identity. I advocate moving from identity politics to a social justice perspective. In this approach, asserting one's identity is not the reason for advocating for rights, freedoms, or protections; rather, the goals are universal justice and the end of discrimination and oppression. All people, whether gender variant or not, will benefit from a broadened acceptance of gender identity, because society will be safer and more just, and all individuals will have freedom to be authentic.

Education, as I said, will be necessary. It does make a difference. Surveys show that people who believe that homosexuality is biological tend to be more supportive of gay rights (Goodman 2005). When people understand that gender variance is also biological (and hence natural), they should be more supportive of trans rights and inclusion.

Visibility also makes a difference. Simply seeing authentic examples can increase people's comfort level with something they know little about. Movies such as *Normal*, *Rent*, *Transamerica*, and *Breakfast on Pluto* plus TV's *L Word*, *Transgeneration*, and soap opera *All My Children* bring the lives of trans-identified people into our living rooms. But it's not only media exposure that matters. Jill (male cross-dresser, transgendered) expressed his belief that familiarity with trans-identified people in real life makes a crucial difference:

the more transgendered people there are out, even if you're just out to your friends, even if it's just one person, I think that's activism. And that's important. It's important for the person, for both people, because the more people know that we are human beings and we're not monsters, we're not evil, that the more people can question their own ideas about gender, I think the more we will learn.

Sae (FtM) agreed that "the way to acceptance and respect for anything is to know more about it." Beth (MtF), too, felt that her visible difference was serving a positive purpose:

I do think it's important that God, the universe, whatever, decided to make me 6' 3" and so masculine-looking so that I am not able to just stop and blend in and disappear into the woodwork after surgery. I'm having to be out here every day at least with people questioning. They might not know exactly, but questioning. So I think that's good.

Many transpeople I interacted with during this study do public speaking in college classes or at other venues as their contribution to increasing acceptance and dismantling stereotypes. DaleLynn (intersex, MtF) educates people about what "intersex" means but also what being human means: "what I speak on," he explained, "are the parallels that we all share. I start with just the simple thing of being born. We're all born. And when we are born we're just beings until somebody says, 'Well, it's a boy or a girl or um. . . .'" Fiona (transgendered) addresses companies such as Anhauser Busch and the Bank of America and organizations including the Centers for Disease Control and the St. Louis Gender Foundation. Robyn (MtF) serves on the speaker's bureau for P-FLAG, has contributed to two books, and is a member of the National Transgender Advocacy Committee (NTAC). Rene (male cross-dresser) speaks to college classes and reported that "we have typical reactions like, 'Wow, we thought cross-dressers were all gay.' We thought we were going to see a RuPaul type person here today.' So they're always quite amazed. Several of us are retired military, as am I, and they're just amazed that macho military guys could be wearing a dress."

Many individuals who are mentioned in this book write letters to their newspapers or their elected representatives (for instance Dee, MtF). They serve on committees and are members of national organizations. Tina (MtF) doesn't identify as an "in-your-face activist," but she is involved in the National Gay and Lesbian Task Force, It's Time Illinois, and It's Time America. Melissa (male cross-dresser) said she "got involved with the New York Transgender Coalition, which is an effort to organize all these local New York groups and at least be able to count us all together as one and say, hello legislator we represent a half a million men in dresses."

Joney (MtF—but wasn't out at work) commented on the irony that a man in her office who followed trans issues "probably knew of Joney Harper, but he didn't know I was Joney Harper. And Joney Harper is an activist. Joney Harper goes to Pride parades. Joney Harper lobbies the NC State legislature and Congress. Joney Harper does this. It's not John sitting over there."

Children Are the Future

More and more schools are seeing children as young as kindergarten age who are gender variant. Whether a child's gender identity turns out to be a phase or a lifelong aspect of the self, teachers and school administrators have found ways to encourage positive development in these students. This may include having children line up by sneaker color rather than gender, as teachers do at the Park Day School in Oakland, California. Teachers at Park Day School are also taught a gender-neutral vocabulary and support all their students (Brown 2006). Children's National Medical

Center in Washington, D.C., has an online support community of two hundred parents of gender-variant youngsters.

California has become one of the most supportive states for gender-variant youth since passage of the California Student Safety and Violence Prevention Act of 2000, which prohibits discrimination and harassment in public schools on the basis of sexual orientation and gender identity. Many children have benefited from the extra steps teachers are taking to respond to needs of gender-variant students. In Florida, the Broward County school system admitted a male-bodied child as a girl, possibly the youngest acknowledged transgender child (Lelchuk 2006). These examples give me hope.

Epilogue: Gender Liberation

I do know what won't work is stuffing our species into two small categories of gender and sexuality (Roughgarden 2004, p. 396).

I do have an agenda. My agenda is to essentially make every individual, whether they're gay, lesbian, bisexual, transgendered or straight, feel like they are a valued person. That's my agenda. (Tina, MtF)

Since so much of a person's self-worth and self-identity in this culture appears to hinge on clear gender identity, the possibility that there are more options is not seen either as an opportunity or as an unfolding of the fascinating diversity of the world, but only and primarily as a THREAT. *(Phillip, metagendered)*

I am walking down the street, and a young person says "Happy New Year" to me while riding past me on a bike. I call out "Same to you!" and notice a bit more: baggy T-shirt, baggy pants, and shoulder-length light brown hair. The voice was somewhat high pitched, which made me think that the person was a female. But now I think, well, maybe a boy who hasn't gone through puberty, so his voice hasn't deepened, or maybe he just has a high voice. As I continue my walk I wonder to myself, why would it matter if that person was a boy or a girl?

I suppose that if I had engaged in a longer conversation, knowing "boy" or "girl" might have helped me choose my topics of discussion. Sports, games, clothes and accessories, music, activities, house chores—these are highly gendered, although some kids (or their parents) switch things around unpredictably. I finally realize that what I'm focusing on is not whether, by mistaking boy or girl, I might have chosen the wrong sport or music group to chat about, but whether there is any right or wrong in the first place. I am not comfortable with the two boxes, and I want more options. I am not alone in this.

Roughgarden (2004) writes that Darwin's theory of sexual selection, as "evolutionary biology's first universal theory of gender . . . has promoted social injustice and that overall we'd be better off both scientifically and ethically if we jettisoned it" (p. 164). For example, contrary to Darwin, males are not universally passionate, nor females always coy. Males do not universally fight to control females. The "best" males and "best" females do not universally fit some hierarchy of genetic quality. Females do not always select males for their superior genetic quality. In truth, the two types of gametes (eggs and sperm) do not always produce bodies of two categories or genders of two categories. Sex roles do not always conform to two sorts of gender roles. Females are not only in search of the strongest sperm, and males are not seeking to spread their "seed" anywhere and everywhere. Same-sex mating behavior is common, though you wouldn't know it from reading the scientific literature. Darwin chose to treat every case that did not fit his binary model of sex and gender as an "exception," meaning that he basically disregarded any evidence that his theory was incorrect (Roughgarden 2004, pp. 169–171). Consequently, a theory of sexual selection based on a binary sex and gender paradigm that is understood to be universal—but is actually contrary to what occurs in nature—has corrupted our view of what is normal and natural. In fact, trans bodies are completely acceptable and normal. It is time we understood that, taught that, and framed our life expectations on new ways of thinking.

The Thomases' dictum "If men [and women] define situations as real, they are real in their consequences" is clearly seen in our societal understanding of gender, based as it is on Darwinian thought. I propose we use the Thomases' premise to create a renewed understanding of gender with new definitions of reality.

A New Conceptualization of Sex, Gender, and Sexual Orientation

The journey I have taken through scores of lives, in gathering this collection of transgender voices, has shown me the inadequacy of a gender binary to capture people's identities. What I learned from this exploration was that a dramatically different perspective is necessary. I no longer believe that the more feminine you are the less masculine you are, or vice versa. I do not believe that biological sex is rigidly male or female. For this reason I propose a different conceptualization that allows for all configurations of bodies, identities, and attractions—a new framework in which all can be explained and understood. It consists of the parallel continuums discussed below (and see the accompanying chart), all of which exist within each individual.

The Sex Continuums. Traditionally, individuals are labeled male or female based on their biological characteristics. The general thinking is that someone is either male or female, not both or neither. However, intersex

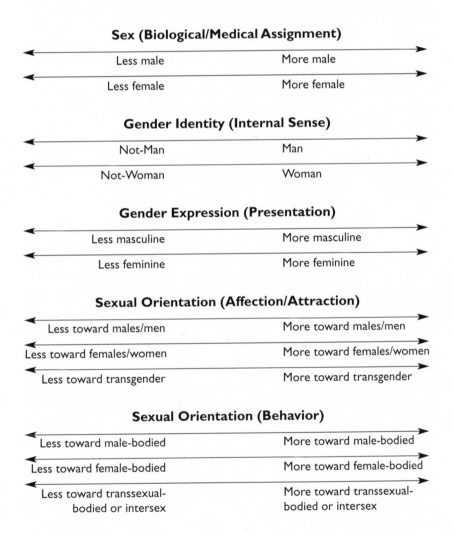

Sex (Biological/Medical Assignment)

Less male — More male

Less female — More female

Gender Identity (Internal Sense)

Not-Man — Man

Not-Woman — Woman

Gender Expression (Presentation)

Less masculine — More masculine

Less feminine — More feminine

Sexual Orientation (Affection/Attraction)

Less toward males/men — More toward males/men

Less toward females/women — More toward females/women

Less toward transgender — More toward transgender

Sexual Orientation (Behavior)

Less toward male-bodied — More toward male-bodied

Less toward female-bodied — More toward female-bodied

Less toward transsexual-bodied or intersex — More toward transsexual-bodied or intersex individuals defy this thinking because they may have a mix of what are usually thought of as unmixable male and female characteristics. Consequently, someone with breasts and a penis, say, or a vagina and a beard, can appear on each part of the two sex continuums (less or more of a male trait, less or more of a female trait) and in a different place on each, not just at one point on one single continuum.

An individual who is transitioning may also have a mix of biological traits such as breasts and a penis, or of secondary sex characteristics such as body hair and a high voice, that does not correspond with traditional notions of sex. The sex continuum I am proposing captures this person's reality. It allows for a more accurate representation of the wide variability of human physiology. And, equally important, it allows for the representation of individuals without portraying them as exceptions or as deviant.

The Gender Identity Continuums. Our internal sense of gender relates to our feelings of being a man, a woman, some combination, or neither. Traditionally it was believed that if you felt masculine you would not feel feminine, and vice versa. But, as we have seen, some people feel differing degrees of masculinity and differing degrees of femininity. Some people do not feel particularly like a man or a woman, and some feel that they have qualities of both. Having an identity continuum where degrees of "man" and degrees of "woman" coexist can help us capture a broader range of gender identity experiences.

It is also important to note that someone could be more male/less female (i.e., "male") or more female/less male (i.e., "female") on the sex continuum and not-man or not-woman on the gender identity continuum. This would be consistent with some trans-identified individuals' experiences. The view that all biological males identify strongly as men is not always true. Other combinations of body and internal sense of gender are also possible, which leads to gender expression.

The Gender Expression Continuums. The manner in which someone presents his/her sense of gender is that person's gender expression. This may or may not be consistent across time (one's youth versus adulthood, for example) or place (one presentation at home, a different one at work). Furthermore, some people may be androgynous and not have a clear masculine or feminine expression; others may clearly express one or the other. The gender expression continuums allow for all expressions to be acknowledged and validated over the full range of other continuums (body types and gender identities), including expressing masculine and feminine traits simultaneously.

The Sexual Orientation Continuums. Sexual orientation has two components, attraction and behavior—that is, to whom one is attracted and with what type of body one is sexual. A person can be attracted to people who are more or less masculine, feminine, or different types of transgender in their gender presentation. A person can also be attracted to different body types, and may can engage in sexual behavior with people who are male-bodied, female-bodied, transsexual, and/or intersex. Thinking about sexual orientation in this way is more congruent with human reality and more inclusive of people with gender-variant identities and gender-variant bodies. For example, a person may be female appearing but have an intersex body; a person who is a cross-dresser may be male-bodied; a genderqueer individual may have a female body.

Once we acknowledge intersex people, transsexuals, and transgenders as people with gender presentations and various body types, a third continuum is added to the "sexual orientation" sections of the chart presented here. This allows us to represent truly every type of person without having to force anyone into an outmoded and inaccurate binary configuration. It is important to note that people who are male or female, and masculine or feminine, also fit into these continuums. They are not excluded but fully accepted as types of human diversity, as are people outside the binary.

If continuums such as these were incorporated into everyday language, teaching, and socialization, people could be comfortable with who they are without feeling that they *have* to go on hormones, have electrolysis, or undergo surgery. There wouldn't be the same emotional, visual, and physical associations with maleness and femaleness that exist now. Acceptance and redefinition could open up a wide range of perfectly legitimate ways to be feminine, masculine, both, and neither. This isn't to say no one would transition in exactly the same ways people do today, but if anyone did, it would be more of a preference than an imperative.

LGBT?

It's been a rough alliance. Lack of acknowledgment of the role of trans-identified people at Stonewall (the name of a gay bar raided by police, in which gays and transpeople fought back, considered the start of the Gay Liberation Movement); lesbian feminists denouncing transwomen in women-only space; macho gay men rejecting femininity in men; butch lesbians transitioning as transmen; androgynous lesbians who reject feminine transwomen; antidiscrimination laws written without including gender identity and expression—these and other political and social clashes over the past forty years have repeatedly raised questions about common agendas, identities, and issues. I believe that we have a common adversary in those who diminish the personhood of LGBT people and see us as "less than." And, while not everyone agrees with this stance, I see sexual orientation as related to gender identity because sexual orientation involves behaviors that are viewed as violations of gender role and gender behavior. I believe that we have more in common to fight for than we have to prevent our alliance.

But as Green (2004) points out, there was a great deal of confusion when many issues burst forth at once—transpeople started to organize themselves and communicate and educate within their own ranks at the same time that intersex people were organizing and articulating their perspectives, while everyone was trying to keep homophobia at bay. As organizations formed, "there was a great deal of confusion about the margins of each organization, each group's issues and goals, and the nature of each group's investment in gender categories because most people, even among gay, lesbian, bisexual, transgender, and intersex (LGBTI) groups, didn't have a clear understanding of each other" (p. 82). Furthermore, Clare reminds us that horizontal hostility extends to the LGBT communities, where marginalized people create internal tensions: "gay men and lesbians disliking bisexual people, transsexual women looking down on drag queens . . ." (1999, p. 92). While relations have improved, there is still a great deal of education to do within the LGBT and intersex communities.

There is much ambivalence over LGBT unity, and these struggles remain unresolved. Nathan (FEM, male) had this to say:

I struggle with [whether the T has much in common with the GLB]. Fundamentally I would have to say no, not really. But then when I look at the facts of the history of the GLBT movement I say most certainly. It was trans and gender queer folks who were targeted and finally revolted in the Stonewalls across the nation. But then if you buy into the notion of gender dysphoria, then there is little relationship between being GLBT and being a transsexual. I think the inclusion creates problems of concepts and understanding of the issue of transsexuality. I get a bit annoyed when people speak of transsexuality as an issue of sexual orientation. It is often assumed, treated as a given. And the inclusion of T in GLB makes it difficult to get people to see transsexuality as something other than having to do with sexual orientation.

Danielle (femme lesbian), too, was really not sure if the T belonged with LGB. She was asked to facilitate a lesbian group.

Now I, I don't know. Some days I feel that if they're lesbian, they're lesbian, and if the transgender issue is something that maybe they would like to disclose, you *know . . . and then there's all these things of marriage and domestic partnership and all of those things going on, and I just, I don't feel that that population should be discriminated against in any way but I think it's almost hard enough to have people accept gay and lesbian. And then to also add another component into the mix makes it even harder.*

November (genderqueer, trans) volunteered for an HIV/AIDS organization and also attended a gender discussion group there. What he heard was LGB people discussing their concerns about reaching out to transpeople and wondering how to provide services. What they didn't realize, November said, was "those transpeople are already in their midst. And they're talking about 'them' to people who identify as 'them.'" Melanie (MtF) ran into problems when she tried to join the Gay and Lesbian Medical Association. "Oh, you're heterosexually identified? We don't want straight people in our organization."

Of course, in addition to the knee-jerk, culturally induced reactions and confusions about how gender identity and sexual orientation interface, there is the issue of where this partnership could lead. Kessler suggests a consequence for sexual orientation categories once gender is rightfully expanded:

One can imagine that just as a heterosexual woman today can legitimately claim not to be attracted to men with excessive body hair, in a newly configured system she could claim not to be attracted to men with penises or to be attracted to men with breasts and a vagina. What then would heterosexual mean? In what sense could a woman with a vagina who is sexually gratified by being penetrated by a "woman" with a large clitoris (that looks and functions like a penis) be said to be a lesbian? If gendered bodies fall into disarray, sexual orientation will follow. Defining sexual orientation according to attraction to people with the same or different genitals, as is done now, will no longer make sense, nor will intersexuality. (2000, p. 124, emphasis in original)

Trans Lives Revisited

This section revisits three of the people whose voices are quoted in this book to see what changes occurred in their lives during the four years since their interviews. It pays particular attention to gender identifications and how they played out during that time.

. . .

Dan was a pre-operative FtM who still lived his life closeted, as a woman, at the time of our interview. He had a singing career he didn't want to give up, family ties he feared losing, and was in a committed relationship with a woman who did not want him to transition. Dan was twenty-five years old and in graduate school. About a year after we spoke, Dan started testosterone shots. As he began to masculinize, his relationship broke up. But something even worse occurred—he became dangerously ill. His illness was mistreated for some time and he continued his testosterone shots, feeling unremitting fatigue, nausea, and an inability to function normally. After Dan had endured five months of debilitating illness, his doctor finally realized that his testosterone levels were more than twice that of a biological male's and that his liver was in distress. Dan stopped getting the hormone shots and tried to continue living as a male. As he regained his health, his features started to soften, his voice stopped lowering, and his periods returned.

After about nine months of being off testosterone, Dan decided to legally resume his female name and his female identity, determined to "make it work this time. I was sick of being the gender outlaw," he explained. "I wanted to live clearly, recognizably and unequivocally as female, and put all of this transsexual business behind me." Dan changed everything about himself—looks, haircut, clothing, toiletries, walk, habits. Still attracted to women, Dan identified as a lesbian.

Dan went through another major change when he met a woman and fell deeply in love. His new relationship "drove all of my suppressed masculinity right back up to the surface, and it all felt very much beyond my control." His partner accepted and encouraged Dan, who began to remasculinize, though without transition.

Dan's story did not end there. About a year and a half after his aborted first transition, he started again. This time, on the proper dose of testosterone, his health is not suffering. He has had chest reconstruction and legally changed his name and documents once again. When I asked Dan what he makes of all this, he could only stress how important it is to live as your true self. About his first attempt at transition, he feels that he wasn't psychologically strong enough to handle his family's rejection and the loss of his singing career. Those shocks, combined with his physical problems associated with the testosterone overdose, caused him to collapse emotionally and physically. His need to be seen as male, feeling that he had the wrong body, and the lack of support had wreaked havoc with his sense of self.

His second transition is different, with its own issues. He is much stronger in his core sense of self, with a supportive partner and a family that is trying to understand, but an unexpected source of pain has emerged. Although testosterone promotes many masculine attributes, such as a lowered voice and body hair growth, the major limitation of T is that it does not create a penis. "I will spend the rest of my life grieving that," Dan predicted. It is an unexpected source of sadness, a pain and grief that he will have to work through.

Jennifer was a fifty-year-old MtF, heterosexual female teacher when we first spoke. She was separated from her wife, and they were planning to divorce. Two years after we had our interview, Jennifer went back to wearing men's clothes and "slowly moved into living as a man." At first, after their separation, Jennifer's wife was doing well. But then her health took a serious decline and she became bedridden, unable to care for herself. If Jennifer proceeded with her surgery as planned, her wife would be taken off Jennifer's health insurance because her workplace did not recognize same-sex marriages. Jennifer "could not live with watching her slowly fall apart and die." With help from her faith and trust in God, Jennifer stopped hormones, changed her name legally, stayed married, and began to live as a man.

Living as a man, though identifying as a woman, Jennifer can see and be with her grandchildren (a treat denied to her before). She is able to care for her wife. She realizes that she is not "cured" of her transsexualism, and she has trouble keeping up her hygiene. "It is hard to bathe when you have to see hair on chest and breasts where once there was none. No point in keeping up eyebrows. Without the hormones the skin has lost its fat and wrinkles deepen unchallenged." Cross-dressing does not ease her pain; Jennifer's only solution would be to live again, at some point in the future, as a woman.

Meanwhile Jennifer has the joy of her grandchildren, and her wife's health is improving. She has, perhaps, made the ultimate nurturing act of the traditional woman—to sacrifice her self so that others she loves can live more comfortably.

November, age twenty-eight, identified as genderqueer or trans when we were first in contact. Female-bodied, he was in graduate school. He didn't apply the words masculine or feminine to himself to describe his gender, though people around him tended to see him more on the masculine side of things. He was okay with female pronouns but more comfortable with

NOVEMBER

male pronouns. Or, as he put it, "I'm completely happy being (as one friend calls himself) 'a dude with a cunt.'"

Sometime after our interview, November finished graduate school, got a teaching job, and got very interested in performing femininity. He would create female characters, with new names and personalities, and accumulated a wardrobe, wigs, and makeup. November found he could do this in ways he never could when he identified as a girl. Eventually, about three years after we first spoke, he decided to resume using female pronouns and incorporate femininity into his, now her, life on a regular basis. "I was very specific," November informed me, "about letting people know that this was not a matter of 'going back' to being a girl or deciding to use female pronouns 'again.' Instead, it was about forward motion: the girl that I became in 2005 was very different than the girl that I was pre-2001 (when I started using male pronouns), and I couldn't have become this new person without the path through a more male identity."

November started a new teaching job presenting as female and identifying as genderqueer. She also moved to a new city where no one had known her as "him." She is now dating a heterosexual man who sees her as female, albeit an unconventional female. She is finding that her students seem more comfortable with her, probably because she is not challenging gender in obvious ways that would disturb them. This makes her job easier.

But this does not mean that November is a girl. "In other words," she explained, "I am by no means saying that I've discovered that 'I'm really a girl;' more accurately, I'm saying something much more qualified: 'at this particular moment, I'm enjoying the experience of being a girl.' So, like I said at the beginning, a lot of things have changed for me, but really, in terms of the way I understand gender to operate in my life, nothing has changed at all."

Reviewing these three cases demonstrates how gender is a "process of discovery" (a comment November made). If people believe that they must fit into one of two boxes, they may force themselves to do so. But given the opportunity—or seizing the opportunity—they may find other ways to express themselves. As we have seen, this can be a lifelong process, and there is nothing linear—or binary—about it.

The evidence is overwhelming that gender identity is an internal sense of self we are born with. We should be able to freely and fully express who we are without fear of negative repercussions. The religious, moral, political, and economic rationales for a gender binary can never justify denying authenticity. Respect for tradition should not be an excuse for laziness, for fear, or for not taking the steps to change what has been understood as natural to what is *actually* natural. We need to define real situations as real, not create a false reality. Once we admit that the gender binary is a lie, we have an obligation to start the wheels in motion toward change. The payoff to our families, our children, ourselves, will be enormous. Gender diversity is the liberation issue of our times and should be put at center stage.

Appendixes

ARE YOU A
GENDER TRANSGRESSOR?

ARE THERE TIMES WHEN YOU ARE TOO FEMALE OR NOT
FEMALE ENOUGH? . . . TOO MALE OR NOT MALE ENOUGH?

DO YOU FEEL YOU'RE NOT MALE <u>OR</u> FEMALE?
OR MAYBE YOU FEEL MALE <u>AND</u> FEMALE?

RESEARCHER LORI B. GIRSHICK, PH.D. IS SEEKING
STUDY PARTICIPANTS TO BE INTERVIEWED FOR A
STUDY ON FEMININITY AND MASCULINITY.

ARE YOU COMFORTABLE WITH THE GENDER BINARY?
LET YOUR VOICE BE HEARD.

FOR A COPY OF THE STUDY QUESTIONNAIRE, CONTACT

LORI B. GIRSHICK, PH.D.
WWC-6124
P.O. BOX 9000
ASHEVILLE, NC 28815

OR download the questionnaire at www.warren-wilson.edu/~lgirshic
OR call (828) 771–3711, OR e-mail lgirshick@mindspring.com

Lori B. Girshick, Ph.D. is a sociologist, writer, and community activist.
Her main areas of work have been domestic and sexual violence, criminal
justice issues, and gender identity. She has written three books. Her
latest book, *Woman-to-Woman Sexual Violence: Does She Call it Rape?*
has just been published by Northeastern University Press.

APPENDIX 2: Survey

DEMOGRAPHICS (GETTING TO KNOW YOU)

(1) How old were you at your last birthday? _____

(2) How do you identify your race/ethnicity?
        White, not Latino/

        Hispanic _____   Asian American _____

        African American _____   Asian/Pacific Islander _____

        Latino/Hispanic _____   Native American _____

        Other (please specify) _____

(3) Sexual identity:
        Transgendered/transsexual (living full-time)

        MtF _____   FtM _____

            pre-operative _____

            post-operative _____

            non-operative _____

        Male _____

        Female _____

        Cross-dresser _____

        Intersexed _____

        Other (Butch lesbian, e.g., please specify) _____

(4) Sexual orientation:

        Heterosexual _____

        Lesbian _____

        Gay male _____

        Bisexual _____

        Polyamorous _____

        Other (asexual, e.g., please specify) _____

(5) Present partner status? _____

(6) What is the highest educational level you have completed?

       Less than high school _____

       GED _____

       High school graduate _____

       Some college _____

       4-year-college graduate _____

       Advanced degree after college _____

       Other certificate program (please specify) _____

(7) What is your occupation/job? _____

(8) What is your annual income (just you, not household) _____

(9) How did you hear about this study? _____

SECTION ON FEMININTY AND MASCULINITY (attach another sheet, if needed)

(10) We live in a society based on a gender binary of female and male. There are generalized ideas of what traditional femininity and masculinity are. Would you please tell me how YOU define femininity and masculinity? (Another way of thinking about this is to ask yourself what the traits of someone you consider feminine are, or the traits of someone you view as masculine.)

(11) What do you think of the idea that females are primarily feminine and males are primarily masculine? Does this make sense to you?

(12) Given the views you've stated above about femininity and masculinity, how would you define yourself? Why do you feel that way (what about you is masculine or feminine)?

(13) If you don't think in binary terms, does the word "androgynous" work for you? Why or why not? If not binary terms and not androgyny, what terms "work" for you and why?

(14) Can you tell me if . . .
   you have ever been perceived as too female . . . or not female enough?
   you have ever been perceived as too male . . . or not male enough?
   When was that? What was the situation?

GENDER ROLE ENFORCEMENT (attach another sheet, if necessary)

(15) I'm interested in how you feel you've learned these ideas of femininity and masculinity. Please look over this list and comment on the aspects you feel have had the strongest influence on your gender ideas.
   religious messages
   verbal comments
   threats of harm
   family roles
   media imagery
   jokes

physical violence (gay bashings, hate crimes)
police harassment
cultural practices (marriage ceremonies, etc.)
forced medical procedures or denial of procedures
discriminatory laws
lack of legal protection for certain groups
other socialization mechanisms for gender you want to mention

(16) Do you think males or females have the harder time in transgressing gender roles? Why?

(17) Are there times when you felt shame about who you are? What societal messages do you feel led you to that feeling?

(18) Have you experienced any hostility or difficult situations at work, in public, or with strangers that created problems for you? What happened?

YOUR GENDER JOURNEY (attach another sheet, if necesssary)

(19) Was there a particular point when you started to question your assigned gender? What happened? What was it like to not feel quite male or quite female?

(20) As you challenged traditional gender roles and norms, how did your blood family respond?

(21) Did/do you have role models for your gender challenges?

(22) How "consistent" do you feel external appearance needs to be with internal identity? Have you felt a need or desire to make any physical changes to achieve a harmony with your identity?

(23) At times have you been referred to by the "wrong" gender pronoun? What happened? Have you been perceived as the wrong orientation, for example, thought to be a gay male when you are a FtM? What happened?

(24) Have alcohol or drugs played a role in coping with stress in your gender journey? Can you tell me about that? Were there other coping strategies you've used (past or present)?

(25) If you take hormones, can you tell me about changes you've experienced?

(26) Is "passing" an issue for you? How? Do you think passing in terms of blending in is the goal of those who alter gender assignment or is the goal to challenge the gender binary?

RELATIONSHIPS WITH OTHERS (attach another sheet, if necessary)

(27) Can you tell me about your intimate relationships with others at different stages of your gender journey? What were your biggest challenges? Your main satisfactions?

(28) How have your relationships with blood family members changed (or not)?

(29) Do you find as you meet potential friends you need to "explain" yourself or tell them about your changes? Or do you see your gender journey as private?

(30) What have been your biggest struggles in intimate relationships?

OTHER

(31) Is there anything else you'd like to mention about gender transgressing that I haven't touched on?

(32) If there is someone you'd recommend I contact about the study, please give contact info:

Glossary

AA: Alcoholics Anonymous

Androgen Insensitivity Syndrome (AIS): Individuals with XY chromosomes, but who are highly feminized. Because of a blockage of testosterone their bodies do not fully masculinize; they usually have internal male organs but female secondary sex characteristics.

Androgynous: To some the term means qualities of both masculinity and femininity within one person; to others it means the person's gender is ambiguous or unclear.

Anti-androgen drugs: Drugs such as spironolactone that suppress the body's production of testosterone.

Autogynephilia: Refers to an individual who eroticizes the feminine. The term reduces male-to-female transsexuality to sexual stimulation rather than including a full complement of humanity.

Berdache: A pejorative term from colonialism referring to Native American people living outside the gender binary and replaced by the term *two-spirit*.

Bi-gender: An individual who identifies as having both masculine and feminine qualities.

Binding: The process of wrapping or compressing the breasts to form the look of a male chest.

Bioman: An individual, assigned as a male at birth based on external male physical characteristics, who also identifies as being a man.

Biowoman: An individual assigned as a female at birth, based on external female physical characteristics, who also identifies as being a woman.

Birth sex: The assignment by doctors at birth of an infant as being male or female according to external genitals.

Butch: An individual expressing stereotypical masculine appearance or behavior; a masculine lesbian.

Camp Trans: The encampment across the road from the Michigan Womyn's Music Festival entrance that began in 1995 to protest the policy of exclusion of transwomen from the festival. Their primary focus is education about trans identity and dialogue about the policy.

Coming out: The process of becoming aware of and telling others about one's sexual orientation or gender identity. This involves assessing levels of risk and making decisions about who to tell, what to tell, and when to tell.

Congenital Adrenal Hyperplasia (CAH): Individuals with XX chromosomes who undergo masculinization at birth or at puberty. This is the only life-threatening intersex condition, and it is caused by a disruption of salt metabolism.

Crico thyroid approximation (CTA): Voice surgery, which attempts to increase the hertz range of a voice, undertaken by some male-to-female transsexuals.

Cross-dressing (also CDing): Wearing the clothing typical of another gender.

Cross-living: Living full-time as the gender an individual believes he/she is. Also referred to as living 24/7.

Daughters of Bilitis: A lesbian rights organization founded in San Francisco in 1955 and important in the early Gay Liberation Movement.

DES (Diethylstilbestrol): A synthetic estrogen that was used to treat a multitude of female hormonal problems including miscarriage, it was later taken off the market when it was found to increase cancer risk in daughters whose mothers took it during pregnancy.

Drag kings/drag queens: People who cross-dress for entertainment and performance.

Diagnostic and Statistical Manual (DSM): The diagnostic manual of the American Psychiatric Association.

Dyke: Another word for a lesbian (a woman attracted to another woman).

En femme: When an individual is dressed in feminine clothing.

Estrogen mimics: These man-made (synthetic) chemicals can change the way the endocrine system functions by mimicking what hormones do and by blocking or triggering natural hormones.

Femme: An individual expressing stereotypical feminine appearance or behavior; a feminine lesbian.

For Ourselves: Reworking Gender Expression (FORGE): A national education, advocacy and support umbrella organization supporting female-to-male transsexuals and transgenderists, and others who were assigned female at birth but who have some level of masculine identification and SOFFAs (Significant Others, Family, Friends and Allies).

FtM: Female-to-male transsexual; a person assigned as female at birth who identifies as a man.

Gametes: Sperm and eggs.

Gender: The assignment of characteristics labeled masculine and feminine expected to correlate to men and women, respectively, in a society's binary system.

Gender bender: Refers to individuals who challenge gender notions through their gender expression and appearance, usually done quite deliberately, and sometimes done as farce or play.

Gender dysphoria: A persistent discomfort with the gender assignment at birth and the resulting expectations of that assignment.

Gender expression: See gender presentation.

Gender fuck: See gender bender.

Gender identity: An individual's internal sense of his/her gender.

Gender identity disorder (GID): The psychological diagnosis found in the Diagnostic and Statistical Manual of Mental Disorders (DSM) IV of the American Psychiatric Association that applies to adults and children who have a persistent discomfort with their assigned birth gender but who may not be impaired or distressed. Many challenge the diagnosis as stigmatizing since it implies the individuals are disordered.

GID Reform Advocates: A group that calls for the removal of GID from the DSM (which is up for revision and publication around 2010), so that difference is not viewed as disease, pathology, or illness.

Gender norms: The acceptable cultural behaviors, ideas, and values associated with different genders.

Gender presentation: The way an individual chooses to present his/her gender to others through dress, speech, actions, and grooming.

Gender Public Advocacy Coalition (GPAC): A not-for-profit organization, which was started, in 1999, to work for the safety and well-being of all people, whether or not they meet social expectations for masculinity and femininity.

Gender roles: The behaviors and ways of thinking and feeling that the culture teaches are appropriate for the different genders.

Gender variant: Individuals who do not match the gender expectations of the gender binary in their gender expression and behavior.

Genderqueer: See queer.

Gonads: Ovaries and testes.

Harry Benjamin International Gender Dysphoria Association (HBIGDA): See WPATH.

He-she: The first word refers to gender identity and the second to birth sex, in this case, a female-bodied, male-identified person.

Hermaphrodite: A stigmatizing word that has been replaced by the term *intersex*.

Heteronormativity: Using heterosexuality as the standard with which to compare any other sexual orientation, where heterosexuality is normal, natural, and right.

Hir: A gender neutral word that means him or her, pronounced "here."

Homophobe: An individual who has an irrational fear and hatred of gay people.

Homophobia: The irrational fear and hatred of gay people.

Human Rights Campaign (HRC): The largest national gay, lesbian, bisexual, and transgender civil rights organization, founded in 1980, in Washington, D.C.

Hypothalamus: The endocrine center of the brain that influences gender identity and secondary sex characteristics.

The International Foundation for Gender Education (IFGE): A nonprofit advocacy organization founded in 1987. Its purpose is overcoming the intolerance
of transvestitism and transsexualism brought about by widespread ignorance.

Intergendered: Individuals who reject any sort of gender system.

Internalized homophobia: When an individual believes or internalizes the negative messages of the culture that homosexuality is wrong or unnatural.

Intersex: Individuals with a variety of nonstandard reproductive, chromosomal,
or sexual anatomies, hormonal blocks or adrenal gland malfunctions.

Klinefelter Syndrome: Individuals who possess XXY or XXXY chromosomes,
which manifest in male genitals, small testes, some breast development, and
sometimes infertility.

Living full-time/living part-time: Living full-time is the same as cross-living (see
cross-living above), while living part-time means that an individual is living as
the gender he/she identifies as only part of the time, usually when he/she goes
to work or is with family members.

Male cross-dresser: Men who dress in women's clothing for fun, self-expression,
erotic stimulation, or for some combination of reasons. Generally the term
"cross-dressing" refers to men because it is acceptable for women to wear
men's clothing.

Metagendered: A term that goes beyond the idea of either combining genders or
crossing/changing between two options, opening up to the possibility of any
number of gender options.

Michigan Womyn's Music Festival (MWMF): The oldest and largest feminist
women's music festival in the country.

Misogyny: The hatred of women in society.

MtF (Male-to-female transsexual): A person assigned as male at birth who identifies as a female.

National Coming Out Day: Observed on October 11, this is an international day
of events to bring awareness about issues of coming out for lesbian, gay, bisexual and transgender people.

National Gay and Lesbian Task Force (NGLTF): Founded in 1973, the NGLTF
works to build the grassroots power of the lesbian, gay, bisexual and transgender (LGBT) community through training activists and supporting community initiatives to work for the complete equality of LGBT people.

National Transgender Advocacy Committee (NTAC): Founded in 1999, NTAC
works for the advancement of understanding and the attainment of full civil
rights for all transgender and gender variant people in every aspect of society
and actively opposes discriminatory acts by all means legally available.

Nellie: A feminine-acting male.

No hormone (no-ho): A trans-identified individual who chooses to not take
hormones.

Non-operative (non-op): Transsexuals who live full-time as another gender
without undergoing any surgery.

Orchiectomy: A type of surgery that reduces the production of testosterone as a result of the removal of the testicles.

Packing: Creating the look of a penis and scrotum in one's pants through using socks, gel-filled condoms, or prosthetics.

Pansexual: An individual who is emotionally, spiritually, physically, and/or sexually attracted to people of many different genders or sexes.

Passing: A concept meaning an individual is accepted as the gender he/she presents as; also meaning acceptance as who he/she really is without question that he/she might be or have been something else.

Polyamorous: Loving many at one time.

Post-operative (post-op): Term for an individual who has had SRS.

Pre-operative (pre-op): Term for an individual who plans to have SRS but has not yet.

Purging: When a cross-dresser collects clothing, dresses, throws everything away, and then repeats the cycle.

Queer: A person who feels his/her gender identity and/or sexual orientation is outside the binary. Queer is a word that has been used negatively but has been reclaimed by some LGBT individuals to describe their gender identity and/or sexual orientation.

Real Life Experience (RLE): A time when the individual lives full-time in his/her true gender in preparation for sex reassignment surgery. The individual needs to demonstrate that he/she can socially and financially function in his/her true gender.

Secondary sex characteristics: Physical characteristics that emerge at puberty such as facial and body hair, voice changes, breast development, and muscle development.

Sex: The biological characteristics of genitals, internal reproductive organs, gonads (ovaries and testes), hormones, and chromosomes. Male and female are the labels for these clusters of biological traits.

Sexism: The belief system that men are better or superior to women, combined with the institutional advantages men have over women to entitle them in law, employment, power, and so forth.

Sex reassignment surgery (SRS): Surgery that allows the body to be more in line with an individual's gender identity, such as surgery that creates a neovagina out of a penis and scrotum, surgery that creates a penis through skin grafts and implants, or surgery that creates a chest through mastectomy and chest reconstruction. Sometimes referred to as gender confirmation surgery or genital reconstruction surgery (GRS).

Sexual orientation: Physical attraction to other people.

She-male: the first word refers to gender identity and the second to birth sex, in this case a male-bodied, female-identified person.

Sie: A gender neutral pronoun to use instead of *he* or *she*, pronounced "see."

Sissy: A male who acts in a feminine manner.

Sissyphobia: A fear and loathing of men who behave in a feminine manner.

Standards of Care (SOC): The protocol used by most doctors in the United States in providing the medical care, including prescribing hormones or preparing for surgery, for transsexuals.

Stealth: When an individual is able to go through life without revealing his/her trans history.

Stone butch: A female-bodied person who is strongly masculine in character and dress, who generally is dominant in sexual relations and often does not want to be touched genitally. Some stone butches identify as lesbians, while others use male pronouns.

Stonewall: Widely considered the start of the Gay Liberation Movement, the Stonewall Rebellion began on June 28, 1969 and lasted several days when gay and transgender bar patrons stood up to the denigration by New York City police who had made a practice of arresting, harassing, and humiliating them.

T: A shorthand way to refer to testosterone.

Tomboy: Females who behave in masculine ways.

Tranny boy: A transsexual male who emphasizes boyish characteristics in expression.

Tranny chaser: A term generally used to refer to an individual who seeks out pre-op MtFs for sex partners.

Transgender (also TG): An umbrella term for gender variant individuals.

Transgenderist: See non-operative.

Trans-identified people (or transpeople): The collective of people who are gender variant in some way, who experience a disconnection to anatomy, gender expression, gender presentation, or gender roles outside the norm.

Transition: A process an individual undergoes to alter his/her gender role, gender expression and physical body to feel greater psychological harmony—measures that are perceived as contrary to birth gender assignment and physical body. A person may or may not take all the steps (hormones, electrolysis, facial reconstruction, breast enhancement or mastectomy, sex reassignment surgery, among others).

Transman: See FtM.

Transperson: See trans-identified people.

Transsexual (also TS): An individual who feels his/her gender identity does not align with his/her physical body, as traditionally defined.

Transexual Menace: A group of activists who organized to promote transgender and transsexual rights, especially inclusion of transgender people in the activism of national LGBT organizations, such as the HRC.

Transvestic Fetishism (TF): A psychological diagnosis found in the Diagnostic and Statistical Manual of Mental Disorders (DSM) IV of the American Psychiatric Association, which labels crossdressing by heterosexual males as a sexual fetish.

Transvestite: Outdated and pejorative word for a male cross-dresser.

Transwoman: See MtF.

Tri-Ess (Society for the Second Self): An international support organization that serves heterosexual male cross-dressers and their partners.

Tuck: Pushing or taping male genitals so they are not noticeable.

Turner Syndrome: Females whose ovaries do not develop, and whose breasts, uteruses and vaginas are underdeveloped.

Two-spirit: A Native American term that refers to individuals who exhibit both masculine and feminine characteristics, or to individuals living outside the gender binary.

Under-dressing: Wearing women's underwear such as bras, panties, stockings, or lingerie under typical men's clothing.

WPATH (World Professional Association for Transgender Health): Formerly the Harry Benjamin International Gender Dysphoria Association (HBIGDA), it is a professional organization devoted to the understanding and treatment of gender identity disorders.

Ze: A gender neutral pronoun that means *he or she*, pronounced "zee."

Bibliography

Arana, Marcus. 2005. *A human rights investigation into the medical "normalization" of intersex people.* A Report of a Public Hearing by the Human Rights Commission of the City and County of San Francisco. San Francisco.

Arizona Daily Star. 2005a. Chemical compound in moms linked to birth defects in boys. May 27, p. A4.

Arizona Daily Star. 2005b. Study: Gays' response to sex chemicals differs. May 10, p. A2.

Bailey, J. Michael. 2003. *The man who would be queen.* Washington, D.C.: National Academies Press.

Berling, Tim. 2001. *Sissyphobia: Gay men and effeminate behavior.* New York: The Haworth Press.

Bloom, Amy. 2002. Conservative men in conservative dresses. *Atlantic Monthly,* April, pp. 94, 96–102.

Bolin, Anne. 1988. *In search of Eve: Transsexual rites of passage.* Westport, Conn.: Bergin & Garvey.

Bornstein, Kate. 1994. *Gender outlaw: On men, women, and the rest of us.* New York: Vintage Books.

Boswell, Holly. 1997. "The transgender paradigm shift toward free expression." In *Gender blending.* Edited by Bonnie Bullough, Vern L. Bullough, & James Elias. Amherst, New York: Prometheus Books, pp. 53–57.

Brown, Mildred L., and Chloe Ann Rounsley. 1996. *True selves.* San Francisco: Jossey-Bass.

Brown, Patricia Leigh. 2006. Supporting boys or girls when the line isn't clear. *New York Times,* December 2. http://www.nytimes.com/2006/12/02/us/02child .html?ei=5070&en=69cd42a41396606e&ex=1165726800&emc=eta1&page wanted=print.

Brownmiller, Susan. 1984. *Femininity.* New York: Fawcett Columbine.

Califia, P. 1997. *Sex changes: The politics of transgenderism*. San Francisco: Cleis Press.

Charon, Joel M. 1989. *Symbolic interactionism*, 3rd ed. Englewood Cliffs: Prentice Hall.

Clare, Eli. 1999. *Exile and pride: Disability, queerness, and liberation*. Cambridge, Mass.: South End Press.

Cook-Daniels, Loree. 2004. Femmes, butches and lesbian-feminists discussing FTMs. http://www.forge-forward.org/handouts/feminismFTM.php. Accessed February 23, 2005.

Crenson, Matt. 2005. Harvard boss may be right on brains. *Arizona Daily Star*, February 28, pp. A1, A7.

Cromwell, Jason. 1999. *Transmen & FTMs: Identities, bodies, genders & sexualities*. Urbana: University of Illinois Press.

Davidson, Megan. 2002, Winter. 'Natural Facts'? Feminism, Transgender, & the Denaturalized Body. *Transgender Tapestry*, 100, pp. 41–44.

DeNavas-Walt, Bernadette D. Proctor, and Jessica Smith, 2006. *Income, poverty, and health insurance coverage in the United States: 2006*. U.S. Census Bureau, Current Population Reports, P60–233, Washington, DC: U.S. Government Printing Office.

Denny, Dallas. 1997. Transgender: Some historical, cross-cultural, and contemporary models and methods of coping and treatment. In *Gender blending*, edited by Bonnie Bullough, Vern L. Bullough, and James Elias, pp. 33–47. Amherst, N.Y.: Prometheus Books.

———. 2002. The politics of diagnosis and a diagnosis of politics. *Transgender Tapestry* 98 (Summer), pp. 3–8.

Devor, Holly. 1989. *Gender blending: Confronting the limits of duality*. Bloomington: Indiana University Press.

———. 1997. More than manly women: How female-to-male transsexuals reject lesbian identities. In *Gender blending*, edited by Bonnie Bullough, Vern L. Bullough, and James Elias, pp. 87–102. Amherst, N.Y.: Prometheus Books.

———. 2002. Who are "we"? Where sexual orientation meets gender identity. *Journal of Gay & Lesbian Psychotherapy* 6 (2), pp. 5–21.

Edgerton, Milton T. 1984. The role of surgery in the treatment of transsexualism. *Annals of Plastic Surgery* 13 (6).

Endocrine Society. 2002. Patient fact sheets. http://www.endo-society.org/pubrelations/patientinfo/estrogens.htm. Accessed August 20, 2002.

Epstein, Rachel. 2002. Butches with babies: Reconfiguring gender and motherhood. In *Femme/butch: New considerations of the way we want to go*, edited by Michelle Gibson and Deborah T. Meem, pp. 41–57. New York: Harrington Park Press.

Ettner, Randi. 1996. *Confessions of a gender defender*. Evanston, Ill.: Chicago Spectrum Press.

Fausto-Sterling, Ann. 2000. The five sexes, revisited. *The Sciences* 40 (4), pp. 18–26.

Feinberg, Leslie. 1996. *Transgender warriors: Making history from Joan of Arc to Dennis Rodman*. Boston: Beacon Press.

————. 1998. *TransLiberation: Beyond pink or blue.* Boston: Beacon Press.

Garber, Marjorie. 1992. *Vested interests: Cross-dressing and cultural anxiety.* New York: Routledge.

Garfinkel, H. 1967. *Studies in ethnomethodology.* Upper Saddle River, N.J.: Prentice Hall.

Gibson, Michelle, and Deborah T. Meem. 2002. *Femme/Butch: New Considerations of the Way We Want to Go.* New York: The Haworth Press.

Girshick, Lori B. 2002. *Woman-to-woman sexual violence: Does she call it rape?* Boston: Northeastern University Press.

Glaser, Barney G., and Anselm L. Strauss. 1967. *The discovery of grounded theory: Strategies for qualitative research.* New York: Aldine Publishing Company.

Goffman, E. 1959. *The presentation of self in everyday life.* Garden City: Doubleday Anchor Books.

————. 1963. *Stigma: Notes on the management of spoiled identity.* New York: Simon & Schuster.

————. 1977. The arrangement between the sexes. *Theory & Society* 4, pp. 301–331.

Goodman, Ellen. 2005. Nature or nurture? *Boston Globe,* December 2. http://www.boston.com/news/globe/editorial_opinion/oped/articles/2005/12/02/nature_or-nurture.

Green, Jamison. 2004. *Becoming a visible man.* Nashville: Vanderbilt University Press.

Halberstam, Judith. 1998. Transgender butch: Butch/FTM border wars and the masculine continuum. *GLQ: A Journal of Lesbian and Gay Studies* 4 (2), pp. 287–310.

Henneman, Todd. 2006. Companies that embrace equality. The Advocate, October 10, p. 59.

Human Rights Campaign. 2006. Workplace. www.hrc.org. Accessed April 25, 2006.

Human Rights Watch. 2001. *Hatred in the hallways.* New York: Human Rights Watch.

Intersex Society of North America (ISNA). 2006. How common is intersex? http://www.isna.org/faq/frequency. Accessed June 22, 2006.

Johnson, Christine. 2004. Transsexualism: An unacknowledged endpoint of developmental endocrine disruption? Master's thesis, Evergreen State College, Olympia, Wash.

Jordan, Judith. 1989. Relational development: Therapeutic implications of empathy and shame. Work in Progress, No. 39, Stone Center Working Paper Series, Wellesley, Mass.

Kaldera, Raven. 2001. Feminist on Testosterone. http://www.cauldronfarm.com/writing/feminist.html.

Kerlin, Scott, and Dana Beyer. 2002. The DES Sons' online discussion network. *Transgender Tapestry* (100), pp. 18–23.

Kessler, Suzanne. 1990. The medical construction of gender: Case management of intersexed infants. *Signs* 16 (1), pp. 3–26.

———. 2000. *Lessons from the intersexed.* New Brunswick, N.J.: Rutgers University Press.

———, and Wendy McKenna. 1978. *Gender: An ethnomethodological approach.* Chicago: University of Chicago Press.

Lake Snell Perry & Associates. 2002. *Public perceptions of transgender people.* Washington, D.C.: Human Rights Campaign. August.

Lelchuk, Ilene. 2006. When is it OK for boys to be girls, and girls to be boys? *San Francisco Chronicle,* August 27. http://www.sfgate.com/cgi-bin/article.cgi?file=/c/a/2006/08/27/MNGL2KQ8H41.DTL&type=printable.

Levitt, Heidi M., and Katherine R. Hiestand. 2004. A quest for authenticity: contemporary butch gender. *Sex Roles* 50 (9/10), pp. 605–621.

Matthews, Robert. 2004. Pregnant women who take slimming pills "are more likely to have gay children." *The Telegraph* (UK), May 12.

Meyerowitz, Joanne. 2002. *How sex changed: A history of transsexuality in the United States.* Cambridge, Mass.: Harvard University Press.

Miller, Jean Baker. 1988. Connections, disconnections, and violations. Work in Progress, No. 33, Stone Center Working Paper Series, Wellesley, Mass.

———, and I. P. Stiver. 1997. *The healing connection: How women form relationships in therapy and in life.* Boston: Beacon Press.

Moir, A., and D. Jessel. 1991. *Brain sex: The real difference between men & women.* New York: Delta.

Munson, Michael. 2004. Survey results. Transgender Sexual Violence Project. For Ourselves: Reworking Gender Expression (FORGE). www.forge-forward.org/transviolence/survey_results.php.

Nagel, Joane. 2003. *Race, ethnicity, and sexuality: Intimate intersections, forbidden frontiers.* New York: Oxford University Press.

Nakamura, Karen. 1997. Narrating ourselves: Duped or duplicitous? In *Gender blending,* edited by Bonnie Bullough, Vern L. Bullough, and James Elias, pp. 74–86. Amherst, N.Y.: Prometheus Books.

Namaste, Viviane K. 2000. *Invisible lives: The erasure of transsexual and transgendered people.* Chicago: University of Chicago Press.

Nanda, Serena. 2000. *Gender diversity: Crosscultural variations.* Prospect Heights, Ill.: Waveland Press.

National Gay and Lesbian Task Force. 2006. Transgender civil rights project. www.thetaskforce.org/our_work/public_policy/transgender_civil_rights. Accessed November 11, 2006.

Nishioka, Joyce. 2002. Transgender: A walk of life. *Asian Week,* September 10.

Oliver, Akilah. 2003. Shifting the subject: An interview with Kari Edwards. *Rain Taxi Review of Books.* http://www.raintaxi.com/online/2003spring/edwards.shtml. Accessed March 24, 2003.

Preves, Sharon E. 2002. Sexing the intersexed: An analysis of sociocultural responses to intersexuality. *Signs* 27 (2), pp. 523–556.

Prince, Virginia. 1976. *Understanding cross-dressing.* Capistrano Beach, Calif.: Sandy Thomas Advertising.

———. 1997. "Seventy years in the trenches of the gender wars." In *Gender blending*, edited by Bonnie Bullough, Vern L. Bullough, and James Elias. Amherst, New York: Prometheus Books, pp. 469–476.

Rich, Adrienne. 1986. Invisible in academe." In *Blood, bread & poetry: Selected prose, 1979–1985*. New York: W. W. Norton.

Roscoe, Will. 1998. *Changing ones: Third and fourth genders in Native North America*. New York: St. Martin's Griffin.

Rothblatt, Martine. 1995. *The apartheid of sex: A manifesto on the freedom of gender*. New York: Crown Publishers.

Roughgarden, Joan. 2004. *Evolution's rainbow: Diversity, gender, and sexuality in nature and people*. Berkeley: University of California Press.

Schecter, Ellen. 2005. Living outside the box: Relational challenges of lesbians in love with men. Working Paper No. 420, Stone Center Working Paper Series, Wellesley, Mass.

Spender, Dale. 1980. *Man made language*. London: Pandora.

Sydney Herald. 2003. Big brothers may make boys gay: New study. March 27.

Thomas, William I., and Dorothy Thomas. 1928. *The child in America*. New York: Alfred A. Knopf.

Valerio, Max Wolf. 2006. *The testosterone files*. Emeryville, Calif.: Seal Press.

Walworth, Janis. 1999. *Working with a transsexual: A guide for coworkers*. Los Angeles: Center for Gender Sanity.

Wilchins, Riki Anne. 1997. *Read my lips: Sexual subversion and the end of gender*. Milford, Conn.: Firebrand Books.

———. 2002. "Queerer bodies." In *GenderQueer: Voices from beyond the sexual binary*, edited by Joan Nestle, Clare Howell, and Riki Wilchins. Los Angeles: Alyson Books.

———, and Taneika Taylor. 2006. *50 under 30*. Washington, D.C.: Gender PAC.